Assessment and Treatment of Non-Suicidal Self-Injury

Assessment and Treatment of Non-Suicidal Self-Injury: A Clinical Perspective is the ideal primer for anyone who works with people who self-injure. Profiling who is affected as well as what their behaviour includes, the book explores the range of factors behind why people self-injure, from the influence of social media to the need for self-regulation, and offers recommendations for both assessment and outpatient treatment.

Throughout, the book is permeated by profound respect for those who use self-injury in an attempt to live a good life, while conveying a deep understanding of the challenges that self-injury presents for family members and treatment professionals. It recognizes that the behaviour can spread in hospital wards or other institutional setting, introducing the concept of *self-injury by proxy*, and assesses the range of therapies available, including CBT, MBT, ERGT and family therapy. Each chapter is complemented by clinical vignettes.

In an era when a great number of professionals will come into contact with someone who self-injures – including teachers, social workers and nurses as well as therapists – *The Assessment and Treatment of Non-Suicidal Self-Injury* is an invaluable resource that examines both the causes and the treatments available.

Bo Møhl is Professor of Clinical Psychology at Aalborg University in Denmark. He holds an MA in Literature and Education and an MSc in Psychology. He has published several articles and books about general psychiatry, psychotherapy, sexology and self-injury. He is trained in Group Analysis, MBT and DBT and has been treating self-injuring patients for more than 20 years. He is a member of the International Society for the Study of Self-Injury.

Assessment and Treatment of Non-Suicidal Self-Injury

A Clinical Perspective

Bo Møhl

Routledge
Taylor & Francis Group

LONDON AND NEW YORK

First published 2020
by Routledge
2 Park Square, Milton Park, Abingdon, Oxon OX14 4RN

and by Routledge
52 Vanderbilt Avenue, New York, NY 10017

Routledge is an imprint of the Taylor & Francis Group, an informa business

© 2020 Bo Møhl
Translated by Dorte H. Silver

British Library Cataloguing-in-Publication Data
A catalogue record for this book is available from the British Library

Library of Congress Cataloging-in-Publication Data
A catalog record has been requested for this book

ISBN: 9781138349797 (hbk)
ISBN: 9781138349803 (pbk)
ISBN: 9780429296352 (ebk)

Typeset in Times New Roman
by Apex CoVantage, LLC

Cover painting: Edvard Weie (1879–1943). A Forest Road (1932). The Royal Collection of Paintings and Sculptures, Copenhagen, Denmark.

Contents

Illustrations

Introduction

Louise was 21 years old when she was first committed to a psychiatric ward. She had attempted to commit suicide by overdosing on medicine, and when she was admitted she showed signs of depression. She did not want to go on living and had become increasingly isolated from friends and family. She had dropped out of college. She spoke of feeling overwhelmed and had no confidence that she would ever recover. She spent much of the time in bed, either watching TV or simply staring into space. She had excelled in school and in her training to become a preschool teacher, but she felt that she had lost her grip when her boyfriend of three years had broken up with her. She had begun to drink, including occasional binge drinking. She mainly drank in bars, and she often went home with men she had just met because she was scared to be alone. She had recollections of very unpleasant experiences with some of these men, and more than once, she had woken up in a strange bed without remembering how she got there, or with whom. After one of these 'desperate nights out', as she called them, when she had been kicked out in the early morning hours by a man she had had sex with, she was overwhelmed by an urge to end it all and take her own life. On her way home she impulsively bought 100 acetaminophen tablets in a kiosk and swallowed handfuls of pills in order to escape the pain that she kept try to escape by means of alcohol and self-injury. Now, she was going to give up on life entirely.

Since she was 16, Louise had been cutting herself in the upper arm, thighs or stomach when she faced adversity or distress. At times she would cut herself almost daily, mostly at night in order to calm herself down before sleeping. In fact, the reason her former boyfriend eventually broke up with her was that he could no longer stand the sight of these physical manifestations of her distress. She had repeatedly decided never to cut herself again but had consistently relapsed when her distress became too intense. In addition to cutting, she had also occasionally burned herself with cigarettes and once, 'in a rage', she had poured scalding hot coffee over her hand. She said that she felt embarrassed and shameful about self-harming, and that she tried her best to hide the marks. She always wore long sleeves and clothes that covered her body, even on hot days. Whenever one of her friends, or the men she slept with, saw her scars and burns, she tried to come up with excuses. Apart from her former boyfriend and the people who had guessed the cause of her scars and scabs, a close childhood friend was the only person who knew about her self-injury.

Louise had grown up with two busy career parents, both academics, and a younger brother, whom she was not close to. Until her parents' divorce when she was 9 years old, the home appeared outwardly 'successful', but the parents had a tense relationship, which also affected Louise and her brother. Louise had witnessed fierce arguments between her parents and offered vivid descriptions of the tense and volatile atmosphere in the home. Louise's mother had reacted strongly to her husband's infidelities, some of which involved his students, and during the time leading up to their divorce, she had developed a drinking problem, which she successfully hid from outsiders, because she was still able to handle her job as a high-school teacher. After the divorce Louise lived alternately with her mother and father, and she recalls these years as being 'very, very difficult', because she was 'constantly anxious and worried', especially for the parent that she was not currently with.

Occasionally, she spent time with her maternal grandparents, with whom she had always been close. They lived not far from Louise's childhood home, and their place had been like a second home to her. Once, while she was staying with them after the divorce, she ran a fever and had nightmares, so the grandparents took her into their bed. During the night she woke up to find that her grandfather had put his hands between her legs and was touching her genitals, but afterwards she felt she could not be sure whether it had actually happened, or if it had been a dream. She never told anyone about it until she was hospitalized and spoke with a therapist.

After the divorce, her father moved in with his girlfriend, whom he had known since before the divorce. Louise's mother had a series of brief relationships, not all of them nice. Louise remembers one of the boyfriends as being particularly unpleasant, because he would make comments about her body in a sexualized tone. One night, when he was drunk, he came into her room and tried to force himself on her. She also kept this experience to herself, not daring to tell her mother, with whom she was having many conflicts at the time.

Louise began to self-injure after the incident with her mother's boyfriend. She had flashbacks and was flooded by distressing emotions, which she found she could reduce by drinking or cutting. After this sexual assault, Louise withdrew and stopped speaking to her mother. She cut herself on a daily basis and later told her therapist that it served both as a form of self-punishment and as a way to get rid of the pain. Cutting calmed her down and offered immediate relief. However, cutting also made her feel shame and self-loathing – feelings that she was able to dampen, again in the short term, by cutting.

While she was hospitalized in the mental health unit she continued to self-injure, and her condition deteriorated. On several occasions she made deep cuts that required stitching and bandaging. She still thought of suicide but found that self-injuring made everything easier to bear. At one point, her self-injury became so severe that she was kept under constant watch. She later said that being prevented from self-injuring made her desperate and intensified her suicidal urges. In addition to placing her under constant watch, the staff only gave her plastic cutlery and cups, because she had previously used the shards of a broken cup to cut herself. While under watch, she ran out of her room one night and grabbed a bread knife from the kitchen and attempted to cut herself. The nurses quickly caught up and wrested the knife from her, but not before she had managed to cut herself. After this incident, she was placed in restraints (confined to her bed with straps around her hands, feet and waist) to prevent further self-injury. Over the coming weeks, Louise was repeatedly put in restraints because she reacted in a self-destructive manner, posing a risk to herself and even to the staff, striking out at them when her restraints were removed. The mood in the ward was increasingly one of powerlessness, pessimism and concern that she might do serious harm to herself, perhaps even take her own life, but also of irritation and anger. Several team members asked not to be assigned to Louise's case, because they felt that she was 'doing it in order to get attention' or 'to punish some of her assigned carers'. Other staff members realized that Louise was experiencing increasing pressure and was reacting to the controls placed on her. 'For every action, there is reaction', as one of her primary carers compassionately put it.

After being hospitalized for a little over four months, during which time her condition had gradually deteriorated, Louise began to see a therapist in the mental health unit twice a week. Louise was very ambivalent about engaging in talk therapy and having to confide in a stranger. She was filled with a sense of powerless self-destructive anger and expressed that 'no one can help me; least of all a man'. However, the therapist was gradually able to establish a connection with her, in part by always going to her room in the ward if she missed her appointments in his office. On an emotional level, however, the contact was not great, and she was often dismissive or distant, as if she were not really there. She continued to self-injure, and the staff attempted to strike a deal with her where she would promise not to self-injure when she went outside the hospital grounds, for example to pick up things from home or to go to the kiosk for cigarettes. Most of the time, she managed to comply and returned to the ward without having self-injured, but sometimes, she had clearly been both drinking and cutting herself.

One day Louise had once again cut herself severely. According to her agreement with the therapist, whenever she had self-injured, that would be the top priority of the session. That involved conducting a chain analysis to describe the course of events leading up to the self-harming act. The intention was both to identify the prompting factors and to discuss what she could have done instead of cutting. She had done this several times previously with her therapist, and this time she may have sensed a certain fatigue and, perhaps, pessimism in his demeanour. At any rate, she reacted with a focused presence in the contact that was in stark contrast to her usual detachment, spontaneously saying, 'I so wish that you could understand what cutting does for me. It's the best drug when I feel bad. You can forget about sedatives and all the skills you want me to use. None of that stuff works when I feel really bad'.

The skills Louise mentions were techniques she learned during the talks with her therapist and in group-based skills training to reduce her inner tension when she was in distress (such as watching a film online, taking a hot shower, using the stationary exercise bicycle in the ward or doing mindfulness exercises). These skills have a documented effect on patients who self-injure and act impulsively, but in Louise's case, cutting was the best way for her to achieve immediate relief. Intellectually, she realized that self-injuring would only offer temporary relief, and that it would ultimately leave her feeling worse, but in the situation, when she felt distress, cutting offered the most effective means of affect regulation.

After telling her therapist how crucial cutting was to her, Louise retreated back into a trance-like, dissociative state, and the session continued as usual – without the freshness and intensity required of a psychotherapeutic contact. Dissociation is a defence mechanism, a filter that makes it possible to endure a physically and mentally painful condition without feeling the pain.

In many ways, Louise's story is typical of a growing number of psychiatric patients. She self-injures both directly and indirectly. She drinks, cuts and burns herself, has sexual encounters with men who are not good for her and is unable to look after herself, but, importantly, she does all these things because she lacks adequate alternatives. She is incapable of managing her inner tension in a way that is more constructive and viable in the long term. Louise is intelligent, but she is unable to rely on her intelligence and insight when she is in distress – when she 'goes over the edge'. Rather than understanding and addressing her problems with herself and others on a psychological level, that is, by mentalizing, she is overwhelmed by her emotions and acts based on impulsive urges and desperation in ways that may provide immediate relief but which exacerbate her condition in the long term. Her ability to look after herself and to rely on her psychological insight is becoming increasingly impaired, her relationships with others are fraying and she risks becoming increasingly lonely in addition to doing physical harm to herself, including infections and scarring.

In 1959, the American psychoanalyst Karl Menninger predicted that in the future, psychiatrists would be seeing many more patients with chronic self-destructive behaviour, such as Louise (Menninger, 1959). By the mid-1960s, the two American psychiatrists Graf and Mallin (1967) were seeing many self-injuring patients ('wrist slashers') suffering from severe chronic conditions that required intensive inpatient care. In their assessment, these patients 'have become the new chronic patients in mental hospitals, replacing the schizophrenics' (p. 36).

Today, psychiatrists are seeing many patients like Louise. This presents new challenges for our understanding of health and illness and for our treatment approaches, in part because patients who self-injure often have varying motivation for treatment and almost always spark very strong emotional responses from their carers. However, not everyone who self-injures is as severely affected as Louise. Most are capable of holding a job or continuing their studies, and only a minority ever come into contact with psychiatric or somatic healthcare services.

Normally, we prefer to avoid and protect ourselves from physical pain. When some people nevertheless deliberately inflict pain on themselves, it is because it has the paradoxical capacity to distract from and soothe psychological pain. Physical pain hijacks our perception, and by subjecting themselves to pain some people achieve a degree of control over their emotions that makes them feel more in control in chaotic and overwhelming life situations. They self-injure in order to feel better. In another paradox, however, self-injury can quickly take on a life of its own and thus pose a severe threat to the individual's general sense of control.

Even if a patient uses self-injury to achieve a sense of control, he or she risks being overpowered by the behaviour, developing a self-destructive pattern with severe long-term consequences, including an increased risk of mental illness and suicide attempts.

Self-injury also affects the patient's family and close friends and the treatment professionals who work with them. Favazza (1998) states that 'the treatment literature on self-injury is basically one of countertransference', referring to the many descriptions of how emotionally draining it can be to be in contact with patients who self-injure, for example from Linehan (1993). Patients who self-injure make a big impression on the professionals who work with them. The American psychiatrist Allen Frances describes how difficult it can be to maintain an understanding and empathic stance in relation to the behaviour of patients who self-injure:

> Of all disturbing patient behaviors, self-mutilation is the most difficult to understand and treat . . . The typical clinician (myself included) treating a patient who self-mutilates is often left feeling a combination of helpless, horrified, guilty, furious, betrayed, disgusted and sad.
>
> (Frances, 1987, p. 316)

This captures the challenging nature of a behaviour that is, in many regards, counterintuitive and thus essentially impossible for most people to understand or empathize with. Experience, however, shifts our mental boundaries, and any curious and sensitive clinician will inevitably learn from his or her patients. After meeting many patients who self-injure, one begins to discern a recognizable pattern that makes it less intimidating to embark on a more detailed examination of how this particular person – this given patient – uses self-injury. Regardless of how much knowledge we may accumulate about a human trait or type of behaviour, we must never forget that we are dealing with a unique person whose behaviour stems from his or her unique history, motivations and emotions.

What I wish to underscore here is the need to adopt a perspective where the individual is placed centre stage, seen with his or her unique individuality and characteristics and not just as representative of a group. Especially when we encounter something that we find it difficult to understand and empathize with, we often generalize and form stereotypes. That certainly applies to patients who self-injure, and my hope with this book is to prevent us from losing sight of the individual human being.

The German writer Rainer Maria Rilke makes a similar point in his novel *The Notebooks of Malte Laurids Brigge* (2008/1910, p. 14), where he introduces the term 'countless singulars':

> Is it possible that one says 'women', 'children', 'boys' without any suspicion (none whatsoever, despite all one's education) that these words have long since had no plural, but only countless singulars?

1 What is non-suicidal self-injury?

Although this book also addresses other forms of self-injury, its main focus is on non-suicidal self-injury (NSSI) as defined by the International Society for the Study of Self-Injury (ISSS) in 2007:

> Socially unacceptable, intentional, and direct injuring of one's own body tissue without suicidal intent.

In this definition, 'direct' implies that the act has immediate physical consequences, such as the wounds resulting from cutting. The definition thus excludes *indirect* self-injury, which refers to a behaviour that may eventually result in physical injury, such as eating disorders, overdosing on medicine, substance abuse, smoking or other behaviours where the injury results from chemical processes within the body.

The self-injury has to be deliberate and 'intentional', in contrast to behaviour that accidentally results in injury to oneself. The definition also specifies that the injury has to affect 'body tissue', although the degree may vary from superficial scratches or bruising to more severe damage, for example as a result of cutting. The act has to be 'socially unacceptable'; this excludes self-injurious behaviour that is more or less culturally sanctioned, such as self-inflicted piercings, tattoos and body modifications and rites of passage that are not addressed here (Favazza, 1996).

The focus in the present book is on acts that defy or deviate from cultural norms and values. However, normalcy and deviation are fluid, contextually defined concepts, and in certain youth subcultures, for example, cutting is socially accepted and more or less a part of the group identity (Young et al., 2014).

Finally, the act of self-injury, under this definition, is not driven by a desire or an intention to commit suicide. If someone cuts their arm with the desire to open an artery in order to bleed to death, that is, naturally, a form of self-injury, but as it must be categorized as attempted suicide it falls outside the definition of self-injury that is applied in the present book.

Direct self-injury

Direct self-injury means that the self-inflicted injury is immediately apparent, for example, in the form of a wound, bleeding, bruising, a scratch or other signs on the skin. The following are the most prevalent methods for NSSI:

Cutting

Cutting may be done with a variety of sharp implements, such as a razor, a knife, a shard of glass or anything else that is sharp enough to penetrate the skin, such as a broken CD or a credit card snapped in two. Numerous studies have identified cutting as the most common method for NSSI (e.g., Victor et al., 2018). Klonsky (2007) notes that 50–90% of persons who engage in NSSI do so by cutting. Other studies have found that 20–30% keep the wound open by picking at it, thus delaying the healing process (Bresin & Schoenleber, 2015), and that some increase the sensation of pain by pouring salt or acidic substances into the wound.

Cutting may be directed at any part of the body, although some parts are more commonly chosen than others. The most commonly endorsed body locations in a 2018 survey (Victor et al., 2018) were arms (88%), followed by legs (60%) and abdomen/stomach (31%); males were more likely to report cutting on their torso/chest. Laukkanen et al. (2013) found that two-thirds of self-cutting adolescents reported only cutting the upper arms, while a third also cut other parts of the body. Cutting on other parts of body than the arms was more common among females and associated with a wide range of emotional and dissociative symptoms and suicidal ideation. Some cut in straight lines or carved words, while others engaged in less structured self-injury by hacking at or even removing parts of the tissue.

> A woman who habitually made superficial cuts in her skin had attempted to block out violent flashbacks by making deep cuts to her arm that eventually ruined the tendons in her lower arm.

Patients who cut their genitals, breasts or face are directing their self-injury against parts of the body that are more emotionally charged, in both positive and negative ways. These patients are typically more severely psychologically affected than those who merely make superficial cuts in, for example, their arms or legs. The genitals may be associated with emotions such as pleasure, joy and pride, but also with shame, guilt or anxiety, perhaps as a result of sexual abuse. A study (Møhl & Rubæk, submitted) found a significant link between having been subjected to sexual abuse during childhood and later developing genital self-injury.

Some cut impulsively in connection with stressful experiences ('triggers'), but many plan the behaviour and wait until conditions are right. They may need to be alone, to avoid being interrupted or discovered; they may plan around what they are going to do afterwards; or they may put off cutting in order to 'have something to look forward to'. Some have even described that they derive pleasure from anticipating the release that comes with cutting. One patient described taking steps to make sure she would not be disturbed and interrupted while cutting. She prepared for the act by getting cotton, plaster and disinfectant ready and regarded these preparations as an almost pleasurable part of the process (Stacy et al., 2018).

The duration of planning and delaying the act of cutting can vary from hours to days or even weeks. One 17-year-old woman described how she had promised her parents to avoid cutting during their three-week holiday, and she managed to keep her promise despite cutting almost daily, sometimes several times daily, as they got close to the departure date. Knowing that she could resume cutting when she returned home was a relief and something for her to look forward to. After returning home she had several severe incidents with NSSI.

Hitting

Hitting oneself with a fist or various objects is the second-most-frequent form of NSSI, mentioned by about one-third of people who self-injure (Bresin & Schoenleber, 2015). A Danish study of NSSI among upper-secondary school students found that 47% of the respondent who self-injured had done so by hitting themselves. Respectively, 64% of the males and 39% of the females who self-injured had done so by hitting themselves (Møhl & Skandsen, 2012). Hitting may also involve, for example, punching a wall or a doorjamb, which may result in bone fractures or other serious injury.

Scratching

Scratching till the blood flows is another frequently used method. In a study among American college students, Whitlock et al. (2006) identified scratching as the most common form of self-injury, and a meta-analysis found that between 21% (males) and 31% (females) who had self-injured had used scratching (Bresin & Schoenleber, 2015).

Burning

Burning oneself with a cigarette or a lighter or by pouring boiling water or coffee over a hand, for example, is a method that is used by 15–35% of people who self-injure (Klonsky, 2007). The result is a painful burn with a high risk of infection. Bresin and Schoenleber (2015) found that 20% of the males and 18% of the females who had self-injured had burned themselves.

Compulsive headbanging

Headbanging, where the person repeatedly bangs their head against a wall, can result in thickened areas in the forehead and temple region and intracranial bleeding. Some report that they mainly engage in headbanging when they are bored, while others do it when they are under stress. A meta-analysis found that headbanging occurs in 28% of males and 24% of females (Bresin & Schoenleber, 2015), but it is more prevalent among individuals with intellectual disabilities or neuropsychiatric conditions, such as Tourette's or Lesch-Nyhan syndrome, where it may serve as a form of auto-stimulation.

Trichotillomania

Hair pulling is an independent diagnosis (trichotillomania) in ICD-10, categorized under Impulse Disorders (F63.3), and in the DSM-5, where it is categorized under OCD (312.39). The condition is characterized by considerable hair loss due to the irresistible, recurring urge to pull out one's own hair. Hair pulling may be directed at the scalp, eye brows or pubic region and often has an automatic character, as a form of distraction, but it may also occur in response to anxiety or stress. It may result in large bald spots. Bresin and Schoenleber (2015) report that 12% of males and 35% of females report pulling hair.

Skin picking

Skin picking, which is another independent diagnosis categorized under OCD in DSM-5 (698.4) (Excoriation Skin Picking Disorder), consists in pulling off skin, either in flakes or by searching for and attempting to remove skin irregularities or impurities; the behaviour may result in severe skin irritation and infections with scabs that the person can maintain by picking at them. These patients often consult dermatologists without coming into contact with psychiatric care. Lifetime prevalence for skin picking is 1.4%, and the disorder is more common among women.

In the novel *Cat's Eye* (1989, p. 113) the Canadian writer Margaret Atwood describes how a young girl self-injures, in part through skin picking, in connection with being bullied by a group of girls from her school:

'In the endless time when Cordelia had such power over me, I peeled the skin off my feet. I did it at night, when I was supposed to be sleeping. My feet would be cool and slightly damp, like the skin of mushrooms. I would begin with the big toes. I would bend my foot up and bite a small opening in the thickest part of the skin on the bottom, along the outside edge. Then, with my finger nails, which I never bit because why bite something that didn't hurt, I would pull the skin off in narrow strips. I would do the same to the other big toe, then to the ball of each foot the heel of each. I would go down as far as the blood. Nobody but me ever looked at my feet, so nobody knew that I was doing it. In the mornings I would pull my socks on, over my peeled feet. It was painful to walk but not impossible. The pain gave me something definite to think about, something immediate. It was something to hold on to'.

Self-inflicted fractures

Rarer methods include self-inflicted fractures or the practice of swallowing objects (such as lighters, teaspoons, hairpins, scissors) that later have to be removed surgically. These practices may be found among psychotic patients or, for example, patients who are incarcerated.

Other methods

As many as 80% of people who regularly self-injure use a variety of methods, often depending on the circumstances and on the specific emotions they are dealing with (Gratz, 2001). For example, a young woman began to hit herself in the face and burn herself with cigarettes or a lighter while she was hospitalized and hence prevented from cutting. For her own protection, the staff had placed all sharp objects out of reach and kept her under constant watch.

Another young woman reported that she would cut herself almost daily, but that she burned herself with a cigarette when she was in severe distress: 'A cigarette hurts more than cutting, and it lasts longer. You can feel it for a long time. That's good when I feel really, really bad. That's why I do it'. None of these methods are really life-threatening unless they are taken to the extreme, which they rarely are by people who self-injure regularly.

Other methods for direct NSSI include biting (16% of the males and 27% of the females); inserting needles or similar objects under the skin (20% of the males and 24% of the females); carving the skin (18% of the males and 27% of the females); sewing the skin with thread; rubbing the skin violently using a rubber eraser to cause burns; pouring acid on the skin; or self-inflicted tattoos (Bresin & Schoenleber, 2015).

Indirect self-injury

Indirect self-injury can be defined as an act that does not lead directly to an injury but instead results in increased risk of an unintended long-term consequence. With indirect self-injury such as heavy drinking or smoking, the actual harm stemming from the behaviour is unclear, and in many cases the harmful effects are a matter of chance. Some people can consume large quantities of alcohol over several years without suffering major long-term effects. Although the habit increases their risk of liver damage, they may still be lucky enough to avoid it. This is an important difference compared to direct self-injury, where the damage is predictable and occurs as an immediate result of the behaviour. Unlike direct self-injury, it can be difficult to define indirect self-injury precisely, except as a behaviour that increases the risk of developing health issues.

Examples of indirect self-injuring behaviour

* Eating disorders, either starving oneself or overeating
* Substance abuse
* Unsafe sex
* Reckless driving
* Getting into fights
* Gambling

Indirect self-injury falls outside the definition that is applied in the present book. It is mentioned here because it often correlates with direct self-injury. Many people

Table 1.1 Overview of different forms of self-injury.

Self-injury is behaviour that causes immediate physical and/or psychological damage or which increases the risk of long-term damage.	
INDIRECT SELF-INJURY is behaviour resulting in increased risk of an unintended long-term consequence; examples include • Alcohol abuse • Drug abuse • Eating disorder (over- or undereating) • High-risk behaviour	DIRECT SELF-INJURY is deliberate behaviour with the purpose of self-inflicted physical damage, such as cuts, bruises or fractures.
SELF-INJURY WITH SUICIDAL INTENT includes • Overdosing on medication • Suicide attempts through strangulation, shooting, jumping from a great height and so forth • Suicide	NON-SUICIDAL SELF-INJURY is self-inflicted injury causing immediate harm to body tissue, such as wounds inflicted without suicidal intent.

who self-injure, for example by cutting, do so while they are under the influence of alcohol or drugs, which lowers the threshold for direct self-injury. A Danish study of self-injury among upper-secondary school students found that 53.9% had experience with one or more types of indirect self-injury defined as 1) alcohol-related blackout, 2) binge eating and purging and/or deliberately starving themselves and 3) use of harder drugs (for example amphetamine, LSD, heroin). We also found a correlation between direct and indirect self-injury in the group overall. Among the male respondents, the correlation was twice as high as it was among the female participants. Thus, direct self-injury implies an elevated risk of indirect self-injury in the form of drug use, alcohol-related blackouts or eating disorders (Møhl et al., 2014). A study (Claes et al., 2015) found that 59% of patients with an eating disorder engaged in at least one type of NSSI (most frequently cutting), with no significant difference in rates of NSSI among eating disorder subtypes.

In a comparison of indirect and direct NSSI, Germain and Hooley (2012) found that individuals who engage in direct self-injury are more critical of themselves and more likely to have a history of suicidal ideation and attempted suicide than those who engage in indirect self-injury. It is, further, a clinical experience that most people who receive treatment for direct self-injury also engage in indirect self-injury, which may make them more susceptible to the loss of impulse control. For example, overeating, drug use or heavy drinking is associated with an increased risk of direct self-injury.

Self-injury by proxy

The ISSS definition of non-suicidal direct self-injury, which is applied in the present book, explicitly describes the injury as self-inflicted, as expressed by the term *self-injury*. The person deliberately inflicts the injury on him/herself. However, clinicians encounter a phenomenon that is not described in the literature, but which I would call *self-injury by proxy*. In the present context, *self-injury by proxy* refers to a situation where the person enlists the cooperation of another person to inflict the injuries. The concept differs dynamically from the related concept of *Munchausen's syndrome by proxy*, where the patient is a parent who harms their child, thus inflicting harm on another person. In self-injury by proxy, the patient actively provokes or encourages someone else to inflict the injury on the patient. This may be done either deliberately or subconsciously and may serve the same purpose as non-suicidal self-injury, for example, as a form of affect regulation or self-punishment.

> An 18-year-old woman, who is hospitalized in a psychiatric youth ward due to severe self-injury, says that she sometimes deliberately breaks a glass or throws a book against the window because she knows that the staff will respond by immediately placing her in restraints. Being held down or restrained with straps gives her the same sense of relief that direct self-injury can provide.

Self-injury by proxy may also manifest as various forms of body modification, for example, piercing of the tongue, nipples or genitals, typically without anaesthesia, or of plastic surgery that is not medically indicated (for example, penis extension or cosmetic alterations of the labia).

> A 26-year-old woman with BPD shared in group therapy that she engaged in several types of self-injury. For several years she had both burned and cut herself when she was under stress. By her own description, she had 'a very short fuse', and sometimes she self-injured several times a day. In addition to this form of self-injury, she had had numerous tattoos, piercings and plastic surgery procedures ('boob jobs'), and she had repeatedly found abusive boyfriends whom she provoked into hurting her. The boyfriend she was currently living with had hit her and burned her, and she had had numerous visits to the emergency room for fractures and other injuries requiring treatment. When she described this abuse in the group, the other group members often expressed both support and care, but she also encountered pressure to leave the boyfriend and, occasionally, anger for staying. Once she did in fact leave him after a dramatic, violent incident. Only a few days later she met and moved in with another man. That relationship only lasted a little more than a month, however; as she explained, he was 'far too nice'. She achieved insight into her own need for drama and, not least, self-injury by proxy.

A 32-year-old man was in treatment for a personality disorder, not otherwise specified, with NSSI, which involved hitting himself (often in the face), burning himself and sticking needles under his skin. During treatment it emerged that he often wound up in fist fights, for example in connection with soccer matches, where he had repeatedly been severely injured after taunting and badgering supporters of the opposite team. He deliberately put himself in situations where he would predictably be injured.

He had also provoked police officers in connection with a political demonstration, which had led to him being hit and painfully cuffed with plastic straps. He had no problem understanding his own behaviour as self-injury by proxy.

Self-injury by proxy is an overlooked phenomenon that plays an important role for some patients. By 'enlisting' others to inflict the injury, the person 1) has an opportunity to engage with others, 2) is able to absolve him/herself of responsibility for the self-injurious behaviour and take on the role of victim ('others are doing this to me'), 3) is able to legitimize and act out his or her anger, which may in itself provide relief, and 4) generates intense drama, which not only results in self-injury by proxy but also in the kind of close and intense engagements with others that many patients with BPD lack due to a feeling of inner emptiness.

In many cases, individuals who engage in self-injury by proxy may have a behaviour pattern reminiscent of the proposed but now abandoned diagnosis *self-defeating personality disorder*. Patients who meet the diagnostic criteria for this condition were described as having a pattern of self-defeating behaviour where they often reject or ruin pleasant experiences; are attracted to situations or individuals that cause suffering; and reject help from others. One of the diagnostic criteria in DSM-III-R was that the individual 'incites angry or rejecting responses from others and then feels hurt, defeated, or humiliated' (American Psychiatric Association, 1987, p. 374) and thus appears as a victim.

The relationship between the parties involved in self-injury by proxy sometimes resembles a sadomasochistic one, as exemplified by the 26-year-old woman who keeps finding abusive boyfriends whom she then provokes into hurting her. In many cases, direct NSSI and self-injury by proxy may be viewed as attempts to re-enact, for example, childhood abuse, where the once powerless victim is now, as an adult, in a position to influence his or her own situation actively by deliberately inciting the abuse. The adult position would appear to imply greater latitude, but this is merely an appearance, since the individual is governed by his or her inner need for re-enactment.

In a study of adolescents who engaged in sex as self-injury (SASI) compared to adolescent with NSSI, Zetterqvist et al. (2018) found that significantly more adolescents with SASI had experience of penetrating sexual abuse and also had more sexual partners compared to those with NSSI. The SASI group also had higher levels of self-reported trauma symptoms, such as dissociation, post-traumatic stress and sexual concerns compared to those with NSSI, suggesting a distinct relationship between sexual abuse, trauma symptoms and engaging in sex as self-injury.

Digital self-harm

Digital self-harm is a fairly new phenomenon, which first was described in 2010. Digital self-harm has also been described in the form of *digital Munchausen's syndrome*, which involves self-inflicted symptoms that are attributed to others and faking illness. In digital self-harm, individuals bully themselves by writing abusive comments and questions to themselves, for example on their Facebook wall. They establish several online profiles and online identities to bully themselves, which makes it difficult for others to discover that the bully or bullies are fictive. Digital self-harm includes exposing one's negative self-image and self-hatred, thus rendering them more 'real' and visible to others and positioning oneself as a victim while still maintaining a degree of control over the nature and extent of the damage. The latter function is similar to physical self-injury. Adolescents who are in distress do not take their aggressions out on others – they take them out on themselves.

Digital self-harm became a focus of attention in particular after a 14-year-old British girl took her own life after being bullied on social media. It later emerged, however, that she had sent many of the abusive comments to herself, thus engaging in digital self-harm.

Patchin and Hinduja (2017) examined nearly 6000 adolescents and found that 6% of them reported anonymously posting negative comments about themselves and 5% reported engaging in cyberbullying against themselves. About half of the respondents reported only doing so once. Adolescents who engage in digital self-harm were found to be more likely to have been cyberbullied by others, to be non-heterosexual, to have depressive symptoms or performed physical self-harm; they were also more likely to report being frequent users of drugs and alcohol.

Digital self-harm may be driven by a variety of motivations, including self-hate, 'a cry for help' or a desire to get attention from adults and peers and get others to worry about them and 'stick up' for them online.

Digital self-harm is a new phenomenon, and our knowledge about it remains limited. There is a considerable need for additional research in this field.

Terminology

Until a few years ago, when a consensus was reached about the definition of NSSI, the terminology related to self-injury was imprecise and inconsistent. Several of the terms that were applied failed to make it clear whether the act in question included suicidal behaviour, or whether it was reserved for non-suicidal behaviour. Vague and inconsistent terminology has led to confusion, which in turn led to problems in relation to both clinical practice and scientific research.

In clinical practice, determining whether the patient has suicidal intentions plays a key role for both risk assessment and treatment planning.

In scientific research, specifically in prevalence studies, it is important to clarify whether the definition of self-injury involves both suicidal and non-suicidal behaviour. Attempted suicide is something different from non-suicidal self-injury.

Some of the research into self-injury is marred by a lack of distinction between suicidal and non-suicidal behaviour. The big multinational CASE study, which involved more than 30,000 respondents from seven countries, found that just over 70% self-injure in order to achieve relief from psychological distress, while as many as 59% are motivated by a desire to end their life. Suicidal intent is the second most-frequent cause of self-injury, and the findings of this study cannot be compared to the findings of studies that deal primarily with NSSI (Madge et al., 2008).

Changing terminology related to self-injury

Until the early 1960s, self-injury was medically categorized as *suicide attempt*. The Danish researcher Bille-Brahe (1982) concluded that individuals who attempt to commit suicide can be divided into two categories: those who carry out a single, dramatic attempt and those who have repeated attempts with methods that are not in fact life-threatening. Kessel (1965) proposed the term *deliberate self-injury* as a substitute for the over-inclusive term *suicide attempt*. A few years later, Kreitman (1969, p. 747) advocated the term *parasuicide* for a behaviour that 'simulates or mimics suicide' but is something other than suicide. It has been used as synonymous with *self-injury*, which has contributed further to the terminological confusion.

In the United States, *wrist cutting* and *wrist slashing* were introduced by Graf and Mallin (1967) and were also used by Grunebaum and Klerman (1967). These terms too are unfortunate, however, because they suggest that self-injury is strictly about cuts to the wrist. Until a few years ago, *self-mutilation* was the most common term, but it is unfortunate because its focus is on damage or destruction: 'inflict a violent and disfiguring injury on' and 'inflict serious damage on' (Oxford Dictionaries online). This focus on physical damage has caused both people who self-injure and researchers and clinicians to abandon the term; moreover, it was used inconsistently about both suicidal and non-suicidal self-injury.

In the United Kingdom, Morgan and colleagues (1975, p. 573) argued that Kreitman's term *parasuicide* 'implies a resemblance to suicide'. They proposed the term *deliberate self-harm* as more apt than Kessel's *deliberate self-injury* because it includes behaviour beyond physical self-injury, such as overdosing. *Deliberate self-harm* or just *self-harm* has been used to refer to direct self-injury and includes both suicidal and non-suicidal intent. The term is particularly widespread in British practice and literature and differs from *non-suicidal self-injury*, which is the term used by the International Society for the Study of Self-Injury (2007). *Self-harm* also includes overdosing on medication or other suicidal behaviour.

In the NICE Quality Standard (2013, p. 6) the term self-harm is used 'to refer to any act of self-poisoning or self-injury carried out by a person, irrespective of their motivation. This commonly involves self-poisoning with medication or self-injury by cutting'.

It is, however, open to debate whether it might not be more helpful to draw a distinction between suicidal and non-suicidal practices. For an in-depth discussion of the use of the term *self-harm* in Britain, see Millard (2015).

Typologies of self-injury

The American psychoanalyst Karl Menninger is often mentioned as the first to attempt to develop a classification and systematic description of self-injurious behaviour, but as early as during the nineteenth century, articles published in psychiatric journals discussed the differences between self-injury with and without suicidal intent, and the early literature includes case reports about self-injuring patients who clearly lacked suicidal intent. As early as 1844, admission papers to the Bethlem Royal Hospital asylum noted whether a patient was 'disposed to suicide or otherwise to self-injury'. The British psychiatrist George Fielding Blandford distinguished between *minor self-mutilations*, such as face or hand-picking, nail-biting or hair plucking, which was 'common among nervous people who are not insane', as he put it, according to Angelotta (2015, p. 76).

In *Man Against Himself* (1938, p. 271), Karl Menninger described self-injury as 'a partial suicide to avert total suicide'; in the book he proposed distinctions between organic, psychotic, neurotic and religious self-injury. This typology never caught on, but it is a historically interesting attempt at imposing order on the incomprehensible chaos that NSSI represents to most people. It sparked both astonishment and interest that he was able, at this early point in time, to say something positive about self-injury in the sense that he described it as a means of avoiding suicide. With this, he anticipated the modern perception of self-injury as a coping strategy aimed, among other purposes, at avoiding the worse option of suicide.

The first modern attempt at a typology was published in 1983, when Pattison and Kahan (1983) categorized self-injury according to three variables: 1) whether the behaviour is direct or indirect, 2) whether it is more or less likely to be lethal and 3) whether it is repetitive, which involves an assessment of frequency and the likelihood of repetition. In the article, they described a deliberate self-harm syndrome involving chronic cutting, which is direct, repetitive and associated with low lethality. Pattison and Kahan's categorization is clinically relevant as a general description of self-injury, but the authors fail to distinguish between suicidal and non-suicidal intentions with the behaviour, which is the most important dimension.

Table 1.2 Typology of NSSI (Kahan & Pattison, 1984).

	DIRECT	INDIRECT
High lethality	Suicide, isolated incident Repeated suicide attempts Repeated incidents	Situational high-risk behaviour Isolated incident High-risk behaviour Late-stage anorexia Repeated incidents
Medium lethality	Atypical or violent self- injury Isolated incident	Acute violent intoxication High-risk sexual behaviour Isolated incident

Low lethality	Frequent self-injury (for
	    example, cutting)
	Repeated incidents
		Chronic substance abuse,
		    bulimia
		Unstable use of, for example,
		    psychoactive medication

Favazza and Rosenthal (1993) have proposed a typology of NSSI that is still used, in a modified form, in both research and clinical practice, although it is largely pragmatic in nature and not very sophisticated. This reflects how difficult it is to develop a systematic, meaningful and helpful typology of a complicated phenomenon such as self-injury.

In the most recent version of the original taxonomy, Favazza (2012) distinguishes between four different types of NSSI: 1) major (or severe), 2) stereotypic and 3) impulsive and 4) compulsive.

1   *Major or severe self-injury* is significant and dramatic, such as eye enucleation and amputation of body parts, and is typically associated with psychotic state. Major self-injury is relatively rare.

A 23-year-old man suffering from schizophrenia was admitted to hospital after failing to take his medicine for about six months. In his psychotic state, where he perceived the world as evil and threatening, he had surgically removed his own eye, using a scalpel and standing in front of his bathroom mirror. He was under the delusion that the procedure would improve his view of the world.

---

2   *Stereotypic self-injury* is characterized by frequent, repetitive, often monotonous and rhythmic self-injury, as seen in patients with autism, intellectual disabilities and syndromes such as Lesch-Nyhan, Prader-Willi and Cornelia de Langes. This type of self-injury has a compulsive character.

An 18-year-old woman with an intellectual disability bangs her head against the wall for hours every day. She has developed a thick, swollen area on her forehead, almost resembling a horn, as a result of this behaviour, which she engages in whenever she feels restless, tense or bored. She lives in an assisted living facility and is repeatedly told that the headbanging may harm her (due to the risk of intracranial bleeding), but she is incapable of giving up the behaviour.

3   *Impulsive self-injury* is the most common form and includes cutting, burning, scratching, hitting and other acts resulting in less severe tissue damage. In particular, the superficial and impulsive form of self-injury is used to achieve quick but short-term relief from inner tension and may thus serve as a means of affect regulation that offers passing relief by reducing the intensity of the painful emotions.

For a number of years, a 19-year-old woman has engaged in impulsive cutting whenever she feels stressed, tense or otherwise distressed. Cutting offers immediate relief and enables her to calm down. At times, she engages in this practice almost daily. She is ambivalent about giving it up and acknowledges that she feels addicted to it. Self-injury has become her main coping strategy whenever she encounters problems as well as sometimes when she feels empty inside.

4   *Compulsive self-injury* is repetitive, often ritualized self-injury such as trichotillomania, nail-biting, skin picking or scratching.

A 17-year-old man bites his finger nails and picks at his fingertips, at times to the extent that they are raw and bloody. He has tried to quit, but failed. He has difficulty identifying why he does it – 'it's just what I do', as he puts it.

Finally, a practice has emerged, particularly among clinicians, to distinguish between mild (low frequency, superficial physical damage), moderate (moderate severity that requires medical treatment, such as suturing) and severe self-injury (frequent, severe, with significant physical damage) (e.g., Whitlock et al., 2008). These levels correspond to other psychiatric diagnoses, for example, depression, with distinctions between mild, moderate and severe depression.

2 Non-suicidal self-injury – an autonomous diagnosis?

In recent years, it has been debated whether non-suicidal self-injury (NSSI) should constitute an autonomous diagnosis. This hinges on whether self-injury should be understood as a *behaviour* or as a *disorder*. In May 2013, NSSI was included in the DSM-5, Section 3, not as a clinical diagnosis but as a set of criteria to be used for research purposes. Further research is required before NSSI can be classified as a proper clinical diagnosis. Before the DSM-5, the only mention of NSSI was as one of the criteria for Borderline Personality Disorder (BPD) in the DSM-III and DSM-IV. Similarly, the World Health Organization's (WHO) diagnostic classification ICD-10 does not include NSSI as an autonomous diagnosis but instead as one of the criteria for Emotionally Unstable Personality Disorder.

However, NSSI is not merely an indicator of BPD. Patients with this disorder do not always exhibit self-injury behaviour, just as the behaviour also occurs in individuals who do not suffer from BPD. Many who use NSSI as a means of affect regulation have no additional symptoms. The strong correlation between NSSI and BPD probably stems from the underlying emotional dysregulation, which affects both patients with this disorder and individuals who self-injure.

The literature shows that NSSI may occur in connection with virtually any psychiatric diagnosis, with the risk being particularly elevated for depression, personality disorders, post-traumatic stress disorder (PTSD), substance abuse disorders and eating disorders. Studies of various aspects of NSSI behaviour (e.g., method, context, causes) have not identified clinical subgroups of patients with self-injury behaviour related to specific psychiatric diagnoses. Thus, NSSI is a transdiagnostic or a *non-specific symptom* that may be present in individuals with no other symptoms as well as in individuals with any of a variety of psychiatric diagnoses.

The non-specific nature of NSSI makes it important to focus on the underlying psychosocial circumstances. Only by focusing on the person rather than, primarily, on the symptom can we hope to gain any insight into the dynamics behind the self-injury.

Categorizing self-injurers in non-clinical populations

There has been an effort to examine and describe distinct subgroups with self-injury behaviour in non-clinical populations. For example, Andover et al. (2005)

found that people who use cutting were more likely to exhibit anxiety symptoms than people who self-injure in other ways. Nock and Prinstein (2005) found that adolescents and young adults who use self-injury for affect regulation are more likely to experience feelings of hopelessness, to attempt suicide and to display symptoms of PTSD than peers who self-injure for other reasons

Findings like these have led to the identification of certain subgroups of self-injurers in community populations. The most important studies are presented in the following.

Klonsky and Olino (2008)

Klonsky and Olino (2008) examined the severity of self-injury and types of psychiatric problems in a group of 205 college students who had self-injured at least once. Using latent-class analysis, the authors identified four subgroups:

Group 1, the 'experimental group', which accounted for 61% of the sample, is characterized by those who occasionally engaged in NSSI and had the lowest occurrence of clinical symptoms. They had 'experimented' with self-injury a few times and their methods tend to vary.

Group 2, the 'mild NSSI group', accounted for 17% of the sample, engaged in self-injury more frequently, had begun earlier and were more likely to practice biting, hitting and pinching; the members of this subgroup had slightly more psychiatric symptoms than the members of the former group.

Group 3, the 'multiple functions/anxious group', which included 11% of the sample, had a higher occurrence of anxiety and used a wider variety of self-injury methods, including cutting, biting, hitting, hair pulling, pinching and scratching; this group heavily endorsed both social and automatic functions (cf. p. 131), suggesting that these behaviours were multiply reinforced.

Group 4, the 'automatic functions/suicidal group', accounted for 10% of the sample; like subgroup 3, subgroup 4 showed more psychiatric symptoms (depression, anxiety and BPD) and were more likely to have attempted suicide (46%). In this group, 32% had required medical treatment as a result of self-injury. Most had cut themselves in private in service of automatic functions (for example, to regulate negative emotions). They were less impulsive and more likely to plan their acts of self-injury than the other groups. The latter group had severe symptoms, matching those found in self-injuring psychiatric patients.

Whitlock et al. (2008)

Whitlock et al. (2008) surveyed a group of 2101 university students, and to assess typologies of individuals for whom NSSI may have become habitual, the analysis was restricted to 282 students who reported two or more incidents of NSSI. As in the study mentioned above, this study too relied on latent-class analysis and identified three separate groups.

Group 1, 'superficial NSSI', accounted for 15% of the respondents, mainly women (74%), who had self-injured fewer than 11 times, using one specific form of self-injury and engaging in fairly superficial self-injury.

Group 2, 'moderate severity NSSI', included 38% of the sample; it consisted mainly of men (59%), who had a low (2–10) lifetime prevalence. The members of group 2 used one to three different methods to engage in self-battery and light tissue damage.

Group 3, 'high severity NSSI', included 47% of the sample, mainly women (71%), who had engaged in more severe self-injury with greater tissue damage. Using a variety of methods, 81% of the members of this group had self-injured on more than 11 occasions and reported a higher occurrence of eating disorders, suicidal behaviour, exposure to abuse and the use of both pharmacological and psychological therapy for psychiatric disorders than members of the other sub-groups. The latter group presented more psychopathology than the others and was found to require different treatment approaches.

Stanford and Jones (2009)

Stanford and Jones (2009) describe a study of 944 students aged 11–21 years, of whom 234 had engaged in self-injuring behaviour. Using cluster analysis, the authors identified three groups with varying degrees of psychopathology.

Group 1, 'the "normal" group', included 43% of the sample, mainly females (75.4%) who engaged in less severe self-harm and had no sign of psychopathology. Recent self-harm is reported by 28.7%. The group had better family relationships and contact with peers than the pathological group.

Group 2, 'the impulsive group', included 32% of the respondents, with equal gender distribution. Recent self-harm is reported by 24.6%.

Group 3, 'the pathological group', included 25%, who showed a higher degree of psychopathology, including symptoms of anxiety and depression. Recent self-harm is reported by 50.9%. The members of the pathological group were more likely to come from broken homes, to have been exposed to bullying, to have lower self-esteem and to be more socially isolated than the others. A larger number self-identified as non-heterosexual (38.2%).

Bjärehed et al. (2012)

Patterns of NSSI were studied in a community sample of Swedish adolescents in a two-wave longitudinal design that made it possible to study the stability of the behaviour over time (one year). The sample consisted of students in grade 7 (mean age 13.7 years) and grade 8 (mean age 14.7 years). Of the respondents, 41.5% had self-injured within the past six months at the beginning of the study (T1) and 42.9% at the end (T2). The authors identified a number of NSSI subgroups similar to those Klonsky and Olino (2008) found in their study. The groups are all about the same size: among the self-injuring girls, 63% at T1 and 60% at T2 belonged to a group corresponding to 'the experimental group'. Among the self-injuring boys, the corresponding Figures are 60% and 67%. The study found that 7% of the self-injuring girls and 10% of the self-injuring boys have a NSSI behaviour at T1 that places them in a subgroup that matches 'the mild NSSI group'. The subgroup that corresponds most closely to Klonsky and Olino's subgroups (3 and 4) with severe NSSI and psychopathology includes about 25% of the self-injuring girls and 14% of the self-injuring boys in the Swedish study.

Klonsky and Olino (2008) concluded that if their results were generalized, it would mean that approximately 20% of young adults who engage in NSSI have heightened psychiatric problems. The Swedish study of adolescents gives a similar percentage averaged across genders.

Additionally, the study found individual stability among the girls, which means that the same individuals tend to show similar patterns from T1 to T2 for both 'low- and high-frequency NSSI', 'cutting', 'preventing wounds from healing' and 'punching'. Among the boys, only 'low-frequency NSSI' and 'preventing wounds from healing' show individual stability.

The authors stress the importance of the finding that girls who engage frequently in certain circumscribed forms of NSSI (e.g., cutting or cutting combined with scratching) suffer primarily from internalizing problems, which suggests that they use NSSI for affect regulation and may benefit from treatment approaches that help them develop better skills for affect regulation (Bjärehed et al., 2012).

In summary, the studies of self-injury among young non-clinical populations cited above identified certain subgroups that vary with regard to the severity of the self-injury and of psychosocial stressors, including psychopathology. Although all the groups display the same symptom, NSSI, they are quite different and have different needs as regards support and treatment. The studies found most people who self-injure do so relatively rarely and without causing severe tissue damage. The incidents often have the character of experimentation or of 'flirting' with a lifestyle where NSSI is part of a group identity or of projecting a particular persona. In addition to this majority group, one finds two subgroups of individuals who use multiple methods and struggle with more severe psychosocial difficulties. Finally, there appears to be a group with many, and more severe, self-injury incidents, who use a wider variety of methods and show multiple psychiatric symptoms, such as anxiety, depression and attempted suicide.

These and other studies document the diverse make-up of the population. One argument in favour of making NSSI an autonomous diagnosis would be it has clinical unity, in the sense that it represents a specific behaviour. Critics have countered this argument by pointing to the diverse backgrounds and diagnoses of the individuals engaging in the behaviour. The same is true of substance abuse, for example, which *is* recognized as an autonomous diagnostic category. Like substance abuse, NSSI is a non-specific symptom that accompanies (if unsystematically) a wide range of psychiatric diagnoses.

A drawback of categorizing NSSI as an autonomous diagnosis is that the individual patient's specific psychosocial background and personality risk receiving less attention, which is unfortunate because these factors determine the patient's treatment and prognosis. It is therefore crucial to continue to conduct systematic research with a view to understanding the diversity and the specific subgroups found among people who self-injure.

Autonomous diagnosis in DSM-5

In the DSM-5 (American Psychiatric Association, 2013), proposed criteria for a Non-Suicidal Self-Injury Disorder was included in Section 3 in the subsection Conditions for Further Study. The diagnosis stresses that NSSI Disorder is not a part of other disorders (e.g., a symptom of BPD) but is recognized as an autonomous diagnosis. The criteria are not designed as a clinical diagnosis but are intended to facilitate consensus about a common definition for use in research studies.

According to the proposed definition, the NSSI must have occurred on at least five days over the past year without intentions of suicide but aimed at reducing negative feelings, resolving an interpersonal issue or achieving a positive feeling state. The self-injuring person experiences relief in connection with the act, and the diagnosis thus implies an underlying motive of achieving a desired psychological change. The behaviour is not socially sanctioned (e.g., body piercing, tattooing) and causes clinically significant distress or disruption in social functioning.

When NSSI is performed frequently, it will be associated with urgency and craving and thus be experienced as a form of addiction. Over time, the self-inflicted damage may tend to become more severe and more extensive. This implies a risk that the condition may become exacerbated over time.

In a review of 16 empirical studies, Zetterqvist (2015) found that the DSM-5 criteria could be used to identify a subset of individuals who had more general psychopathology and impairment than both clinical controls and those with NSSI who did not meet the DSM-5 criteria. The study found that DSM-5 criteria can also be used for differentiation in relation to patients with BPD and thus seem to constitute a valid and constructive diagnostic construct. There is an ongoing discussion, however, about the relevance of the different criteria in DSM-5. Ammerman et al. (2016) found it clinically relevant to use the proposed criterion A for NSSI disorder (i.e., that the individual has engaged in NSSI on five or more days during the past year), while Muehlenkamp et al. (2017) argue for a higher cut-off score. They found that individuals who have engaged in NSSI on 25 days or more over the past year are likely to experience a range of mental health problems, such as depression, BPD features, substance abuse and suicidal ideation. This distinguishes them significantly from youth reporting NSSI on 5 to 24 days who thus meet the proposed criterion A for NSSI Disorder.

It is important to clarify the relevant criteria for the diagnosis of NSSI Disorder, in part in order to distinguish NSSI Disorder from other, related diagnoses.

Differential diagnoses

Attempted suicide

One of the most important differential diagnoses is attempted suicide or suicidal self-injury. Although clinicians have not always distinguished between suicidal and non-suicidal self-injury, it is important to treat them as different phenomena.

The American Centers for Disease Control and Prevention defines attempted suicide as

> a non-fatal, self-directed, potentially injurious behavior with an intent to die as a result of the behavior; might not result in injury.

There is a considerable overlap between NSSI and suicidal attempt, in that many who self-injure also attempt suicide and vice versa. As many as 70% of individuals who have self-injured are going to attempt suicide at some point, and in a sample of college students, Klonsky and Olino (2008) found that respondents who had engaged in NSSI were 25 times more likely to attempt suicide than those who had not. A study of Swedish adolescents found that 86.7% of those who had attempted suicide reported at least one incidence of NSSI (Zetterqvist et al., 2013). Studies of both community and clinical samples have found that NSSI increases the risk of attempted suicide, constituting a risk factor that serves as a stronger predictor of future suicide attempts than previous attempts (Muehlenkamp, 2014).

The association between NSSI and suicide attempts is evident from a Scottish study with participants aged 18–34 years, which found that 11.3% and 16.2% reported a lifetime history of suicide attempts and non-suicidal self-harm (NSSH), respectively. Of those who attempted suicide, 57.3% had also engaged in NSSH, and of those who reported NSSH, 39.7% also had a history of attempted suicide. It is noteworthy that many of the participants had engaged in the behaviour repeatedly, and indeed there seems to be a parallel course. Of those who had attempted suicide, 60% reported doing so more than once, while 80% of those with a history of NSSH had harmed themselves more than once, and the age of the first episode of NSSH tended to precede the first suicide attempt by about two years (O'Connor et al., 2018). This supports Joiner's (2005) assumption that NSSI lowers the threshold for attempting suicide and thus leads to acquired capability for suicide. Through recurring NSSI the person gets used to confronting pain and bodily harm, which normally serve as a barrier that inhibits the suicidal impulse. Joiner sees this as part of the explanation for the link between self-injury and attempted suicide (the gateway theory).

Some researchers have proposed a continuum for degrees of self-injury. At one end of this continuum one would find indirect, relatively harmless NSSI, such as occasional binge drinking; next, one would find direct, moderate NSSI, such as scratching or hitting oneself; followed by direct, more severe NSSI, such as cutting and burning oneself; and finally, actual suicide attempts or suicide. This gradual scale suggests that a given person may engage in various forms of self-injury, either during the same period or at different times. Both frequency and number of methods have been associated with increased risk for suicide attempt (Matney et al., 2018).

As described by Menninger as early as 1938, self-injury may serve as a form of self-medication that allows the person to avoid determined suicide attempts. One of the common functions of NSSI is to prevent suicidal behaviour (the anti-suicide function), and research suggests that suicide attempts among people who regularly self-injure are often made during periods when self-injury is not being used to manage suicidal behaviour (Gratz, 2006). However, their risk of suicide increases if the affect-regulating function of self-injury diminishes or disappears entirely.

The primary factors distinguishing NSSI from attempted suicide are:

1   *Intent*, which is the most important factor distinguishing NSSI from attempted suicide (Nock & Kessler, 2006). The suicidal intent may be more or less determined or ambivalent, and it can therefore be difficult to distinguish between attempted suicide and self-injury. A subsequent conversation with the patient is crucial for determining the underlying intention and, potentially, for intervening to protect the person (e.g., hospitalization).

2   *Methods and severity of injury* such as cutting, scratching or burning one's skin damages the body but is rarely life-threatening. This stands in contrast to suicide attempts, which are often more severe with regard to methods, injury and risk of death. Approximately 90% of suicides in the United States involve firearms, suffocation or poisoning (Centers for Disease Control and Prevention, 2018). Several studies have found that people who committed suicide used methods that were different from their prior NSSI methods.

3   *The frequency of NSSI versus attempted suicide.* Usually, attempted suicide is a rarer occurrence than NSSI, which some people engage in frequently. While approximately 50% of individuals engaging in NSSI do so only once or twice, some self-injure more than a hundred times. Although suicide attempts may occur frequently for example in connection with a personal crisis or psychiatric hospitalization, few people have several repeated attempts in short order.

4   *Hope versus hopelessness.* Studies show that individuals who attempt to kill themselves are more likely to feel hopelessness than people who self-injure without suicidal intent. Compared to people who have attempted suicide, people who engage in NSSI generally experience significantly greater attraction to life, more reasons for living, more positive future thinking and less hopelessness (Muehlenkamp, 2014).

5   Finally, there are differences in the *individual's reactions* after self-injury with suicidal intent versus NSSI. The latter produces a sense of relief by either regulating negative feelings or inducing positive feelings, which is not the case after an attempted suicide. As Walsh (2006) puts it, the intent behind an attempted suicide is to *terminate* consciousness, while the intent of NSSI is to *modify* it to make it easier to go on living.

It is nevertheless important to maintain a distinction between self-injury with and without suicidal intent. Failure to distinguish between suicidal behaviour and NSSI can lead to inaccurate case conceptualization, risk assessment, treatment and iatrogenic hospitalization (Zetterqvist, 2015). In working with an individual patient, it is thus important to examine the intent behind the self-injuring behaviour.

Borderline Personality Disorder

NSSI has long been regarded as a symptom of BPD, and historically, NSSI was considered as pathognomonic of BPD. 'Recurrent suicidal behavior, gestures, or threats, or self-mutilating behavior' is one of the diagnostic criteria for BPD (301.83) in DSM-5, and 'tendency to self-destructive behaviour' is the corresponding formulation for one of the diagnostic criteria for Emotionally Unstable Personality Disorder, borderline type (F60.31) in ICD-10. Studies have found that up to 80% of patients with BPD have engaged in NSSI at some point in their life (Andrewes et al., 2017), but most people performing NSSI do not have BPD. Patients with BPD who engage in NSSI have more frequent problems with emotion regulation and use NSSI to cope with symptoms of their disorder, including dissociation and suicidal ideation, and as a form of self-punishment (Bracken-Minor & McDevitt-Murphy, 2014).

It is thus important not to base a diagnosis of BPD exclusively on the occurrence of NSSI. Besides the 'tendency to self-destructive behaviour', the essential features of Borderline Personality Disorder are a pervasive pattern of instability of affect, interpersonal relationships and self-image and marked impulsivity. Persons with BPD struggle with intense negative feelings and have significant problems with mentalizing, affect regulation and self-regulation, which makes them extremely vulnerable to NSSI.

Factitious Disorder

In ICD-10 (F68.1) and DSM-5 (300.19), Factitious Disorder is defined as a condition where the patient deliberately (fully or partially consciously) produces recurring or persistent symptoms, sometimes by means of self-injury (e.g., self-embedding behaviour, which is the repeated insertion of objects, such as sewing needles, pins and staples into the soft tissues of, for example, the abdomen or the breast).

Although Factitious Disorder or Munchausen's Syndrome is a form of self-injury, it differs from NSSI in that the patient has a more or less conscious intent of pretending to others that the injury is not self-inflicted but rather the result of somatic illness in a traditional sense, as in the following example:

> A 43-year-old nurse came into a somatic emergency room for treatment of a severe infection in a persistent wound. After a wound swab she was prescribed penicillin and told to contact her own doctor if the infection did not abate. A few days later she contacted her own doctor who found that her CRP (C-Reactive Protein) count was elevated; she also had a fever and her general condition was impaired. Her doctor performed a blood culture and prescribed a different type of antibiotics. A few days later, she presented at the emergency room again, now with signs of sepsis. After

being hospitalized for two days and receiving penicillin intravenously, she improved and was discharged. A few days later, she saw her own physician again, now showing signs of severe infection, and she was hospitalized again for diagnosis and treatment. During her stay, the hospital examined her patient history, including her file from a hospital in a different part of the country, where she had grown up. The file showed that she had been hospitalized repeatedly in both psychiatric and somatic wards due to self-inflicted infections contracted by injecting faeces into her own bloodstream.

Patients who self-injure or pretend to have conditions that require medical treatment are often believed to do so in order to receive care and nurturing (Bass & Halligan, 2014).

Sadomasochism

Sadomasochism is a sexual disorder revolving around ritualized dominance (sadism) or submission (masochism) that may involve pain, humiliation or bondage (ICD-10, F65.5). DSM-5 operates with autonomous diagnoses for, respectively, Sexual Masochism Disorder (302.83) and Sexual Sadism Disorder (302.84).

Both individuals who self-injure and individuals who derive sexual pleasure from sadomasochistic practices experience growing tension before the act, followed by a sense of calm and relief afterwards. Some people who self-injure may act out both masochistic and sadistic impulses, where they feel alienated from their own body (perhaps as a result of dissociation), which may become the object of a veritable sadist attack during the self-injury practice. Thus, they may simultaneously take on the role of acting subject and passive object in a sadomasochistic practice directed at their own body. This fusion of libidinous and aggressive feelings and the objectification of the target of their sexual desire – in this case, their own body – is a characteristic feature of actual perversions or paraphilias.

The self-injuring act in itself is rarely associated with actual sexual arousal. In a study of 250 individuals with chronic self-injury, Favazza (1996) found that 2% were sexually stimulated by the act of planning self-injury, while 3% were stimulated by the self-injuring act, and 20% reported sometimes using NSSI to avoid unpleasant sexual feelings.

There are several spectacular examples of a link between self-injury and masochism. One of the best known is Kirby Dick's documentary about Bob Flanagan (1952–1996), *Sick: The Life and Times of Bob Flanagan, Supermasochist* (1996), which shows Flanagan engaging in a masochistic relationship where he was subjected to extreme physical torture, including having his lips sewn together, having needles pushed through his penis and taking hundreds of blows to his body.

An important part of Flanagan's personal background is that he was born with cystic fibrosis with expectations of an early, painful death. His sadomasochistic performances re-enacted transgressive events from his childhood, where he was held down while doctors subjected him to painful examinations and treatments.

Flanagan's self-injury may be interpreted as a way of achieving some form of control over his childhood traumas, but precisely because the traumas remained unchanged and unprocessed, he was compelled to repeat the self-injuring behaviour over and over again. Although Flanagan characterized himself as a masochist, it may be debated whether his behaviour represents what I have called self-injury by proxy or masochistic practices for sexual gratification, if it even makes sense to draw that distinction in this case.

3 Epidemiology and gender differences

NSSI is a major public health issue, particularly among young adults. Studies from USA, Europe, Australia and other Western countries show that one in five young adults has, at some point in their life, deliberately self-injured without having an intention of suicide. In the United Kingdom, self-injury was one of the top five causes of acute medical admission (Royal College of Psychiatrists, 2006). With this prevalence, self-injury can no longer be explained exclusively as an individual phenomenon that springs from the sufferer's personal background. Although NSSI appears to have become so widespread that it now must be considered a social or a cultural phenomenon, it is called 'the hidden illness' because only a small fraction of people engaging in non-suicidal self-injury get in contact with healthcare professionals (Geulayov et al., 2018).

Around the turn of this century, a number of countries, including the United States, Canada, Australia and the United Kingdom, declared 1 March the official Self-Injury Awareness Day in response to the growing prevalence of NSSI over the past 30 years. The event is marked with lectures and talks by people who have self-injured, and it is possible to buy bracelets and other items to signal sympathy with the cause of prevention and destigmatization. A variety of organizations are involved in marking Self-Injury Awareness Day, and in the UK, for example, LifeSigns (Self-Injury Guidance & Network Support) has a website with information about the organization's efforts (www.lifesigns.org.uk/).

There is good documentation that NSSI is on the rise, and that it is more prevalent today than it was 20 or 30 years ago, but for a number of reasons it is difficult to determine the occurrence of NSSI in various population groups. Thus, we cannot say with any certainty whether the self-injury epidemic has peaked, or whether the prevalence may continue to grow.

The lack of a clear consensus on terminology and definitions of NSSI is a major obstacle for the research effort. Some studies simply fail to define what they mean by self-injury, some apply a definition that includes suicidal acts and yet others focus exclusively on NSSI. That makes it difficult to compare findings across studies.

Moreover, the data collection methods are not always stringent or comparable across studies. Some studies simply ask respondents whether they have ever performed NSSI, without defining the term more specifically. Generally, studies relying on yes/no questionnaires produce a lower prevalence rate than studies that ask the participants to consider a list of specific NSSI methods.

In a meta-study of prevalence research, Muehlenkamp et al. (2012) found a lifetime prevalence of 12.5% in studies asking respondents to mark 'yes' or 'no' to the question 'Have you ever hurt yourself on purpose?', compared to a lifetime prevalence of 23.6% in studies requiring the respondents to consider checklists of specific self-injury behaviours. That is a significant difference.

It is also important to consider the population in question. NSSI among hospitalized psychiatric patients has been reported to lie between 40% (Darche, 1990) and 82.4% (Nock & Prinstein, 2004), while the rate for non-clinical populations averages 18% (Muehlenkamp et al., 2012), with approximately 17% among adolescents (Swannell et al., 2014). The difference may be explained by a greater occurrence of negative emotions among psychiatric patients, which may lead to NSSI, and by the 'social contagion effect', which means that contact with someone who self-injures increases the risk of developing self-injury behaviour. Other factors include the affiliation with alternative subcultures, such as Goths or Emos (Bowes et al., 2015), or LGBT-persons who have an elevated risk of NSSI (Fraser et al., 2018).

Another point to consider is how the respondents were recruited, and how representational the sample is; for example, whether the study was conducted within the framework of an internet forum for young people struggling with emotional problems, or whether it was a questionnaire survey among all the students at a particular educational institution.

Ethnic or national characteristics, gender and geographic distribution also influence prevalence rates. The European multi-centre CASE study, which was carried out in the early 2000s, examined the prevalence of self-injury (including self-injury with suicidal intent) among 15–16-year-olds in the UK, Ireland, the Netherlands, Belgium, Norway, Hungary and Australia. The study found significantly lower rates in the Netherlands and Hungary than in the other countries, which suggests that national characteristics influence the occurrence of self-injury behaviour (Madge et al., 2008). Differences have also been found in the prevalence of NSSI and self-harm in different ethnic groups in the UK (Ali-Sharifi et al., 2015).

The time interval involved in a study has a significant influence on the findings. Some studies look at lifetime prevalence ('have you ever hurt yourself on purpose?'), while others inquire about NSSI within the past 6 or 12 months.

In addition to these methodological questions, there is a tendency to underreport NSSI because many consider it shameful and embarrassing.

The problem of vague and inconsistent definitions of NSSI was diminished with the introduction of NSSI Disorder in the 2013 edition of the Diagnostic and Statistical Manual of Mental Disorders (DSM-5). This newly proposed disorder identifies those with more frequent NSSI (at least five days over the past year) who experience significant distress or interference in one or more areas of life due to their self-injury (cf. pp. 803–805) (American Psychiatric Association, 2013).

Studies using the NSSI-Disorder definition will find a lower frequency of NSSI. In community samples of adolescents, 3.1–6.7% have been found to meet

NSSI-D criteria (Manca et al., 2014; Zetterqvist et al., 2013a) as compared to about 18%, which is the prevalence found in studies using the traditional definition of NSSI (Swannell et al., 2014). These findings indicate that adolescents with NSSI-D are more severely affected by NSSI than the larger group of adolescents who self-injure.

Prevalence in different age groups

A few studies have examined the prevalence of NSSI in a broad age span of the general population. These studies have revealed varying prevalence levels, perhaps because they were conducted at different times, in different cultures and using different methods and time intervals. Four studies have included a representative sample of the general population: Briere and Gil (1998) found that 4% of Americans had self-injured on at least one occasion; a few years later, Klonsky (2011) found a prevalence of 5.9% in the American population; and a Danish study found a lifetime prevalence of 11% (VIOSS, 2015). Finally, Plener et al. (2016) found that a history of at least one occurrence of NSSI was reported by 3.1% of a representative sample of the German population. The methodological variations between the four studies are too big to warrant direct comparison.

Prevalence rates vary greatly across different age groups, which will therefore be discussed separately.

Children

There are few systematic studies of self-injury among children, but there are indications that NSSI may begin in early childhood, perhaps as early as the age of 4 years (Yates et al., 2008). In a community sample of children, Barrocas et al. (2012) found that 7.6% of children in third grade report NSSI and about 5% of college students with self-injury behaviour report that their self-injury began before the age of 10 years (Whitlock et al., 2006). Ross and Heath's (2002) study of self-injury among high-school students found that 25% had begun to self-injure before the age of 12 years. Early onset of NSSI increases the risk of problems later in life. Muehlenkamp et al. (2017) found that individuals who began self-injuring at or before age 12 reported significantly more lifetime acts of NSSI, greater method versatility and more medically severe NSSI than those with later onset.

Further, an increasing number of statements from preschool teachers and child psychologists reflect a growing prevalence of self-injury among children. However, we lack systematic studies of the phenomenon. Children with autism, developmental impairments and other psychosocial problems are at elevated risk of developing self-injury (Whitlock & Selekman, 2014).

Among younger children, biting, scratching or hitting oneself are the most common self-injury methods, while older children and teens use the same methods as young adults (cutting, hitting or burning themselves).

Adolescents

Adolescence is a time of profound changes in a young person's life. This is the time when one develops one's own identity, leaves childhood behind and moves towards a new degree of independence in a new phase of life. To a vulnerable young person, this can be a challenging time. Stress factors have been suggested as part of the explanation why many begin to self-injure between the age of 12 and 18 years.

In a systematic review, Cipriano et al. (2017) found that 7.5–46.5% of adolescents in non-clinical samples had performed NSSI (or self-harm), and in another systematic review, Swannell et al. (2014) estimated that the overall pooled NSSI prevalence was 17.2% among adolescents. A Swedish community study of young people aged 15 to 17 in the general population found much higher Figures: 35.6 % of the adolescents reported having engaged in NSSI at least once during the past year. Of these, 14.2% reported only one episode of NSSI, 30.8% reported 2–5 episodes, 13.8% reported 6–10 episodes and finally 41.2% reported more than 11 NSSI episodes. Lifetime prevalence of NSSI at least once was reported by 41.6% of the adolescents (Zetterqvist et al., 2013)

Follow-up studies generally show that many who self-injure during adolescence are at increased risk of suicide attempts, depression and other psychological disorders as adults (Chesin et al., 2017). However, most adolescents experiment with NSSI without developing significant problems later in life.

Young adults

Studies of college, university and upper-secondary school students have found that at least one in five has experiences with self-injury. In a systematic review, Cipriano et al. (2017) found that nearly 40% of university students had performed NSSI. A large study of NSSI among American college students found that 17% had self-injured at least once, and 75% of this group reported repeated incidents (Whitlock et al., 2006). In the same study, 38.6% reported that they began their self-injury behaviour in their late teens.

The prevalence of self-injury is elevated among psychiatric patients; a study of young adults who were psychiatric inpatients found that 68% had self-injured over the past 12 months (Guerry & Prinstein, 2010).

Elderly people

In an Australian community study, Martin and Swannell (2016) found a significant decline in the incidence of NSSI after the age of 25 years: 4.1% of people between 60 and 69 years of age had performed NSSI within the prior 12 months, while the same was true for 1.4% of people older than 70 years. Other studies conclude that self-injury among elderly people is closely associated with attempted suicide. Somatic and mental illness, divorce and economic and work-related problems appear to constitute common risk factors (Hawton et al., 2013). This is confirmed by a British study which found that self-harm is a major risk factor for suicide, with people over 65 years of age reportedly having greater suicidal intent than any other age group (Morgan et al., 2018).

Onset, course and prognosis

Most of the young people who self-injure initiate the behaviour between the ages of 11 and 16 years, but different studies have led to different findings. Gillies et al. (2018) found that the mean age of initiating self-injury was 13 years, and Plener et al. (2015) reported that the prevalence of NSSI steadily increases from the age of 12 years and peaks between 14 and 16 years of age; by the age of 18 years, the prevalence of NSSI appeared to decrease. In a meta-analysis, the probability of onset peaked around the age of 14–15 years, and a second peak was observed around the age of 20, while NSSI was less likely to begin after the age of 21 years (Gandhi et al., 2018)

However, other studies have found that the variation in age of onset appears to follow a normal distribution, where about 25% begin between the ages of 10 and 14 years, 27% between the ages of 15 and 16 years, and 38.6% between the ages of 17 and 24 years (Whitlock et al., 2006). Some begin even earlier, and some later; thus, the age of onset varies considerably.

Martine is referred from a rape crisis centre because she has begun to cut herself in different parts of her body after she was raped in a doorway early one morning by a man she had met in a bar. At the time of the incident she was 27 years old. Already the day after the rape she made a deep cut in her wrist, and she explains that when it happened, she was thinking about taking her own life by cutting her small artery. Ultimately, she was too scared to go through with it, but she experienced that the pain of cutting temporarily extinguished the thoughts and emotions associated with the assault, because it forced her to concentrate on something else: staunching the bleeding and finding a plaster to bandage her wound. Martine was referred for a session at the rape crisis centre soon after the rape, but she still relived the situation over and over, although she was now able to disrupt her flashbacks by cutting. She had never previously deliberately self-injured.

Although most young people who self-injure experience spontaneous remission before they reach adulthood, and most have only engaged in the behaviour a few times, the risk of repeating the behaviour is considerable, and many continue once they have begun. Approximately 50% of individuals engaging in NSSI do so only once or twice, while for others, the behaviour has a chronic course (Whitlock et al., 2006). Another study found that 25% have self-injured just once and 32%

two to three times, while 20% have more than four occurrences of self-injury over the past 12 months (Muehlenkamp & Gutierrez, 2007). A similar pattern is seen among Danish upper-secondary school students: Møhl and Skandsen (2012) found that 28.9% had self-injured just once, 32.3% had done so two to five times, 12.4% six to 20 times and 9.3% more than 20 times within the past 12 months.

Risk factors for persistent self-injury behaviour include bullying, school-related stress, problems in relation to friends and parents, alcohol, drugs, sexual identity issues and psychiatric symptoms (cf. p. 91 ff.) for a description of additional risk factors.

Many begin after hearing about self-injury from a friend, and the closer the relationship is, the greater the risk of 'social contagion'. Many report that they initially self-injured in connection with a specific conflict or stressor, but that they did so because they had encountered the practice online (for example on Instagram). Yet others report that the inspiration for self-injury came from copying a popular musician or other celebrity.

For an overview of studies of self-injury prevalence, see Gillies et al. (2018) and Swannell et al. (2014).

Gender differences

The existing literature is inconsistent with regard to the presence of gender differences in the prevalence of NSSI, with some studies showing a higher prevalence for women compared to men and other studies showing no difference.

A number of studies have found that women are more likely to self-injure. A meta-analysis of 172 community-based studies of self-harm among 12-to-18-years-olds conducted between 1990 and 2015 in 41 countries found that females were 1.7 times more likely than men to self-harm (Gillies et al., 2018), and Monto et al. (2018) found that nearly twice as many upper-secondary school girls than boys had performed NSSI. In a meta-analysis of 120 studies concentrating on NSSI, Bresin and Schoenleber (2015) found significant heterogeneity in the effect size across studies; however, overall they found that women are 1.5 times more likely than men to report NSSI. The authors describe this as a small effect size in epidemiological studies. They found that the gender differences were higher in clinical samples, which could affect the overall result of the survey.

The European multi-centre CASE study found a larger share of women than men self-injuring in all seven countries (Madge et al., 2008); 13.5% of the women and 4.3% of the men had self-injured at least once in their life, and 8.9% of women, compared to 2.6% of the men, had self-injured within the past year. One explanation for this over-representation of women could be that the study involves all types of self-injury, including overdosing on medicine. Heath et al. (2009) point out that any study that includes overdosing in its definition of self-injury will find a larger share of women, while studies that only look at physical damage to body tissue, such as cutting, burning, scratching and hitting oneself, will find an approximately equal prevalence of self-injury among women and men.

Other studies, however, have not found significant gender differences in the prevalence of NSSI (e.g., Gratz et al., 2002; Hilt et al., 2008; Møhl & Skandsen, 2012; Andover et al., 2010).

It seems to be a persistent assumption that only women self-injure; this perception may have been fuelled by some of the early descriptions in the scientific literature of self-injuring patients, which overlook or exclude men.

Graf and Mallin's (1967) description of a typical cutter is often quoted and has undoubtedly contributed to perpetuating the image of the self-injuring person as a women:

> an attractive, intelligent, unmarried young woman who is either promiscuous or overtly afraid of sex, easily addicted and unable to relate to others. . . . She slashes her wrists indiscriminately and repeatedly at the slightest provocation, but she does not commit suicide. She feels relief with the commission of her act.
>
> (Graf & Mallin, 1967, p. 41)

Angelotta (2015) points out that the literature that identified the prototypical cutter as young and female simply ignored male cutters. In a study of 21 'wrist slashers' from 1964, the one male patient was excluded because the authors 'felt that he was atypical' (Graf & Mallin, 1967). Another study from 1972 of patients with a history of wrist cutting included 24 women, while the 11 males with histories of cutting were excluded because 'the findings were so different than those of the women' (Rosenthal et al., 1972, p. 47). The exclusion of men was contested in at least one article in 1971 by the psychiatrists Clendenin and Murphy. They examined the distribution of male and female cutters based on St. Louis police reports. There were 65 cutters in total, 40% of whom were men (Clendenin & Murphy, 1971). The finding that 40% of cutters were men was replicated in a study of cutters admitted to the emergency department at Yale New Haven Hospital (Weissman, 1975). A review of all published cases of low lethality, repetitive self-harm between 1960 and 1980 found that of the 56 individual cases identified, 27 were men and 29 were women (Pattison & Kahan, 1983).

It is interesting that this perception of self-injury is so reflective of stereotypical gender perceptions that the researchers deliberately *chose* to exclude men from the early studies, thus confirming their preconceived notions. Sarah Chaney (2017) points out that this gender bias stems from the Victorian era, when female hysteria was used as a psychological explanation model to understand the manipulative 'needle girls'. The link between 'hysteria' and 'self-mutilation' was so entrenched in the mind of the male researchers that their a priori assumption was that a cutter is, by logical necessity, a woman.

This gender bias has probably been perpetuated by a variety of factors: 1) there is a preponderance of woman who report having injured themselves in studies that include overdosing on medicine, as outlined above; 2) far more women than men seek treatment for self-injury. This reflects a general tendency for women to seek professional help when they have a problem. Thus, there are far more female than male psychiatric patients who self-injure; 3) further, the healthcare system finds what it looks for; if we expect to find indications of self-injury in women, we find it, and, conversely: if we do not expect to find self-injury in men, it will go unnoticed; and 4) finally, it may make a difference that women and men tend to self-injure in different ways. The general difference is that women cut themselves, while men often self-injure by punching a wall or giving themselves a black eye. The injuries men inflict on themselves may be more difficult to diagnose unambiguously as self-injury, while injuries or scars from cutting are more easily identified as such. With the gender matrix that continues to dominate in the healthcare sector, it will be easier for a treatment professional to spot that a bruise or other signs of physical damage may be the result of self-injury.

Women cut; men hit themselves

Many studies of NSSI have found that men and women use different methods for self-injury. In a study of high-school students, Møhl and Skandsen (2012) found cutting to be the most common method of self-injury among women, used by 62.3% of the women who had self-injured, while the most common form of self-injury among the men in the study was hitting themselves, used by 63.8%. However, 25.9% of the men in the study cut and 32.1% burned themselves. For the women, 39% hit themselves, and 48.6% self-injured by scratching their skin.

The men continue for longer and have more incidents of self-injury than the women, who tend to have a decreasing number of self-injury incidents during their upper-secondary school years (Møhl & Skandsen, 2012). This matches Claes et al.'s (2007) finding that men who self-injure have more incidents per day than women who self-injure.

As described above, injuries and scars from cutting are unambiguous signs of self-injury and are often associated with profound feelings of shame. Generally, women seem to put in a greater effort to hide their self-injury than men do. Most women are alone when they self-injure, while a relatively larger share of men self-injure while others are around (Whitlock et al., 2011). Women also focus more on wearing clothes that hide signs of self-injury and on avoiding social situations where the body is exposed (for example going to the beach or showering with others) (Hodgson, 2004). The decrease in self-injury incidents found in the study referenced above (Møhl & Skandsen, 2012) may occur because the self-injury becomes harder hide, for example, from a lover. The men, on the other hand, continue their self-injury behaviour, including by hitting themselves, and it is easier for a young man to explain a bruise or a fracture as the result of a sports injury or a brawl than it is for a woman to explain wounds or scars from cutting. The sort of physical injuries that men may incur after hitting themselves may even be viewed as a sign of masculinity and strength (Claes et al., 2007). (For an overview, see Bresin & Schoenleber, 2015.)

The stated gender differences reflect prevailing gender stereotypes in the Western world. Under emotional pressure, women are generally more likely to internalize their emotional reactions and to turn their anger against themselves, with the result that they develop depressions or cut themselves, while men are gener-ally more likely to externalize their emotional reactions. Thus, they turn their anger outwards, acting it out on others. Saying that 'women injure themselves, while men injure others', is obviously not an absolute truth when it comes to self-injury. However, pounding a wall and thus injuring one's hand may be seen as a compromise, where the man directs his aggression simultaneously outwards and at himself.

Ted is a 26-year-old university student who is referred for treatment for self-injury. He uses a variety of methods to self-injure, depending on how he feels. He has burned himself with cigarettes, cut himself, scratched him-self until he bled and bitten himself. However, the most frequent form of impulsive self-injury is to pound the wall with his fist or to hit himself. In the weekly therapy sessions, however, it was easy to see how his past week had been; if it had been a bad week he would show up with bruises in his face, and once he had a split eyebrow after punching himself.

A literary example of a man who self-injures

Some men practice a form of NSSI that is clearly about self-directed aggression. An insightful literary example is found in Sadie Jones's novel *The Outcast* (2008). In the following scene Lewis, who has a traumatic background, which includes losing his mother and never having been close to his father, considers putting his hand through a window pane so that he can cut himself on the shards:

> He put his hand onto the cold glass pane. He felt far away from himself. He imagined putting his fist through it and the jagged hole in the pane and the points of glass still attached to the wood. He imagined dragging his wrist and his arm against them so they would cut into him. He didn't think he would feel it.
> [. . .] He closed his eyes to stop imagining it, but it was the same, picturing the glass going into him, needing to do it. His heart started going quickly, pushing the cold blood around. [. . .] He realised he'd been scraping his arm and stopped doing it. (p. 142)

Lewis senses the powerful need to self-injure but initially manages to control his urges and merely scratch his arm. Later, he actually does injure himself:

> He went into the bathroom and shut the door and locked it. He stood at the mirror, and looked, and the need to damage himself took over. All he could think of was hurting himself and how to do it. He picked up his father's razor. It was an old-fashioned one, the kind you open. He opened the razor and

looked at the blade. He knew he wouldn't feel it if he were to stick it right into himself – but the sight of the blade stopped him for a second. [. . .] He held out his left arm and pushed up the sleeve with the hand holding the razor. He pressed the blade against the skin immediately, just at the feel of the sharp blade on the skin, his heart went quicker and blood came back into him. He was breathless with wanting to do it. He could taste the need to hurt himself in his mouth, and when he did, he cried with the relief of it. He made a long cut down his forearm and the red line of filled with bright blood very quickly and started to run. He was frightened of the blood and trying not to cut too deep, hurting himself just enough – and it did hurt, and he held his arm over the basin and rested his forehead on the edge of the basin, and the sadness and the hurting were comforting to him because he could feel them.

[. . .]

He felt pathetic and small and stupid now. What a stupid crazy sick thing to do, he told himself; if they know about this, they will put you in a special school, they'll put you in a hospital.

(Jones, 2008, pp. 142–143)

4 Self-injury as a sign of the times?

In many ways, Louise's story from the introduction of this book is characteristic of the current manifestation of self-injury that is becoming increasingly common among adolescents and young adults today. NSSI has been called the 'the new pathology' of our time, and indeed, any historical period has its own specific pathologies reflecting its particular challenges. This raises the interesting question of why certain pathologies arise, as patients 'choose' their symptoms from the cultural pool of symptoms.

During the 1970s and 1980s, eating disorders became prevalent in the Western world and quickly came to dominate in the media discourse as the current scourge. From the mid-1990s NSSI, in particular cutting, came to dominate the pathological landscape.

The common factor for individuals with eating disorders and NSSI is their attempt to control their lives by controlling their bodies, thus turning the body into an arena for social and psychological deformation. The language of the body is tangible and physical. Hence, the disorders of any historical period enter into a dialogue with contemporary culture, and the key symptoms are never arbitrary, although they are also not necessarily predictable.

Eating disorders became a major concern in the Western world after the economic boom times of the 1960s. With food shortages and malnourishment eradicated, the problem now was how to make healthy choices, given the abundance of food and variety in shops and restaurants in the Western world and the near-fetishist treatment of food in gastronomic books, magazines and TV shows. NSSI, in particular cutting, is similarly gaining prevalence at a time when the consumption of pain medicine is seeing explosive growth, and the ability of medical science to manage pain is extremely effective. Most surgical procedures can now be performed virtually pain-free. We have developed an instrumental understanding of pain as something that can be reduced or removed with a pill or a shot. Even toddlers are consuming large amounts of paracetamol (acetaminophen) and other over-the-counter drugs, given to them as a quick fix by their parents. Just a few years ago, headache in young children was viewed as a non-specific symptom that was often best treated by snuggling up in mom's or dad's arms. In parallel with the development of a pain-averse culture we are seeing a growing fascination with various self-imposed painful practices, such as sadomasochism, sexual bondage, extreme sports, tattoos and piercings. 'Jackass' stunts and train-surfing may also be seen as potentially self-injuring behaviours that cause pain. This is certainly not the whole story about the 'epidemic' of self-injury, but it may be an important element.

Both the manifestations of the pathologies and our understanding of them are shaped by historical and cultural factors. This leads to variations both in symptomatology – what ails people – and in our interpretations of these common conditions. The perception of self-injury varies considerably across different cultures and historical periods.

Gilman (2013) wrote that much of the existing literature on the history of self-injury falsely presents it as a transhistorical category, rejecting the view held by other scholars, who view self-injury as a universal human phenomenon that has existed across historical periods and cultures and has involved virtually all parts of the human body. In 1871, Darwin thus described self-mutilation as a universal behaviour: 'hardly any part of the body, which can be unnaturally modified, has escaped' (1871, p. 336; quoted from Gilman, 2013). In a contemporary context, Favazza (1996) has pointed out that the only organs of the human body to escape voluntary, ritual mutilation are the anus and the eyes. However, Favazza's observation is already outdated: anal tattoos are now being performed, as evidenced in YouTube videos, and the recent emergence of cosmetic ink injections into the sclera, or white, of the eyes may be seen as a form of culturally accepted but extreme self-injury involving the eyes.

To understand the meaning of different forms of self-injury in different cultures and at different times, it is important to view any specific form of self-injury in the context of contemporary culture. For example, Chaney (2017) notes that voluntary self-castration became more common during the second half of the nineteenth century as a form of protection against masturbation, which was then considered an illness ('self-abuse') and as a cause of insanity, blindness or even death. 'Masturbatory insanity' was a frequent cause for admission to mental hospitals at the time. Similarly, bloodletting was a standard medical practice during the sixteenth and seventeenth centuries, and many people applied self-performed bloodletting for therapeutic purposes, including Elizabeth T., who is introduced below. Thus, bloodletting during the sixteenth and seventeenth centuries should not primarily be seen as a manifestation of self-injury or mental illness, as it is today, where some use bloodletting with a syringe as a form of self-injury that is more easily concealed. The point is that the self-injury *has a function*: people self-injure in order to feel better, to avoid feeling worse or because they cannot find any other form of relief. Thus, self-injury should be understood as a coping mechanism where the person uses the body as a way to deal with life.

In the following, I briefly mention certain specific forms of self-injury as they are described in literature in order to illustrate the diversity and social context of the phenomenon of self-injury.

Historical descriptions of self-injury

Cleomenes

The oldest detailed description of self-harm associated with mental illness, according to Favazza (1996), comes from Herodotus, who ca. 450 BCE described how the captured Spartan Cleomenes in desperation took a knife and 'sliced his flesh into strips, working upwards to his thighs, hips, and sides until he reached the belly, which he chopped into mincemeat' (quoted from Favazza, 1996, p. 18). Cleomenes is evidently out of his mind, and today we would probably say that he was in a psychotic state during this self-assault.

Religiously motivated self-injury

The Bible contains multiple examples of self-injury. One, in the New Testament, deals with a man who was 'possessed by a legion of demons'.

> This man lived in the burial caves, and no one could bind him anymore, not even with a chain. For he had often been chained hand and foot, but he tore the chains apart and broke the irons on his feet. No one was strong enough to subdue him. Night and day among the tombs and in the hills he would cry out and cut himself with stones.
>
> (Mark 5:1–5)

When asked his name, he answers, 'My name is Legion . . . for we are many' (Mark 5:9).

Apart from the fact that he is described as 'possessed', we do not know anything about Legion, but he comes across as a desperate, suffering man, and in modern terms we might call him psychotic. Perhaps he is hearing voices telling him to cut himself with stones?

The words of the Bible may be taken literally, and throughout history, atonement of Christ's suffering has been a frequent motivation for self-injury.

> If your hand or your foot causes you to stumble, cut it off and throw it away. It is better for you to enter life maimed or crippled than to have two hands or two feet and be thrown into eternal fire. And if your eye causes you to stumble, gouge it out and throw it away. It is better for you to enter life with one eye than to have two eyes and be thrown into the fire of hell.
>
> (Matthew 18:8–9)

This text might have inspired the 48-year-old widow who, in 1846, gouged her eyes out, walked the streets naked, asking anyone and everyone to marry her and requested that the doctors amputate her hands and feet. We do not know, but a literal reading of the Bible has frequently led to concrete acts. During the second and third centuries of the Common Era, voluntary self-castration was a well-known practice, both as a pagan ritual and in early Christian religions; in the latter case it served as a way of realizing the words of the Bible (Chaney, 2017).

> For there are eunuchs who were born that way, and there are eunuchs who have been made eunuchs by others – and there are those who choose to live

like eunuchs for the sake of the kingdom of heaven. The one who can accept this should accept it.

(Matthew 19:12)

During medieval times, several forms of religiously motivated self-injury arose, including asceticism, isolation, fasting and self-induced pain, for example through flagellation, which became a widespread practice during the later Middle Ages in Europe as a literal embodiment of the suffering of Christ. Chaney (2017) notes that there was a strong performative element to religious flagellation, and groups of flagellants would travel from town to town to engage in group rituals. 'The flagellants used the body as an instrument of penance and devotion, to expiate sin and to praise God' (ibid., p. 38).

Flagellation as a group activity was eventually outlawed by the church because it became too popular and spectacular and thus challenged the dominant role of the official church. Perhaps this is an early example of self-injury spreading through 'social infection', as it is spreading today through social media?

Bloodletting

As mentioned above, bloodletting was for centuries a common and approved healing practice, which spread as a means for ordinary people to handle mental suffering. Chaney (2017) writes about the 38-year-old housewife Elizabeth T., who in 1860 was admitted to Bethlem Royal Hospital diagnosed with acute melancholia. Elizabeth had sought her own treatment prior to the admission, in part by drawing 'blood which she fancies would relieve her'. On one occasion, she had rushed into a chemist's shop and asked to be cupped immediately, 'as the only means to relieve the distress of the head'. When admitted, she had wounds on her right temple and left hand, both self-inflicted with a pair of scissors, and she insisted that her actions were intended therapeutically. Elizabeth's behaviour was interpreted as a symptom of mental distress, but only because a 'supernatural voice' had commanded her to 'go and be cupped'. In fact, Elizabeth was merely following the advice of a famous contemporary book: Isabella Beeton's *Book of Household Management* (1861) contained instructions on the performance of bleeding to be used at home in 'cases of great emergency' that rendered her behaviour meaningful.

The needle girls

Many of the early medical descriptions of self-injury are found in spectacular patient histories published in medical journals or monographs. The case of the young Jewish woman Rachel Hertz became known worldwide. From 1807 to 1826, several doctors followed her closely due to a series of inexplicable symptoms, including stomach aches, fatigue, headaches and insomnia. Later, she vomited blood and had violent seizures, numbness and urine retention. The doctors perceived her condition as critical, and Dr Herholdt discovered a tumour in her abdomen that caused acute spasms when touched. 'Being of the opinion that the patient was at death's door', Dr Herholdt made 'a deep incision into the tumour at the tender spot and discovered a narrow, hard foreign object, which turned out to be an oxidized sewing needle' (p. 4). Over the course of the following years, Herholdt surgically removed a total of 389 needles from inside her body, and a few years later, observations through a hidden spyhole in a door to her room revealed her suffering to be self-inflicted. She was accused of deception and faking illness and entrusted into the care of a priest who was to oversee her moral and religious education. One of my own ancestors, Dr N. C. Møhl, who also saw Ms Hertz, wrote in a letter to the Danish scientist P. W. Lund that she,

> for whose autopsy knives were being sharpened mere days before the discovery of her deception, has now recovered with such rapid haste that only a few months later she was occupied with domestic chores – ironing, laundry and raising her host's young son.
>
> (Michelsen, 1989, p. 24)

Today she would probably have been diagnosed as suffering from Factitious Disorder or so-called self-embedding behaviour (Mannarino, 2017). Many descriptions followed of similar 'needle girls', as this new type of patient became known. They received considerable attention in medical journals during the mid-nineteenth century. In December 1850, the English Dr Budd published an article in *The Lancet*, 'The mania of thrusting needles into the flesh', describing a patient who was admitted to King's College Hospital suffering from stomach pains and fits of vomiting. Dr Budd discovered the cause when he examined the outside of her stomach and felt 'hard and resisting bodies' below and 'little white scars . . . scattered about' (p. 676) on the surface of the skin. Over the following ten days, about 50 needles were removed from the patient's abdomen. In the article, Dr Budd discussed whether the act was committed 'under the influence of hysteria' or whether it should be understood as a symptom of madness. Over the next four decades, doctors increasingly came to favour the former explanation. The American doctors Gould and Pyle stated that the 'needle girls' engaged in a 'peculiar type of self-mutilation . . . sometimes seen in hysterical persons' of 'piercing their flesh with numerous needles or pins' (Gould & Pyle, 1897; quoted from Chaney, 2017). Interestingly, ever since this discovery, self-injury has been perceived as a female phenomenon – to this day, it remains a frequent misperception that only women self-injure.

Miss A – the first modern description of self-injury

One of the first descriptions of a self-injury in a non-psychotic psychiatric patient was published in 1913 by Dr L. E. Emerson, who held a PhD in experimental psychology from Harvard University. His treatment of the patient was psychoanalytic, and he offered many interesting reflections on the case. The subject was the 23-year-old female factory worker Miss A, who

> came to the Hospital with a self-inflicted cut on her left arm. Her arm had many other scars, and there was one on her breast: she said she had cut herself

twenty-eight or thirty times; and on the calf of her right leg was a scar forming the letter W.

(p. 42)

In a scuffle that occurred when 'her cousin [. . .] attempted a sexual assault', she accidently cut herself with a bread knife and discovered that cutting offered relief from a headache and from a 'queer feeling' which she could not describe. After this incident she began to cut herself intentionally in order to achieve relief from depression and other painful feelings.

> When I had cut my arm the bad feelings went away. [. . .] Before I cut myself I had what I called a crazy headache, and after I had let blood my headache went away, and I thought that the cutting of my wrist, and letting the blood flow had cured it.

Bloodletting remained a popular and widely used therapy well into the nineteenth century, and it is understandable that she would consider bloodletting a cure. Bleeding was viewed as a regular natural process that aided the healthy function of the body (Chaney, 2017). Miss A's menstrual cycle was irregular, and hoping that cutting could '*help* [her] *to menstruate regularly*', she would cut herself every four weeks.

She describes trying – and failing – to control the urge: 'I tried hard not to cut myself again'. Sometimes she cut to induce a positive feeling. She frequently thought about self-injury and was preoccupied with the act before engaging in it. 'I had tried hard to control myself' but then changed her mind: 'I did not want to try not to cut myself. What was the use, nobody cared' (p. 47). 'At last I could not stand it any longer' (Emerson, 1913).

Miss A had a troubled childhood with a cruel father who terrorized the entire family, and between the ages of 8 and 14 she was sexually abused by an uncle, who 'was accustomed almost daily to masturbate her'. When she was 12 years old, he attempted to rape her. She was offered money to have sex with her brother, and the analyst wrote that 'her family's sexual morality is suggested by the fact that she said all her brothers but one asked her for "connections" (i.e., coitus)'. Emerson noted 'the multiplicity of motives' for her self-mutilation and remarked that 'the "indispensable condition" for the later self-mutilation was the psychosexual trauma of childhood' (p. 50). Emerson also pointed out that 'the patient was not afraid of pain, but she was unable to bear mental anguish' and noted a 'strong component of masochism', a sadistic identification with the aggressor, and 'sexual relief through symbolical masturbation' (i.e., cutting). She had the 'will to live a full life', as demonstrated by her almost overwhelming desire to have a child; this prevented her from committing suicide and compelled her to get by, instead, with partial self-destruction. Emerson treated her successfully, stating that at the time of writing she had gone 14 months without cutting herself, although he stressed that 'it is too short a time upon which to base any prophecy of the future, yet it does give a certain ground for hope' (Emerson, 1913, p. 54).

Although there are differences between Miss A and Louise from the case described in the Introduction, there are also similarities in the underlying dynamics behind their self-injury. Both use cutting as a form of affect regulation and as a way of escaping a painful reality. They self-injure in order to achieve immediate relief. Both have intense self-hatred and have difficulty describing the emotions that prompt their self-injury. Both have been subjected to sexual assault, and in both cases, their self-injury is driven by an urge for independence. Both dream of a good life – and who among us doesn't? However, it may be difficult for outsiders to look past the self-injurious behaviour, which will appear inexplicable to most people.

A major difference between the two women is that they live in different historical eras, and thus, their self-injury occurs in different contexts. Louise lives in a world where self-injury is widespread – one in five upper-secondary students self-injures – and the object of considerable media attention. Almost everyone in the Western world knows about cutting and have an opinion about it. Thus, the people around Louise inevitably attribute meaning to her self-injury and perceive as a statement about who she is.

Skin

Slicing through one's own skin with a knife, a razor blade, a shard of glass, a corner snapped off a credit card or any other sharp object is the most common form of self-injury. It is remarkable that the most common form of NSSI involves injuring the surface of the body – the skin – as this practice leaves such obvious marks. Perhaps it is less surprising when we consider that we live in a time when self-fashioning and self-promotion play such a crucial role in social interactions. Moreover, the skin plays both a concrete and a symbolic role in delimiting the self.

The skin is the boundary between the individual and the world – between me and not-me. This is where the self meets the environment, where inner meets outer. Infants are psychologically awakened by sensory contact through the skin and receives some of their most important stimuli via the skin: warmth, caresses and the physical sense of being held and contained. If the infant does not receive this stimulation, early death is a real risk. Skin contact is vital to our survival and forms the basis for our earliest conscious memories of intimacy and physical contact (cf. Chapter 6). Held in the mother's arms, the infant senses her physical presence, warmth and emotional state – whether she is tense and nervous or calm and relaxed.

Our skin reveals our feelings. We blush or pale, get goose bumps when we are cold and get damp with sweat when we are hot. We also use our skin as a means of self-expression: we spend hours lying in the sun to get a tan, we use moisturizers and we wear make-up to signal who we are, or who we would like to be. The American anthropologist Mary Douglas (2003, p. 143) writes that 'what is carved in the human flesh is an image of society', thus pointing to the implied cultural signals in our symptoms and behaviours.

By decorating or mutilating our skin, for example through body art or cutting, we convey a message that relies on cultural codes. It is culture that imbues the imprint on our skin with meaning. That includes wrinkles, marks, tanning, scars, piercings and tattoos, all of which tell part of our story and are often used deliberately to frame that story.

The skin is like a canvas we can use to express our inner world. Thus, in more than one sense, it is a highly sensitive organ that most people who self-injure choose as their target or medium. Cutting, hitting or burning oneself can alter one's mood, offer distraction from inner pain or communicate one's inner feelings to oneself and others. Self-injury is thus not just a way of acting out inner pain by taking it out on the body but also a means of communication and of styling the body that goes far beyond simply inflicting pain.

Late modern society

Over the past 50 years, life in the Western world has moved towards ever greater personal freedom and individualization. Traditions, family, religion and social class no longer determine the organization of a person's life. This cultural liberation has provided unprecedented possibilities for choosing and shaping our own lives or, paraphrasing Ulrich Beck: individuals living in late modern society have the ability to construct their own *biographies*.

In the Western world, we have moved from a society shaped by destiny to one shaped by choice, where identity is no longer inherited but is instead shaped by individuals themselves, based on the countless options provided by a given culture. Recipes for 'the good life' are offered by commercials and lifestyle magazines covering diet, fashion, sex and family life, interior design, travel and other ingredients in the formation of modern human identity in a consumer society. Anthony Giddens (1991) argues that people living in late modern society are subject to a *reflexive project* that involves the most intimate aspects of existence. This reflexivity extends to the body itself, which can be moulded and used in a self-fashioning project. The body is no longer a passive object but has become an active part of an action system and is made to represent whatever the individual is or strives to be. This freedom to shape ourselves and our own identities inevitably causes us to compare ourselves with others; in this comparison, we often fall short of our own idealized images of what and who we strive to be.

However, freedom of choice and the ability to fashion our own selves not only represent possibility and freedom but have become the relentless requirements of modern society, along with self-realization and the *obligation* to unfold our potential. If we falter or fail in this project, in our own and others' eyes, the responsibility is entirely our own. Hence, the other side of the coin is the responsibility to make the *right* choices.

Modern life may offer advantages for resilient and flexible individuals who have the psychological and social ability to manage this freedom and benefit from it, but is less positive for those who do not have what it takes to construct 'the good life' for themselves. Social isolation, loneliness, substance abuse, divorce, anxiety, depression and self-injury may be regarded as signs of suffering that afflict individuals and are thus viewed as individual problems, to be addressed or solved as such. People who fail to build a meaningful and coherent life risk developing symptoms, including self-injury. Giddens (1991) points out that with increasing freedom comes an added need for ontological security, a stable sense of identity.

It is not helpful, however, to make each individual solely responsible for dealing with his or her own problems, when these involve important cultural and social dimensions, as is the case with self-injury. It is not sufficient to address isolated incidents in an individual's life, since the culture and the larger environment have a dynamic of their own, which makes NSSI a public health issue.

Bauman (1997) notes that living in late modern societies means living in *liquid modernity*, where rapid social change also leads to a yearning for the opposite: firm, predictable forms and structures. Bauman has compared the human condition in late modern society to a game where the rules are subject to recurring and unpredictable changes. In both our work and our personal lives, it is therefore best to avoid getting too firmly settled and to preserve our flexibility, mobility and readiness for change. Hartmut Rosa (2010) describes how the increased efficiency brought about by technological advances has only, paradoxically, made it harder to find time and space for contemplation. Modern society requires us to move ever faster in order to keep up, and this accelerated pace results in disorientation and alienation.

This disorientation and unpredictability are stress factors that require a high degree of internal structure and stability, and in contrast to earlier, more traditional societies, this does not only affect young persons who are in the process of discovering themselves and forming an identity. Today, identity formation is a lifelong project that may foster uncertainty about who one is, and whether one is good enough.

Navigating in late modern society is a daunting task, and to some, it is overwhelming. Individualization, reflexivity and the erosion of many of the integrating norms and values that have traditionally held the individual's life and identity together require a new level of flexibility for individuals to adapt and, ultimately, succeed.

When perfect becomes the new normal

In an editorial in the BMJ titled 'Adolescent mental health in crisis', Gunnell (2018) wrote about the worrying mental health status among young people in the UK. The authors refer to studies finding that young people's mental well-being is very low. For example, Universities UK reports a fivefold increase in the number of students disclosing mental health conditions since 2007 (from 9,675 in 2007–2008 to 57,305 in 2017–2018) and growing pressures on student mental health services, despite a modest rise in student numbers. Another study finds a 68% increase in hospital self-harm presentations in 13–16-year-old girls from 2011 (45.9 per 100,000) to 2014 (76.9 per 100,000) (Morgan et al., 2017). The poor mental health state is correlated with some of the stress factors that affect young people in modern life.

An increase in stress and stress-related symptoms is also found among younger people. According to a survey conducted by YouGov on behalf of Barnardo in 2018, nearly half of 12-year-olds in the UK (48%) feel sad or anxious at least once a week, with only 2% in this age group saying they never do. By the age of 16, 70% report feeling this way at least once a week, with more than a fifth (22%) having negative feelings as often as once a day. A majority of 12-to-16-year-olds report that school is their main cause of stress (65%), followed by thoughts about their future (42%), problems at home (31%), their weight (26%) and offline bullying (25%). By the age of 16, stress at school is a worry for 83% of children in England, and 80% worry about their future. Social media is an issue for 11%, who worry about getting enough likes or replies on social media, 12% are concerned about online bullying, while 15% say they have been troubled by something they had seen on social media. Online bullying is a concern for 12%.

The report does not identify the specific causes of this negative trend in young people's mental health, but it seems obvious to look to the rise in the prevalence of stress, which is quite high among young people today. Among 10–24-year-old Danes, almost one in five reports feeling stressed often; one in four feels stressed once a week; and 1–8% experience stress daily. The share of young women experiencing stress in everyday life more than doubled between 1987 and 2005 (Christensen et al., 2014). A 2013 study found that 26% often or very often felt nervous or stressed (ibid.). The trend seems to be the same in the rest of Europe.

The prevalence of stress among young people may stem from an everyday life characterized by increasingly high performance demands in the bodily, social and academic/educational arenas. Social media postings showcase idealized self-presentations, shifting the norms for what it takes to be perceived as 'good enough' by others and, not least, oneself. Intense competition, demands for perfection and high performance requirements afflict both sexes, in particular young women, who, according to studies, are the group most severely afflicted by stress.

A further consequence of the many choices postulated by mass media in late modern society may be that many young people worry about the risk of making the wrong choice. Choosing one thing means *not* choosing something else, and this existential position may be an excruciating burden to some. Many make plans for their future education and career at an early age, often in consultation with teachers or guidance counsellors, thus setting up expectations and, not least, an expectation of control. It is an implied assumption in Western culture that success depends largely on one's own individual competences and networking skills. The German psychologist Hartmut Rosa offers a very precise description of some of the consequences for the individual's self-concept: 'All failures and shortcomings directly fall back on the individuals. It is exclusively our own fault if we are unhappy or fail to stay in the race' (Rosa, 2010, p. 114).

Thus, choosing and staging the 'perfect life' becomes an individual, personal responsibility. If someone fails to achieve the job or the career he or she had in mind, the explanation lies not with the economy or the job market. As the

Danish sociologist Bjørn Holstein put it in the Danish newspaper *Politiken* (27 September 2014),

> We are living in a time when the individual perspective dominates over the collective. When society focuses more on individuals than on what we can achieve together, it places greater demands on the individual. The young are living a liberalist individualist nightmare.

Self-injury as social pathology

Few among us enjoy a sense of meaning, order and control over our life. Individualization means seeing oneself as detached from the collective community in order to achieve self-realization. NSSI may thus be seen as a meaningful act that is used either as a way of severing the ties to the community or as a lifestyle where cutting and other forms of self-injury are a means of self-actualization that actively use the body in a late modern reflexive process. Thus, body modifications are viewed as a statements about the individual that enter into a larger, meaningful discourse (Giddens, 1991).

By using NSSI as a compensatory strategy that also addresses the inability to live up to late modern demands for rationality and clarity, the individual may be seeking to attain a sense of control over the body or, perhaps, self-punishment for failing to live up to his or her own or others' expectations. The individual thus identifies him/herself as a loser, and to make matters worse, regards this failure as entirely self-inflicted.

The shame associated with failing to live up to the demands of late modern society may result in a feeling of *inadequacy*, which may provide further motivation to self-injure. Self-injury may, however, also intensify the sense of shame, self-loathing and the urge to cut, and thus, the feeling of shame locks the person into a self-perpetuating process (cf. the model on p. 140).

Moreover, maladaptive affect regulation and a reduced mentalizing capacity become social and personal impairments in a world driven by accomplishments and a capacity for self-control and goal-oriented efforts. Thus, NSSI may be seen as both a *stress response* and as a *coping strategy* in the face of the lack of control over events in one's own life. NSSI may represent an attempt at regaining a sense of control, only now in the form of symbolic control over one's own body.

Honneth (2009) has used the term 'social pathology' about a psychosocial disorder that has become so widespread in a culture that it becomes a public health issue. Although NSSI may be perceived as an individual phenomenon by the person engaging in the practice, as described above, it is influenced by a collective cultural dynamic and must therefore be characterized as a social pathology.

Demedicalizing and normalizing self-injury

NSSI may also be used as a form of self-fashioning and thus as a way of embracing an identity, for example as a cutter, or of marking one's membership of a community where cutting and, perhaps, 'uglification' are used as means of expressing one's identity (for example punks, Emos, Goths) (Young et al., 2014). This involves using the body as an alternative reflexive medium in an attempt to live up to the demands of late modernity of being *something* or *someone*.

The American sociologists Patricia and Peter Adler (2007; 2010) conducted a qualitative study of cutters that led them to conclude that cutting is not necessarily a sign of psychopathology or mental problems. On the contrary, they see cutting as a coping strategy – an explicit rejection of bourgeois norms and a tangible, externalized expression of inner pain. Adler and Adler (2007, p. 537) view cutting as a 'voluntarily chosen deviant behaviour' framed by a social context, a statement of the cutter's identity. The majority of the 80 cutters they interviewed said that their primary motivation for taking part in the study was to send a message to other cutters that they are not alone or 'crazy'. They wanted to explain something about their self-injury that might shed light on the phenomenon and remove the stigma.

Adler and Adler describe how cutting has spread from people with mental illness to structurally disadvantaged populations, such as young homeless people, and to subcultures, such as Goths, before ultimately becoming an almost mainstream practice, part of a lifestyle among young people from the middle class, including upper-secondary and college students. Adler and Adler thus seek to depathologize cutting, but they also point out that young people living in late modern society face demands and expectations that are higher, or at least harder to meet, than those faced by previous generations – a perspective that is also put forward by other scholars and lifestyle experts.

The spread of cutting and other forms of NSSI to privileged groups, such as middle-class student populations, has coincided with the spread of other types of body modification, such as piercings and tattoos, which have also migrated into the mainstream after once being the mark of a marginalized status embraced by bikers, criminals, prostitutes, sailors or, from around 1980, rock musicians and others who use their bodies to signal alternative values.

Whether the body modifications involve plastic surgery, strenuous physical exercise, make-up, hairdos, clothing or cutting and other forms of self-injury, the body conveys statements that are assigned meaning in a given cultural context, and so the body becomes a social signifier.

Social media

Virtually everyone in the Western world has access to the internet, and most young people, who are statistically the group most likely to self-injure, are daily users of social media, such as Instagram, YouTube and Facebook. Social media have radically changed the way young people form an identity and how they relate to each other.

Young people in general are virtually always online and are constantly assessing and being assessed by others. There is a relentless demand for performance and perfection (with perfect becoming 'the new normal') across all domains of life. Social media constitute a condensed social universe where the number of likes and friends is an indicator of success; hence, being ignored or bullied online can be profoundly traumatic. Unlike previous times, there is no refuge, nowhere to hide, and if someone is labelled as being a *misfit* or a *loser*, the label is immediately picked up by a much larger group. In the modern world, the young person's identity is the product of other people's gaze. Being seen and reflected in the social mirror is a condition for *being someone*, and being surrounded by an idealized version of reality in the form photo-edited images of other people can lead to a distorted perception of reality and normality. Many edit photos of themselves before posting them on social media, and that can make it difficult to maintain a realistic self-image. In addition to the performance pressure and the need to acquire likes that many young people experience, the media also portray a dazzling and exciting image of endless possibilities that can instil a sense of stress over FOMO – Fear Of Missing Out.

Instagram, which has been rated as the most important social network among adolescents in the United States, is a particularly popular site for young people to share photos of their own self-injury and to meet others who self-injure. The internet is an attractive meeting place for people who would otherwise practice self-injury in isolation, because it enables anonymous contact (Brown et al., 2018a).

In a systematic review of the relationship between internet use and self-harm among young people, Marchant et al. (2017) find that there is significant potential for harm from online behaviour for vulnerable young people due to normalization, triggering, competition and contagion but also potential benefits in the form of crisis support, reduction of social isolation, delivery of therapy and outreach.

Lewis and Baker (2011) have conducted a study of YouTube videos of self-injury. The 100 videos included in their study were among the most frequently viewed on YouTube at the time, with more than two million viewings. There are also several forums that offer advice on how to self-injure and how to conceal wounds or scars. These pro-self-injury forums, which legitimize and even promote self-injury, are similar to Pro-Ana (pro-anorexia) or Pro-Mia (pro-bulimia) sites promoting a positive image of eating disorders as a lifestyle choice.

Whether self-injury is viewed as a time-typical non-pathological youth phenomenon, a 'voluntarily chosen deviant behavior' (Adler & Adler, 2007, p. 537) or as the manifestation of a social pathology (Honneth, 2009), it has reached a prevalence level that calls for different analytical methods than before, when NSSI was viewed as an individual, relatively rare phenomenon found mainly among psychiatric patients (Graf & Mallin, 1967).

Investigating the social psychology of NSSI is an important research task. What cultural factors lie behind the high current prevalence of NSSI? How can we devise campaigns to prevent the spread of NSSI? The main issue is to shift the research effort from an isolated focus on individuals to a wider perspective that incorporates the sociocultural circumstances in modern society.

5 Historical theories and new models for understanding non-suicidal self-injury

Most people will be able to empathize with the notion of being in so much anguish that suicide seems like the only 'solution'. By contrast, self-injury – deliberate self-inflicted pain – seems counterintuitive and difficult to grasp. Perhaps that is why there have been so many speculative theories and attempts at identifying the causes of self-injurious behaviour and a years-long search for a 'hidden' meaning that would explain why some embrace this practice. As these theories reflect a clinically observable condition, namely the patient's self-injurious behaviour, some of them do contain a rational core and thus hold some explanatory value. However, the theories discussed in the following have no supporting evidence in a modern sense of the term.

Historical theories

Several of the early theories about self-injury sprang from a psychoanalytical understanding of death drives and aggression management. The first article about self-injury in a non-psychotic individual is L. E. Emerson's (1913) case study, which is interesting because it contains several elements that are found among young people with NSSI today (cf. p. 21).

Twenty years later, Lillian Malcove (1933) published an article about the link between learning to eat using knives, forks and spoons in early childhood and the practice of cutting in adulthood. According to Malcove's analysis, the child identifies with the food that is being cut up and may come to re-enact this mutilation as an adult by cutting his or her own body. Malcove viewed both acts as the expression of a primitive, aggressive and even cannibalistic urge. To a modern reader, these early articles seem curious and speculative, reflecting the persistent difficulty for psychiatrists of attributing meaning to self-injury.

In an article from 1935 and in his 1938 book *Man Against Himself*, the psychoanalyst Karl Menninger established a theoretical framework proposing to explain the meaning of self-injurious behaviour. Menninger based this work on Freud's theoretical construct of inherent death drives (Freud, 1955/1920) and saw self-injury as a *compromise* between life and death instincts and thus as a way of preventing an actual suicide attempt. In this view he differed from the prevailing perception of self-injury as failed or half-hearted suicide attempts. On the contrary, he argued that

> local self-destruction is a form of partial suicide to avert total suicide, and in this sense it represents a victory, even though sometimes a costly one, of the life instinct over the death instinct.
>
> (Menninger, 1938, p. 271)

Firestone and Seiden (1990) later followed up on Menninger's assumption with their view of self-injury as possible 'microsuicides', which may even create an 'illusion of mastery over death'. Menninger's basic view of self-injury as a way of averting total suicide corresponds to the current notion of NSSI as a form of affect regulation and is further related to the observation that the risk of suicide increases significantly when the individual, for some reason, is barred from using NSSI as a means of regulating inner tension.

A related theory, which was similarly rooted in the psychoanalytic drive model, regards self-injury as a way of reducing general psychological tension. According to this theory, the psyche has an optimal tension level; if this level is exceeded, it will be perceived as unpleasant, and the individual will seek to reduce it by various means, including cutting. In a discussion of this theory, Favazza (1996) points out that many patients perceive cutting as a means of affect regulation and report that cutting has a similar effect to popping a balloon or lancing a boil.

Other theorists suggest that cutting represents negative reactions to and symbolic attempts at controlling menstruation (Doctors, 1981); a way of expressing and controlling forbidden thoughts, urges or sexual impulses (Emerson, 1913; Lane, 2002); or an unconscious, symbolic attempt at destroying the genitals as the seat of forbidden urges, only displaced to a different part of the body (Friedman et al., 1972).

Bruno Bettelheim (1955) refers to the anthropologist Géza Róheim, who described how self-inflicted damage to the penis (so-called ritual subincision) leaves a wound that is perceived as a vagina or 'penis-womb'. Róheim mentions that the men engaging in this practice 'are offering an artificial vagina as compensation for the real one' (Bettelheim, 1955, p. 106). In this analysis, self-injury stems from a sort of envy of female genitalia. Others see elements of self-punishment and masochism in self-injury, a way of expressing unacceptable aggressive and violent impulses towards both him/herself and internalized representations of others (Bennum, 1984). According to these theories, self-injury is an expression of aggression towards others that is redirected towards the self as a safer option than confronting the other, who might retaliate. The theories of a negative introject may also help to explain the persistent feelings of shame, self-blame and alienation that plague many patients who practice self-injury.

Kernberg (1995) also focuses on the interpretation of self-injury as a manifestation of powerlessness and aggression in an attempt to exercise control over others. He views self-injury as a behavioural manifestation of the existence of a fragmented personality that lacks a clear distinction between the internalized representations of self and other. Stone (1987) focuses especially on patients who suffered abuse as children, explaining self-injury as an attempt at punishing the abuser. The patients use their own skin as a symbolic representation of the abuser. Other scholars too have interpreted self-injury as an attack on a destructive or aggressive introject (Figueroa, 1988). Several authors have described self-injury as a symbolic and controlled way of re-enacting the sexual abuse the patient was subjected to during childhood (Bennum, 1984). The patient thus transforms his or her childhood position of powerless victim into an active position that implies some degree of symbolic control.

Doctors (1999) and Pao (1969) have both applied object relation theory in descriptions of self-injury as an attempt at delimiting the self and thus counteracting the sense of dissolution and loss of self. According to this view, the patient has become fixated in the separation–individuation phase and is stuck in a dynamic where he or she on the one hand has a primitive desire of returning to a fused state with the archaic mother Figure and, on the other hand, seeks separation and independence. Because the separation–individuation phase was not completed, the individual's boundaries are vague and fragile. As a result, in stressful situations or close personal relationships the person may feel anxiety about being swallowed up or disappearing – an anxiety that is essentially about the fear of losing oneself. Self-injury makes it possible to sense one's own boundaries and thus regain a sense of autonomy. Kafka (1969, p. 209) has described how self-injury may activate a transitional object in the form of blood: 'as long as one has blood, one carries within oneself this potential security blanket capable of giving warmth and comforting envelopment'. Self-injury and blood thus hold the capacity to recreate the lost sense of security.

In a review, Suyemoto (1998) discusses various functions and theories pertaining to self-injury. She outlines a number of different paradigms (cf. box p. 82) and emphasizes that it is not possible to find one *universal* theory to explain self-injury, in part because self-injury is contextually complex. Self-injury likely has multiple functions and motivations, all active at the same time, and thus it is necessary to involve different paradigms to understand why people hurt themselves.

NSSI paradigms

- *The environmental model* focuses on the relationship between the self-injuring person and the environment. The environmental model is grounded in both behavioural and systemic developmental traditions.
- *The drive model* is grounded in psychoanalytic drive theory and considers self-injury an attempt to repress life, death and sexual drives.
- *The affect-regulation model* views self-injury as a way of managing and reducing the intensity of painful and overwhelming emotions.
- *The dissociation model* views self-injury as a way of either causing or ending a dissociative state with the ultimate goal of preserving the self. The dissociation model is grounded mainly in self-psychology.

> •   *The boundaries model* views self-injury as a way of affirming the boundaries between self representations and object representations (self and other). This model is grounded in object relation theory.

Emotion dysregulation and three theoretical models

Since Suyemoto's (1998) article, there has been an intensive research effort directed at understanding why people purposefully and directly hurt themselves. Today we know that a wide range of factors contribute to the dynamic of self-injury, including biological, psychological, social and cultural factors, and this research has informed new models for understanding NSSI.

The Experiential Avoidance Model is focused on emotion dysregulation and was developed by Alexander L. Chapman and colleagues (Chapman et al., 2006). The next model we will look at here is the Integrated Model developed by Mathew Nock (Nock, 2009); and the third is the Benefits and Barriers Model developed by Jill M. Hooley and Joseph C. Franklin (2018). (Nock & Prinstein's (2004) Four-Function Model will be reviewed on p. 131.)

Emotion dysregulation

Persons who engage in NSSI typically have low distress tolerance and lack effective adaptive coping strategies. Low distress tolerance means that they have a lower stress threshold than others. Moreover, they often rely on dysfunctional coping strategies such as avoidant and distracting behaviour, including drinking alcohol, taking drugs, overeating or NSSI. Thus, emotion regulation is a major problem for people who engage in NSSI. Emotion dysregulation is a key component of NSSI (e.g., You et al., 2018; Hasking et al., 2016) and an important concept in any theory about the development and maintenance of NSSI. Most people who self-injure appear to struggle with emotion regulation. They may be prone to mood swings and intense and rash emotional reactions that are out of proportion with the situation. Whitlock et al. (2011) noted that 81% of those who reported using NSSI endorsed that it served an emotion regulation function. Emotion dysregulation occurs in response to intense and overwhelming emotions. The inability to regulate these emotions puts the person at risk of resorting to dysfunctional strategies, such as NSSI, drugs, binge eating or binge drinking.

Most of the people who engage in NSSI are over-reactive to emotional stimuli, experience high levels of negative affect and are unable to regulate or modulate their emotions. A study (Bresin, 2014) found that people who self-injure experience more intense negative emotions, lower positive affect, greater variability in their emotions and multiple concurrent negative emotions (e.g., anger, sadness, worry). Another study, focusing on the prevalence of emotion dysregulation in both self-injuring and non-self-injuring college students, found a significantly higher degree of emotion dysregulation in those who self-injure than in those who do not (Gratz & Roemer, 2004).

Linehan (1993) was the first clinician to focus on emotion dysregulation as a cause of NSSI. Her theory has had a major impact on the treatment and understanding of NSSI. According to Linehan's biosocial theory, emotion dysregulation stems from an innate vulnerability combined with growing up in an invalidating environment (cf. Chapter 6). An invalidating environment increases the risk of developing ineffective interpersonal skills and inadequate emotion regulation, which in turn increases the risk of developing maladaptive coping strategies, including NSSI.

Klonsky (2007) notes that there is evidence to support Linehan's assumptions about emotion dysregulation as a background factor for NSSI. There is also documentation that a hostile climate and a poor relationship between child and parents during childhood is a risk factor for developing self-injury (Hilt et al., 2008).

Emotional dysregulation may manifest in a variety of ways; the following examples are not exhaustive. Some persons are short-tempered, have a short fuse and may be prone to losing their composure in a verbal or physical show of aggression. People who lose their temper in this way are often very shameful afterwards when the clouds lift, and they are able to think clearly again. Usually, what they experience is a veritable impulse breakthrough, where the fight-or-flight mechanism takes over (cf. p. 117).

Rachel is a little overweight and finds her mom to be overly focused on how much she eats. One evening at the dinner table, Rachel's mom tries to dissuade her from having another plate of food: 'Surely, you've had enough'. Infuriated, Rachel screams at her mom, and when her dad asks her to tone it down, she yells at him too, then slams her glass into her plate, breaking both. She storms out of the dining room in tears, slamming the door behind her, and goes to her room where she makes deep cuts into her upper arm. When she sees her therapist in a scheduled session a few days later, Rachel is still very angry but also sad and embarrassed.

These angry outbursts often involve rash decisions with far-reaching consequences, which lead to shame and remorse once reality sinks in. These feelings can linger for a long time.

Rita relates an incident in the café where she worked. Her supervisor had told her to slice the cucumber a little thinner when she made sandwiches. She perceived his tone to be sharp and bossy. Rita was furious and quit on the spot without pausing to consider whether his criticism might be justified

> or what the consequences would be of being without a job. A few hours later, after telling her boyfriend what happened, she was overwhelmed by shame and felt useless and embarrassed, which caused her to cut herself.

Some individuals with emotional dysregulation are unable to identify, name or modulate emotions and turn almost reflexively to self-injury as a way of making negative emotions go away. In other words, they fail to sense their feelings before reacting impulsively, for example by cutting. They simply feel overwhelmed by intolerable and unbearable distress and resort to self-injury in order to calm down.

> Sean is in his final year of upper-secondary school. In therapy, he describes how he said something in class that made everyone laugh at him, including the teacher. Without fully realizing how the incident affected him, he abruptly left the classroom and went straight to the school lavatory where he cut himself. Because he is unable to name the emotion he is feeling, he is easily overwhelmed and feels powerless to act by considering how he might manage his feelings of shame and embarrassment.

Persons with emotion dysregulation are easily swept up in their emotions, are quick to lose their composure and often find that their emotional reactions create problems for themselves and in their relations with others. Although they realize that their actions are often impulsive and destructive, they are powerless to act differently in the situation.

Emotion dysregulation is painful both for the dysregulated person and for the people around him or her, who often struggle to understand the person's reactions and what might trigger the next 'eruption' (as described in Mason and Kreger's (2010) bestselling book about living with a person with a borderline condition and affective dysregulation, *Stop Walking on Eggshells*).

The Experiential Avoidance Model of NSSI

One of the first attempts to understand why NSSI is so important for emotion regulation was the Experiential Avoidance Model developed by Alexander L. Chapman, Kim L. Gratz and Milton Z. Brown. The model is based on the premise that NSSI is a negatively reinforced strategy for reducing or terminating unwanted emotional arousal (e.g., anger or anxiety). The Experiential Avoidance Model describes how a stimulus triggers an unwanted aversive emotional response, in turn causing the person to experience an urge to avoid or remove the emotion. Lacking better skills and more adaptive responses, the person engages in NSSI. The experience provides instantaneous but temporary relief by reducing or

THE EXPERIENTIAL AVOIDANCE MODEL (EAM) OF
DELIBERATE SELF-HARM

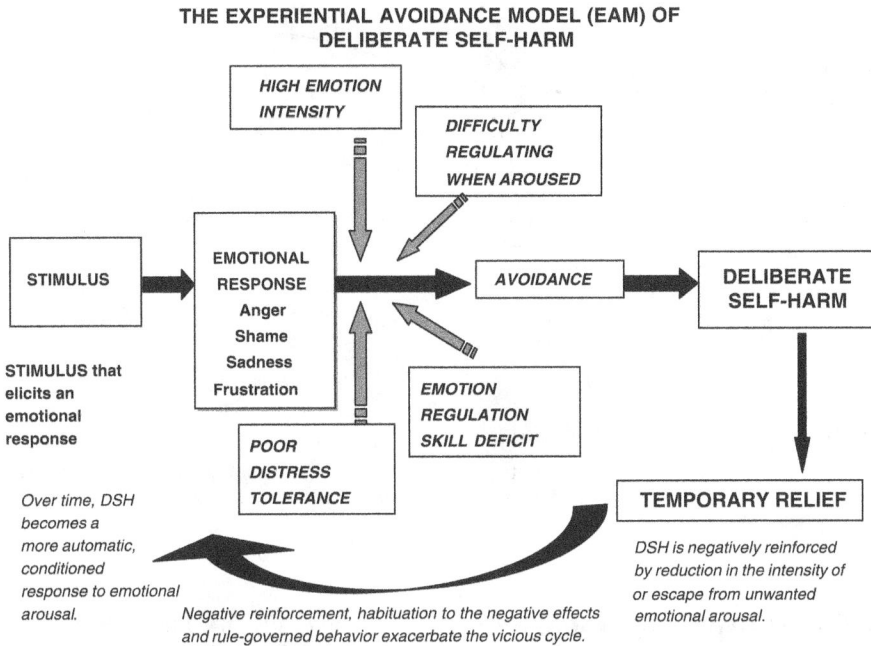

Figure 5.1 Experiential Avoidance Model.

Source: Chapman, A. L., Gratz, K. L., & Brown, M. Z. (2006). Solving the puzzle of deliberate self-harm: The experiential avoidance model. *Behaviour Research and Therapy, 44*(3), 373. Copyright © 2006. Reprinted with permission from Elsevier.

suppressing the emotional arousal and thus serves as an effective way to avoid the unwanted negative emotion. Through recurring negative reinforcement, the association between unwanted unpleasant emotional arousal and NSSI is strengthened, and as a result, NSSI becomes an automatic escape response (Chapman et al., 2006).

The Experiential Avoidance Model makes good sense in a clinical context, but only in relation to persons who use NSSI as a means of emotion regulation. Emotion regulation is also included in other models, for example the Four-Function Model (Nock & Prinstein, 2004), which is outlined below p. 131).

Mathew Nock's Integrated Model of NSSI

In 2009, Mathew Nock developed an integrated model in which he included findings from several different areas of research (Figure 5.2). According to this model, NSSI is a means to regulate affect, not only by offering a way to avoid the aversive emotion but also by regulating social situations. Nock also includes *distal* factors (such as genetic predisposition for high emotional/cognitive reactivity,

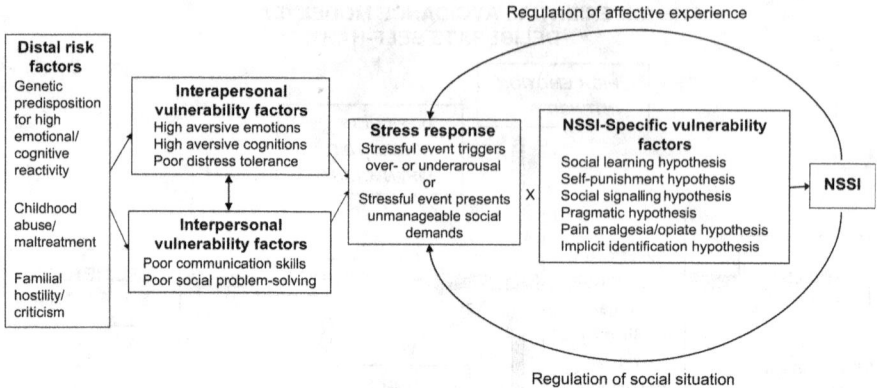

Figure 5.2 Integrated Model of NSSI.

Source: Nock (2009) Why do people hurt themselves? *Current Directions in Psychological Science Journal,* *18*(2), 79. Copyright © 2009 by Mathew K. Nock. Reprinted with permission from SAGE Publications, Inc.

childhood abuse/maltreatment and family hostility/criticism) that may lead to both intrapersonal and interpersonal vulnerabilities (for example, poor distress tolerance and poor communications skills) and ineffective responses to stressful life events (for example, inability to effectively communicate the need for help). The model further includes *proximal* factors that may affect vulnerable individuals, for example that they learn NSSI from peers or the media or that NSSI fills a need for self-punishment, serves as a cry for help or offers an identity, for example as a *cutter.* Finally, there are *pragmatic* factors, meaning that the person finds that NSSI works or is an easy solution compared to other possibilities (Nock, 2009).

The model is helpful and has good explanatory power in clinical work, since unlike the Experiential Avoidance Model, it is not focused exclusively on the here and now but also considers the person's childhood and youth (*distal* factors). Many persons with NSSI have suffered adverse childhood experiences and may, as a result, have developed an attachment disorder that severely hampers their psychosocial function during their youth and into adulthood.

The Benefits and Barriers Model

In the Benefits andd Barriers Model of NSSI (Figure 5.3), Hooley and Franklin (2018) summarize benefits offered by NSSI, which may be regarded as risk factors, and the barriers or protective factors that someone has to overcome before they begin to use NSSI. The core tenets of the model are that 1) NSSI has the potential to provide benefits for nearly everyone, but that 2) most people do not try to attain the benefits associated with NSSI because certain physiological, psychological and social barriers keep them from doing so. Although NSSI provides affective benefits, it is a behaviour with considerable physical and psychological costs.

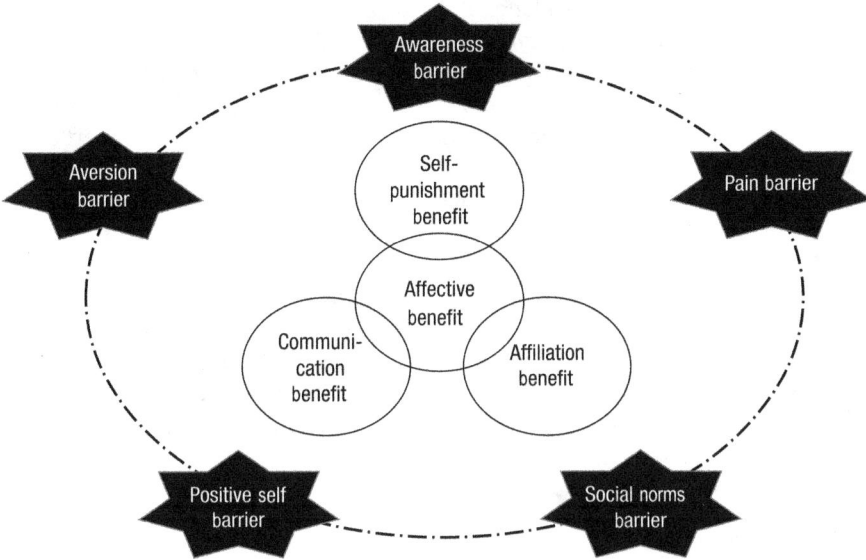

Figure 5.3 Benefits and Barriers Model of NSSI.

Source: Hooley & Franklin (2018). Why do people hurt themselves? A new conceptual model of non-suicidal self-injury. *Clinical Psychological Science*, *6*(3), 437. Copyright © 2018 by Hooley, J. M., & Franklin J. C. Reprinted with permission from SAGE Publications, Inc.

Benefits of NSSI

Hooley and Franklin mention four benefits of NSSI that may motivate self-injury:

1   *NSSI improves affect*: Research has documented that affect regulation is the most frequent motivation for self-injury. NSSI can reduce negative affect but also stimulate positive affect. Among the active factors, Hooley and Franklin (2018) mention that the gratification of self-punishment desires may improve affect and that the pain associated with self-injury distracts from negative thoughts and feelings. Finally, they mention so-called pain-offset relief: by cutting, for example, the person experiences pain, followed by relief when the self-injury stops. The removal of pain thus increases positive affect and reduces negative affect and physiological arousal (Bastian et al., 2014).

2   *NSSI gratifies self-punishment desires*: Persons who self-injure are more self-critical, have a more negative self-image, are more perfectionistic, are self-critical because they fail to live up to their own high standards and are more prone to feeling shame. Hence, it is no surprise that the desire for self-punishment is a common motivation for NSSI. When a person has a negative self-image and feels that he or she deserves to be punished, it is not only distraction from the negative feelings that has an affect-regulating effect. The negative self-image may be a result of abuse and maltreatment during

childhood, and it is maintained by NSSI, because it is associated with shame and self-criticism (Schoenleber et al., 2014).

3   *NSSI provides peer group affiliation*: Some individuals may engage in NSSI in order to attain or maintain affiliation with a peer group. There are many indications that NSSI can promote group belonging, and studies show that self-injury is present in certain subcultures, where it may even be a part of the group identity (Young et al., 2014). Moreover, studies show that adolescents who self-injure know more people who self-injure than adolescents who do not engage in this practice.

4   *NSSI can communicate distress or strength*: Although most who self-injure do so when they are alone and conceal the practice from others, studies show that NSSI also serves as a form of communication that is more direct but less specific than verbal communication (Nock, 2009). The exposure of fresh wounds and scars often takes place in social media. A study found that NSSI acts that were revealed to others were followed by increased perceived social support (Turner et al., 2016).

Barriers to NSSI

Hooley and Franklin (2018) mention five barriers that prevent most people from self-injuring. They found that the presence of a single barrier is sufficient to prevent a person from self-injuring.

1   *Lack of awareness about NSSI*: Someone who has never heard about self-injury, the authors argue, is not going to start. Today, however, it is almost impossible *not* to have heard of self-injury, because it is exposed in social media, websites, newspapers, film and TV, literature and songs, just as some celebrities have also spoken publicly of their self-injury. Self-injury is a prominent topic in the public realm. Contact with peers is also important. If one of the cool kids in class begin to self-injure, there is a real risk that others will follow suit. Exposure to self-injury may serve as an immediate trigger.

2   *Positive self-attitude*: Above, it is mentioned that NSSI is associated with a negative self-image. Conversely, a positive self-image and self-love makes it more likely that the person will try to protect him/herself physically and mentally, in part by looking after his or her body.

3   *Physical pain*: Most people will try to avoid pain, which is undoubtedly a survival skill. NSSI is only possible if the person is able to able overcome his or her fear of pain. Studies show that persons with NSSI generally have a much higher tolerance to pain and a higher pain threshold, which may stem from both physiological and psychological factors. A high pain threshold is not in itself a risk factor for developing NSSI, but the painful qualities of NSSI attract highly self-critical individuals to NSSI (Fox et al., 2017).

4   *Aversion to NSSI stimuli*: Most people have an aversion to blood, wounds and so forth, which is less pronounced in persons with NSSI – sometimes, it is even replaced by a fascination. In persons with NSSI, aversion stimuli can

trigger self-injury because they are associated with a positive feeling of relief when they stop.

5 *Social norms*: In most cultures, engaging in NSSI is not acceptable, and the practice will be met with fear and repulsion. Certain subcultures, however, may share and thus reinforce NSSI because it represents a rebellion against the prevailing social norms (Young et al., 2014).

In most initial episodes of NSSI, a broad range of distal risk factors generate major proximal risk factors. The proximal factors lower the barriers to NSSI and carry specific affective benefits. Over time, this 'affective engine' further lowers the barriers to NSSI and becomes the primary motivator of NSSI episodes. Given its role as perhaps the most common motivator of initial NSSI episodes, the negative self-attitude should be a primary treatment target. Similarly, given its role as a primary barrier to NSSI, diminished aversion to NSSI stimuli should also be a primary treatment target (Hooley & Franklin, 2018).

Hooley and Franklin (2018) offer the following example to explain the relationship between a negative attitude towards the self, physical pain and NSSI.

A negative attitude towards the self (negative self-association) (Figure 5.4) can generate 1) the desire to escape this unpleasant affective state, 2) the belief that one deserves pain and punishment and 3) access to and identification with self-injury. In turn, these factors engender the motivation to select and endure painful self-injury, which leads to NSSI behaviours. In effect, a negative self-attitude removes both the positive self-association barrier and the physical-pain barrier

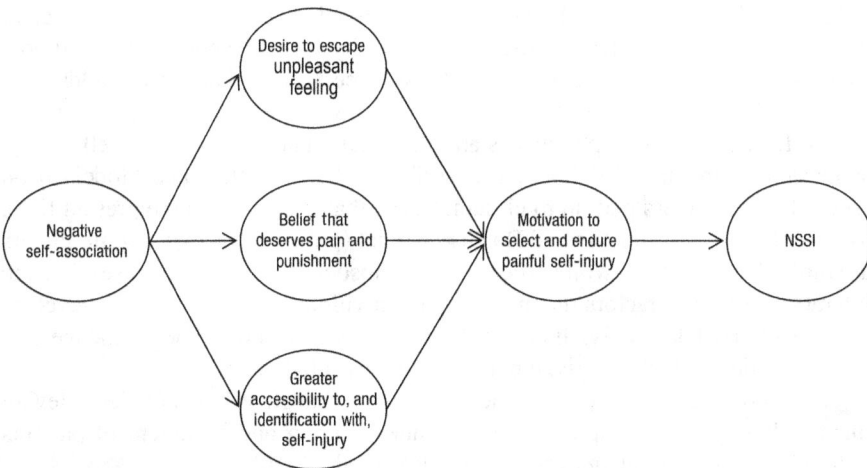

Figure 5.4 Example of the relationship between a negative attitude towards the self, physical pain and NSSI.

Source: Hooley, J. M., & Franklin J. C. (2018). Why do people hurt themselves? A new conceptual model of non-suicidal self-injury. *Clinical Psychological Science, 6*(3), 439. Copyright © 2018 by Hooley, J. M., & Franklin J. C. Reprinted with permission from SAGE Publications, Inc.

of NSSI and motivates the selection of NSSI over behaviours that carry similar benefits (for example binge drinking or binge eating).

In order to engage in NSSI, the person must overcome all barriers to NSSI. Given that barriers discourage most people from engaging in NSSI, it is likely that building or re-establishing these barriers will reduce the risk of NSSI in people who are vulnerable to NSSI.

The Benefits and Barriers Model differs from the traditional models (for example the Experiential Avoidance Model or Nock's Integrated Model of NSSI) by focusing not only on the positive effect of NSSI but also on the barriers that protect against the development of NSSI. Interventions framed by the traditional models focus on helping the self-injuring person to find better means of affect regulation, while the barriers-focused interventions aim to increase the barriers to NSSI. The latter perspective is probably new to most clinicians working with NSSI, although many in their treatment seek to build a kind of barrier to NSSI, for example by helping the patient avoid keeping razor blades or other items around that they normally use in their self-injury practice.

Vulnerability and resilience factors for the development of self-injurious behaviour

Each of the models mentioned above sheds light on the dynamics behind NSSI and may thus offer clinicians an overview of the factors involved in NSSI. However, models can never be allowed to detract attention from the individual NSSI patient who is seeking help. Every human being is unique, and human behaviour can never be put on a formula.

In extension of the Benefits and Barriers Model, with its focus on protective or resilience factors (barriers) versus vulnerability factors (benefits) we will now examine some of the vulnerability and resilience factors that are not addressed in the model, but which are often described in connection with the development of NSSI. There are multiple factors and thus many paths that lead to self-injury; some stem from early childhood, as described in Nock's Integrated Model (distal factors), while others pertain to circumstances that are closer to the present time, as described in the Benefits and Barriers Model (proximal factors). Some factors are biological in nature, while others are psychosocial, and in many cases, it is the interaction of these factors that make a person vulnerable or resilient to developing self-injury. Ultimately, the balance between vulnerability and resilience factors determines whether a given person develops self-injury.

The following review of risk factors is not exhaustive but includes relevant themes that are often important in the understanding and treatment of patients with NSSI (for a complete overview, see Fox et al., 2015).

Risk factors

Emotional neglect and abuse

Neglect, maltreatment and sexual abuse during childhood are risk factors for developing NSSI because they often create a negative attitude towards the self

(Swannell et al., 2012). More than 70% of people with NSSI in a representative sample of the German population have experienced emotional abuse during childhood (Brown et al., 2018). Especially the trauma symptoms (e.g., depression, anxiety, anger, disgust, guilt, shame, self-derogation and dissociation) may play an influential role in understanding the development of NSSI (Smith et al., 2014).

Some researchers suggest that people who have suffered neglect and sexual abuse tend to use self-injury as a coping strategy. Noll et al. (2003) found that sexual abuse victims repeatedly 're-enact the experience' through NSSI, but this is not a general feature, as many individuals who self-injure have *not* experienced sexual abuse.

Camilla was in her late twenties when she began treatment for NSSI, which was manifest especially in the form of cutting. She was acutely aware that, in a sense, her self-injury represented a re-enactment of traumatic sexual abuse from her childhood. She was occasionally overwhelmed by flashbacks but also by unbearable feelings of guilt and shame. She used cutting to block her flashbacks but more frequently as a means of self-punishment: 'Essentially, I feel that what happened is my fault'. She thus repeats the abuse, but now from a position where she decides when and how the 'abuse' occurs and experiences a degree of control over the act. Thus, she moves away from the powerlessness she experienced as a child and into an active position, where she may be driven by an irrational and destructive compulsion to repeat what happened, but where she has also seized some degree of control.

In discussing the function of self-injury, Suyemoto (1998, p. 541) describes the potential dynamic at play when someone like Camilla self-injures after childhood sexual abuse: 'Self-mutilation is [. . .] an attempt to turn passive into active, taking control of penetration and sexual impulses'.

Low self-esteem and a negative self-image

Low self-esteem, self-loathing, negative self-image, putting oneself down and being highly self-critical all seem to be significant risk factors and motives for developing self-injury (Forrester et al., 2017). 'I do it to punish myself' or 'I do it because I deserve it' are frequent explanations when people describe their motives for self-injuring (Klonsky, 2009).

Low self-esteem and negative self-image may stem from a fundamental feeling of irrational guilt or shame, but it may also be the result of bullying and psychological distress (National Council for Children, 2016). The majority of people who practice NSSI report feeling emotional pain, shame, guilt, sadness and anger directed at themselves immediately after self-injuring (Klonsky, 2009). These feelings may either make it more difficult to establish a treatment alliance, because the patient does not feel that he or she 'deserves it', or because 'others are more deserving of the therapist's time'.

Sarah is a 28-year-old woman admitted for a severe depression after a suicide attempt. She has been cutting herself for a number of years and has also engaged in extensive indirect self-injury (bulimia, random and mindless sexual encounters with strangers, alcohol and cannabis abuse). During her stay in hospital, where the main treatment focus is on her depression, she cuts herself severely and has several serious suicide attempts. After being hospitalized for 18 months without showing any real improvement, she is referred to an in-hospital therapist for intensive psychotherapy focused on her self-injury. During the first weeks of her treatment she refuses all contact, but gradually the relationship improves, probably because the therapist insists on having twice-weekly sessions in his office; when she fails to show up, the sessions are conducted in Sarah's hospital room. Over and over, she repeats that she cuts in order to punish herself, and that she does not deserve to receive treatment from the therapist, who, in addition to teaching DBT skills (Dialectical Behaviour Therapy) is very supportive and direct in the contact. After spending almost one more year in treatment, she is released for continued outpatient psychotherapy, during which she feels increasingly entitled to receiving help.

Many people who practice NSSI are extremely perfectionistic. They set exceedingly high standards for themselves and are highly performance-driven. High levels of perfectionism may also facilitate high levels of self-criticism (Daigle et al., 2018).

Attachment disorders and reduced mentalizing capacity

Children who experience neglect and sexual abuse are generally at an elevated risk of developing attachment disorders, which not only increases the risk of NSSI but also of psychopathology in general. Early attachment experiences form the basis of inner working models which have a considerable impact on personal relations throughout the lifespan, including the relationship with the therapist. In the longitudinal Minnesota study, Yates (2009) found that disorganized attachment stemming from childhood trauma was associated with more than a threefold increase in the risk of developing NSSI.

Ambivalent and disorganized attachment, which manifests as 'contradictory biologically channelled propensities to approach and to take flight from the parent' (Hesse & Main, 2000, p. 1099), is frequently found among those who self-injure (Wrath & Adams, 2018).

While Frida was growing up, her parents were emotionally distant or, frequently, physically absent. They were both focused on their demanding creative jobs and had no time or energy for Frida. She recalls how she had to 'act adult' and was generally ridiculed or ignored when she expressed childish emotions. When she was sad or angry, she found that her parents rejected her and even occasionally threatened to abandon her. She has a profound anxiety of abandonment. She has always had a hot temper, which she sometimes struggles to control. Quick to take offence, she reacts strongly to slights or rejection and has trouble forgiving the 'offender'. However, she struggles to describe exactly what emotions the experience triggers in her: aggression? Abandonment anxiety? Vindictiveness? Sadness? Powerlessness? She simply cannot tell. If she feels that a friend has been inconsiderate, for example by cancelling an appointment, she can spend days thinking about how to get even. In those situations, she feels the urge to cut or bite herself in order to calm down and let the feeling go. She may also cut or bite herself, to the point of drawing blood, if she is overwhelmed by negative feelings and has the opportunity to do so.

Sexual minority youth – LGBTQ

In recent years there has been a growing interest in studying marginalized young people who to some degree live in a separate subculture. Studies show that individuals who identify as gay, lesbian, bisexual, transgendered or gender-queer (LGBTQ; gender minority) are more likely to experience adversities such as child abuse and neglect, maltreatment, violence, sexual assaults and rejection and separation from family and dropping out of education, and they report higher rates of drug use, psychiatric symptoms, suicidal ideation, suicide attempts and NSSI compared to their heterosexual and cisgender (self-affirmed gender matches natal sex) peers (Marshall et al., 2016). Sexual minority youth who are open about their sexual orientation or gender identity are more likely to be bullied. Further, more than half of youth with sexual minority status feel unsafe at school, which can lead to feelings of vulnerability and low self-esteem; sexual minority youth are three to five times more likely to engage in NSSI compared to their heterosexual peers, and among college students, 62.8% reported lifetime NSSI (Muehlenkamp et al., 2015). A study of adult LGBTQ persons (mean age 34.5 years) in the United States found that 41.9% reported a history of NSSI, which is much higher than among heterosexuals (26.4%) from the sample. Participants who identified as queer report levels of NSSI that are higher than the average for the full sample (62.3%) (Dickey et al., 2015).

These elevated Figures for NSSI among LGBTQ persons suggest that a non-majority sexual and gender identity is a major risk factor for NSSI. The high rates are probably associated with individual stress, for example internalized homophobia, but also with social contagion, a factor that may play a key role in less open environments (Jarvi et al., 2013).

Mental illness

Mental illness is another important risk factor for developing self-injurious behaviour, but the reverse is also true, in that self-injury may be a risk factor for developing mental illness (Wilkinson et al., 2018).

NSSI is a transdiagnostic or non-specific symptom and is associated with most mental disorders (Zetterqvist, 2015). In a systematic review, Hawton et al. (2013) found that psychiatric (Axis I) disorders were identified in 83.9% of adults and 81.2% of adolescents and young adults presenting to hospitals following self-harm. The most frequent disorders were depression, anxiety and alcohol abuse; in younger patients, additionally attention deficit hyperactivity disorder (ADHD) and conduct disorder. Personality (Axis II) disorders were found in 27.5% of adult patients.

NSSI co-occurs most commonly with BPD and depressive disorders. Between 49% and 90% of BPD patients engage in NSSI and nearly half of psychiatric patients who performed NSSI had a diagnosis of major depressive disorder (Peters et al., 2018; Glenn & Klonsky, 2013). The link between NSSI and depression may be explained by a highly negative self-image and low body regard.

Eating disorders appear to be risk factors for NSSI; 22% of patients with anorexia nervosa and 32% of patients with bulimia nervosa had histories of NSSI. Researchers who have investigated the relationship between NSSI and eating disorders suggest that both behaviours are related to difficulties in emotion regulation (Cucchi et al., 2016).

Anxiety disorders, especially generalized anxiety disorder (Zielinski et al., 2018) and PTSD, are found to co-occur with NSSI. Studies indicate that about half of the patients with dissociation and flashbacks use NSSI to decrease dissociative symptoms, such as depersonalization and numbing, and to block upsetting memories and flashbacks. In other words, some use NSSI as a way of breaking the sense of isolation and '*getting back in touch* with reality'. However, other patients self-injure in order to achieve a dissociative state, splitting the 'observing self' and the 'experiencing self', thus shielding themselves from physical and psychological impressions (Ford & Gómez, 2015).

The co-occurrence of substance abuse and NSSI is high. Moran et al. (2015) found that nearly half of those who had engaged in adolescent self-harm met criteria for a dependence syndrome, and one in six met criteria for multiple dependence syndromes. The correlation between substance abuse and NSSI may reflect the capacity of both types of self-injury to serve as a coping strategy in relation to psychosocial stressors; further, the use of drugs or large quantities of alcohol may lead to increased impulsivity as well as a lower threshold for self-injury.

The reviewed selection of risk factors is not exhaustive but captures the most important ones. In a meta-analysis of risk factors for NSSI, Fox et al. (2015) found that a prior history of NSSI, hopelessness and cluster B (e.g., BPD) had the strongest effect. Others are mentioned in the list below.

Risk factors for developing NSSI

- Sexual abuse and maltreatment
- Growing up in an invalidating environment
- Hostile and critical family climate
- Loss of parent(s)
- Emotion dysregulation
- Alexithymia
- Attachment disorder and reduced mentalizing capacity
- Low self-esteem, perfectionism and negative body image
- Mental illness and substance abuse
- Problems with peers, bullying, isolation
- Perceived abandonment, for example a break-up
- LGBTQ
- Sleep disorders

Resilience factors

We know less about protective or resilience factors in relation to developing NSSI than we do about the risk factors. However, some factors have a well-documented protective effect against psychopathology in general: intelligence and good verbalization skills, optimism and high but realistic self-esteem, internal locus of control, a sense of meaning and purpose in life, productive activity and the ability to form attachments to others (Rotolone & Martin, 2012)

Some of the factors that offer protection against developing NSSI are the polar opposite of the risk factors; for example, a good and stable mentalizing capacity offers protection against self-injury, while a vulnerable, unstable mentalizing capacity increases the risk of a failure to mentalize and of self-injury.

Perceived social support has long been considered an important protective factor against the negative consequences of physical and psychological trauma and other distressing experiences during childhood. Studies found that children who have had traumatic experiences are at increased risk of developing self-injury, but that social support from someone they feel close to reduces this risk (Christoffersen et al., 2014). Also later in life, a close and cohesive family situation is a protective factor against self-injury. Young people who self-injure generally perceive themselves as having less social support than others, and they are more likely to feel lonely, have a less-developed social network and have poorer contact with their parents (Arbuthnott & Lewis, 2015).

That social support and a sense of connectedness offer protection against developing NSSI is also evident in the fact that young people who experience bullying and group exclusion are at increased risk of developing NSSI but adolescents who experienced bullying or victimization were less likely to go on to engage in NSSI when they perceived their parents to be supportive (Claes et al., 2015a). In studies of young people's ideas about what might prevent the development of self-injury, most respondents point to social support in the form of having someone to talk to.

In preventing the development of NSSI, for example in schools, it is important to use the existing research-based knowledge about barriers to the development of self-injury (Hooley & Franklin, 2018), including social support as a protective or resilience factor. Social support and a culture that aims to prevent bullying and develop positive methods for stress management and emotion regulation seem to be key in this regard. Social support from both adults and peers promote an adaptive development in the young person and offer protection against the development of NSSI and other types of self-harm, such as eating disorders, alcohol and drug abuse.

Factors that offer protection against developing NSSI

- Secure attachment and a good capacity for mentalizing
- Interpersonal skills
- Ability to handle negative emotions
- Good and flexible skills for emotion regulation
- Support from the family and others while growing up
- Positive view of the self
- Sense of coherence

Different forms of NSSI may be associated with different risk and protective factors. For example, cutting one's face or genitals is associated with a higher degree of sexual abuse during childhood and psychopathology than cutting one's arm or leg (Møhl & Rubæk, submitted).

6 Attachment, affect regulation and growing up in an invalidating environment

In this chapter, the focus turns to the background for developing some of the vulnerability and resilience factors in relation to self-harm that were mentioned in the previous chapter: early attachment between mother and child, which has far-reaching consequences for affect regulation and mentalizing. The chapter also addresses Linehan's theories about the impact of growing up in a so-called invalidating environment, which is another documented risk factor. The developmental perspective in this chapter provides a basis for understanding the development of NSSI and a background for the discussion of Dialectical Behaviour Therapy (Chapter 11) and Mentalization-Based Therapy (Chapter 12).

Attachment

Infants depend on care from others for their psychological and physical survival. Although both parents are important caregivers for the infant, the relationship with the mother is especially critical during the first few months of the child's life. Presumably, the infant's ability to form an attachment with the mother is an innate instinct, which triggers the activation of the *attachment system* when the child feels insecure or stressed. The system is deactivated once the infant feels safe and comfortable again.

The child's attachment behaviour is seen, for example, in smiles, crying, eye contact and attempts at physical contact with the mother. The mother is probably genetically disposed to respond to the infant's attachment behaviour based on a complementary *caregiving system* that animates her to provide the safe, nurturing and caring environment that the infant needs to survive and remain physically and emotionally regulated. Her mere presence has a soothing effect on the infant, but if the infant becomes distressed or anxious, she needs to pick the child up and provide comfort through physical contact (Bowlby, 1988).

The attachment system is activated when the infant feels insecure and requires protection and care; it is deactivated once the infant feels secure again. The dynamic between the attachment system and the caregiving system revolves around regulating proximity and distance and providing the sense of security the infant needs to explore the outside world. Bowlby (1988) introduced the notion that parents have to provide a *secure base* for the child, arguing that the experience of having a secure base is crucial for the development of mental health and the capacity to approach one's environment with a curious, open and explorative stance.

Adults also display attachment behaviour when they feel threatened or unsafe. In people with BPD in particular, the attachment system is on a hair trigger, which means that they are sensitive to any perceived rejection, for example a telephone call that goes unanswered, a cancelled appointment, a friend, lover or therapist leaving town, an averted face, an inattentive conversation partner, an argument or simply a disagreement. Separation anxiety and a hyperactive attachment system are common factors behind acts of NSSI.

Early interaction experiences are reflected in the infant's attachment patterns, which are internalized to form what Bowlby (ibid.) calls *internal working models*. These internal working models are mental representations that have developed based on interactions with the caregiver: 'Evidence shows that during the first two or three years the pattern of attachment is a property of the relationship', but 'as the child grows older, the pattern becomes increasingly a property of the child himself, which means that he tends to impose it, or some derivative of it, upon new relationships' (ibid.).

As the patterns of attachment are gradually generalized, the internal working models come to reflect the child's expectations of interpersonal interactions that serve as a matrix for the child's later relationships with others. Research finds that nothing is more important for children's development than the way they are treated by their parents or other caregivers. One reason for this is that the infant's brain undergoes a tremendous growth period and is thus shaped by 'the early social environment, medicated by the primary caregiver, directly influences the final wiring of the circuits in the infant brain that are responsible for the future social and emotional coping capacities of the individual' (Schore, 2003).

Internal working models

According to Bowlby (1973), the internal working models may be more or less accurate, but they are largely realistic. They are stored in specific memory systems in the brain as either *explicit* or *implicit* representations. The explicit models lie within our conscious awareness and represent experiences we can talk about, for example, 'my dad could be really unpleasant, and I was scared of him when I noticed a certain look in his eyes'. Implicit models, on the other hand, are unconscious and embedded in the so-called procedural or implicit memory, where they manifest as automatic procedures that govern our behaviour outside our conscious awareness. The implicit models in our procedural memory system are stored in the same way as, for example, the ability to ride a bicycle. Once a skill has been acquired, we apply it more or less automatically and never forget it. In a sense, the body remembers.

The *emotional memories* that are part of the implicit internal working models are partially stored in the amygdala (cf. Chapter 9). They are active and accessible on the perceptual motor level, where they may be activated in certain situations or by specific *cues*. Thus, someone who has a sensitive amygdala may have inappropriately intense, impulsive and unexpected reactions in situations that happen to reactivate painful emotions, such as fear of abandonment or a sense of violation. Such an experience may activate an emotional storm, which in turn may trigger an act of NSSI.

The parts of the internal working models that are stored in the implicit memory are relatively stable but may be modified, for example when they are identified and addressed in psychotherapy. They may also be modified by changes in meaningful relationships that give rise to *corrective emotional experiences*.

Longitudinal studies from infancy to adulthood have documented a significant degree of continuity in the patterns of attachment but have also documented the impact of environmental stimuli (Grossman et al., 2005). For example, if an adult experiences a psychological trauma in an interpersonal relationship, this experience may cause the person's pattern of attachment to change and become insecure. On the other hand, a stable and secure long-term attachment will help the person modify his or her internal working models, enabling the person to engage in close intimate relationships without feeling threatened or needing defence mechanisms. It is easier, however, to lose the basic trust in connection with a psychological trauma than it is to establish an internal working model characterized by trust and a sense of security. The key point is that our internal working models are characterized by both continuity and flexibility.

The Strange Situation and patterns of attachment

The Canadian psychologist Mary Ainsworth, who worked with Bowlby for several years, designed and conducted the Strange Situation experiment. In this procedure the young child (9–18 months of age) is observed during play while the caregiver and a strange person enter and leave the room. Three different infant attachment patterns are identified: *secure, ambivalent/resistant* and *avoidant* attachment (Ainsworth et al., 1978). Later, Mary Main and colleagues (Main et al., 2005) identified a fourth pattern: *disorganized* attachment, which combines features from the other three.

An infant with a *secure attachment* will begin to play with the toys, perhaps with the mother or the stranger (exploration behaviour). When the mother leaves the room, the infant responds with varying degrees of distress but is, to some extent, able to be comforted by the stranger. At the second separation from the mother, the infant has a stronger reaction and needs more comforting. When the infant is reunited with the mother, he or she seeks physical contact and closeness, is soothed and calms down and is then able to resume playing. Mothers of securely attached children are characterized by being sensitive and responsive to the infant's needs.

A child with an *ambivalent/resistant attachment* reacts strongly to separation. When reunited with the mother, the infant is clingy and demanding but also refuses to be comforted. This ambivalence can be quite explicit, for example when the child wants to be picked up but wriggles free from the mother's arms while continuing to cling to her. The infant is clearly distressed but simultaneously so frustrated that he or she cannot be soothed.

Mothers of children with an ambivalent/resistant attachment are typically inconsistent or dismissive when the infant wants to be comforted. Ainsworth et al. (1978) interpreted the infant's objections and anger as an attempt at provoking the mother to make her provide care. In ambivalently attached children, the attachment system is hyperactive, and when the mother eventually gives the infant the attention he or she craves, she effectively rewards the behaviour, thus teaching the child to repeat the strategy of intensifying his or her efforts in order to get the mother's attention. The infant remains ambivalent, however, and thus, the desire for care and closeness is associated with frustration, anger and bitterness.

An infant with *avoidant attachment* does not show much outward reaction when the mother leaves or returns. The infant appears to have developed emotional self-reliance, because of the repeated experiences of being rejected by the mother. Studies show that the infant displays physiological signs of stress (increased heart rate and elevated cortisol levels), however, which suggests that the infant over-regulates his or her emotions. Ainsworth found that mothers of infants with an avoidant attachment pattern typically appear discreetly dismissive, emotionally reserved and irritated, and that they tend to minimize physical contact with the infant. Infants with an avoidant attachment style have had to deactivate their attachment needs and get by on their own.

Infants with a *disorganized attachment* style may have brief episodes of 10–30 seconds' duration during which they react unpredictably and irrationally with no clear purpose or goal. Mary Main and her colleagues, who identified and described this pattern of attachment (Main et al., 2005), explain the behaviour as a reaction to an unresolved conflict, which stems from the caregiver being simultaneously the source of anxiety and security. The conflict arises because the caregiver is the person the infant turns to for care and comforting but also the person who causes anxiety. When the child feels anxious, and the attachment system is activated, the infant automatically seeks to be close to the caregiver; when the caregiver merely increases the level of anxiety, the attachment system is further activated. This poses an impossible dilemma for the infant, who therefore grows up with a basic sense of powerlessness and hopelessness, which are some of the fundamental emotions behind NSSI.

Disorganized attachment is often seen in children who have been subjected to physical or sexual abuse or other trauma but also in children who have experienced more subtle forms of disrupted emotional communication and a lack of affective attunement with the mother (Allen, 2013).

Allen (2013) points out that disorganized attachment is a sign of attachment trauma, where the child has repeatedly been left to him/herself in unbearable emotional pain (for example in connection with abuse or mistreatment). In itself, disorganized attachment may be understood as a failure of integration or as a dissociative reaction in connection with a painful and irresolvable conflict. In dissociation, the painful experience is split off from the conscious mind, which may give the infant temporary relief. Studies have found that disorganized attachment is correlated with dissociative and NSSI later in life.

Persons who engage in NSSI often show attachment disorders in the form of either ambivalent or disorganized attachment. This is in part because their capacity for affect regulation and mentalizing is severely compromised, and because the attachment disorder makes them sensitive to experiences of betrayal, violation and invalidation, which heightens the risk of conflict, especially in intimate relationships.

Mind in mind and affect regulation

The quality of the early attachment relationship is crucial for the infant's mental and emotional development and thus for the risk of later NSSI. The infant needs the calm mental space provided by a stable and secure attachment to be able to explore both him/herself and the caregivers. A child with an attachment disorder is in a constant state of alarm and therefore lacks the capacity and the focus to engage in exploration and learn what it is like to be a human being in relation to other human beings.

Daniel Stern (1985) described the affective and psychophysiological attunement that continuously unfolds between mother and infant from the moment the child is born. With her care, she is able to regulate the infant's physical and mental arousal to keep it from exceeding the infant's capacity and thus leading to overwhelming distress in the form of anxiety or frustration. As she provides care for the infant, she also mirrors the infant's mental state. When she sees and responds to the infant, keeping the infant's 'mind in mind', as Peter Fonagy phrased it, she mirrors the infant's inner states.

Mary Ainsworth et al. (1978) and, later, Daniel Stern (1985) emphasize how important it is that the mother is able to mediate secure attachment by displaying 'sensitive responsiveness', which means picking up on and reacting to the child's mental state. In doing that, she creates an inner representation, which she hands back to the child in a modified version by means of facial expressions, prosody, words, tone of voice and gestures. By internalizing the mother's mirroring response, the infant gets a *second-order representation* of his or her emotional state. The mother does not hand the infant's anxiety back to the infant; what the infant receives is *the mother's image* of the infant's anxiety. This is the beginning of what later develops into concepts for emotional states.

It is important that the mother's mirroring is adequate, but a number of factors may cause her mirroring to be 'off' or inadequate, for example because she is stressed, under the influence of drugs, suffering from depression or other mental disorders or simply because she is constantly distracted by her mobile phone or iPad.

Congruent and marked mirroring

When an infant looks at the mother's face, 'what the baby sees is himself or herself', and when the mother looks at the baby, 'what she looks like is related to what she sees there' (Winnicott, 1971, p. 131). The mother reacts to the infant, and the infant reacts to the mother. The infant learns that the mother's reactions mirror the infant's own inner state and thus comes to life in his mother's gaze. The mother needs to be able both to perceive the infant's state and mirror it correctly and to sense her own emotions and regulate them. This emotional attunement is characteristic of *congruent* mirroring.

Congruent mirroring means that the mother is able to see and convey the child's emotional state in accordance with the infant's own experience. If the infant is distressed, for example, that is the emotion she mirrors with her voice and her facial expressions while comforting the infant.

A predominance of *incongruent* mirroring prevents the child from adequately identifying and managing his or her emotions. This may lead to a compartmentalization where one part of the personality adapts to the external world: the mother; while another part adapts to the internal world: the child's own emotions. The child will experience the emergence of an environmentally oriented *false self*: *false* because it does not contain the child's actual emotions. As a result of the lack of mirroring and recognition of the child's own emotions (*authentic self*), the child risks developing a sense of emptiness and/or anxiety and shame over being 'wrong'. Because the false self is an empty self, the result is a lack of coherence between the child's own experiences and the meaning that the environment attributes to these emotions. The result of this *invalidation* may be a lack of integration between *pretend mode* and *psychological equivalence mode*, which increases the risk of developing a low capacity for affect regulation and of developing NSSI. By contrast, the mother's congruent mirroring of the child's emotions results in highly charged moments, essentially 'giving back to the baby the baby's own self' (Winnicott, 1971, p. 138), which lets the infant experience vitalization and coherence.

Marked mirroring means that the mother reflects and reproduces the infant's emotions in a way that differs from the infant's own expression. The mother typically has a remarkable ability to signify when she is reflecting the infant's emotions rather than expressing her own. For example, she may clarify that she is reflecting the infant's internal world in her mirroring by exaggerating or understating the infant's contributions, thus representing them with a little twist. If the infant is upset and crying, she does not begin to cry but might say 'there, there' in a slightly sad but light tone way while comforting the infant. This lets the infant know that she has picked up on his or her emotional state, and at the same time she makes it clear that her expression is a response. To provide marked mirroring, the mother has to be able to sense and manage her own emotions without being overwhelmed or panicking and scolding the child. She has to be able to contain and process the infant's emotions and hand them back in a metabolized form.

When the mirroring is not marked, the mother reacts with the same or perhaps even greater intensity, in which case her reactions may *intensify* the infant's emotions. This may give the infant a sense of being abandoned, unable to regulate his or her own affects. A predominance of unmarked mirroring may prevent the infant from learning to identify and regulate his or her emotions. The infant risks being stuck in *equivalence mode* (cf. p. 113) without any perceived difference between the internal and the external world. Unable to regulate these emotions, the infant is overwhelmed, which increases the risk of later NSSI.

The alien self

Winnicott (1971) wrote that when the infant does not find himself in the mother's gaze, he finds the mother. The infant is biologically inclined to internalize the caregiver's mirroring stance, and this internalization also occurs when the caregiver fails to mirror the infant's state. Fonagy et al. (2002) write that the infant cannot help but internalize the representation of the mother's state of mind, but this representation is then anchored as a non-integrated alien part of the self – the so-called *alien self.*

> Inaccurate mirroring will lead to the internalization of representations of the parents' state rather than of a usable version of the child's own experience. This creates what we have termed an alien experience within the self: ideas or feelings are experienced as part of the self which do not seem to belong to the self.
>
> (Bateman & Fonagy, 2004, pp. 88–89)

Although the internalized alien self becomes part of the child's self, it is not integrated, nor is it part of the child's *experience* of having a coherent self. Especially in connection with sexual abuse, the non-integrated aspects may even be experienced as destructive and threatening. When the aggressive alien representation has become internalized, the child will attempt to create a coherent self by consistently seeking to externalize the alien representation and get rid of it by projecting it onto other people. The purpose of this is to protect the self from the destructive introject and to regulate the inner tension and achieve a sense of calm; this sense of calm disappears, however, when the relationship fails to allow for this sort of externalization.

Thus, the person becomes dependent on others to receive the alien self via projective identification. If there is no one around to receive the projected alien self, the person is going to try to preserve the experience of a coherent self by projecting the alien aspect into an *isolated* part of the body where the person can attack or attempt to *destroy* it through *self-injury.*

Characteristically, most self-injury incidents occur when the person is alone, which lends support to Fonagy and his colleagues' theory about the link between the alien self and self-injury (ibid.).

A man in his late 30s had been subjected to recurring sadistic sexual abuse from his stepfather in his early childhood. With fear, he recalls the lust in the stepfather's eyes and the physical pain of anal penetration. As an adult, he repeats this pattern in self-destructive relationships; in the receiving position in homosexual anal intercourse, he has found himself losing touch with himself and becoming completely incapable of saying no when he encounters the lust in the other man's eyes. As an adult, he has therefore allowed himself to be subjected to painful sadistic abuse, which he later regrets. He describes

how he senses a part of himself that is 'not a part of me' – a part characterized by violent aggression mixed with sexual desire that leads him into self-
destructive and sometimes dangerous relationships with other men.

When he wakes up in the morning, he generally has an almost physical sensation of anxiety and frightening aggressions 'occupying and taking over' his
body, manifesting as severe headache and pain in his pelvic region. He feels
defenceless against these feelings and has to soothe them with prescription
drugs or hard physical exercise. This aggression shapes his relationships with
others, and he repeatedly finds himself in situations where he feels violated
and victimized. When he is violated, he reacts with intense aggression, which
he has trouble controlling, and therefore he may appear threatening, for example to the therapists and other patients in a therapy group.

This case concerns a patient who has internalized a controlling alien self, and who
describes the feeling of having something inside that is not really part of him.
At one point, he worried that he might be 'going crazy', and he feels that lacks a
'personal core'. His identity diffusion sometimes verges on dissociation, where he
is not only in doubt about who he is but actually feels like someone else, someone
who is alien to the person he normally feels like.

All relationships between caregiver and child have some degree of non-
congruent mirroring, where the child internalizes alien elements. In the normal
course of development of the mentalizing capacity, alien elements that are not
anchored in internalized mirroring of self-states are integrated in a coherent self
structure. If the mentalizing capacity fails to develop sufficiently, however, the
person will continue to need to externalize the alien self via projective identification. The fragmentation of the self that accompanies the alien self is manifest as
an insecure or even a diffuse sense of identity, as we see in many who self-harm
as a means of affect regulation (Bateman & Fonagy, 2004).

Mentalizing

> For a relationship between any two individuals to proceed harmoniously, each
> must be aware of the other's point-of-view, his goals, feelings and intentions, and
> each must so adjust his own behaviour that some alignment of goals is negotiated.
> This requires that each should have reasonably accurate models of self and other
> which are regularly up-dated by free communication between them.
>
> (Bowlby, 1988, pp. 147–148)

What Bowlby describes here is really mentalizing or mentalization, a term that
Peter Fonagy first used in 1989 in article about *theory of mind* and borderline
states (Fonagy, 1989). Later, Fonagy incorporated the concept of mentalizing
into a comprehensive theory of attachment and mentalizing together with his colleagues at the Anna Freud Centre in London (Fonagy et al., 2002). The term has

roots in French psychoanalysis, where it has been described as a psychological mechanism that translates drives and affects into symbols and in the work of the English psychoanalyst Wilfred Bion, who developed a theory of thinking and what he called *the alpha function* (Bion, 1970)

Mentalizing is the capacity to understand one's own and others' behaviour as meaningful based on mental states such as desires, intentions, feelings, fantasies or expectations. This understanding is normally intuitive and *implicit*, as we 'read' someone else and grasp the motivations underlying his or her actions or statements. Mentalizing may also be *explicit*, when we ask questions and put our understanding of the other's mental state into words, but usually this is only done as a way of aiding intuitive, implicit mentalizing.

Mentalizing thus involves directing attention at one's own and others' mental states and imagining the underlying intentions motivating a given behaviour. Mentalizing helps us achieve coherence and meaning in our own internal world as well as in our external, social world. When we mentalize, we experience and treat ourselves and others as individuals with varying capacities for psychological thinking. We keep *mind in mind*.

When we mentalize, we are aware that our thoughts are thoughts about an independently existing reality, and we are able to reflect on the relationship between our thoughts and reality. This includes our understanding that these thoughts are individual and represent one among several perspectives on reality. Different people have different experiences of reality, and one person's perception does not carry any greater validity than anyone else's. Mentalizing also means being able to understand the concept of misunderstandings (see Figure 6.1).

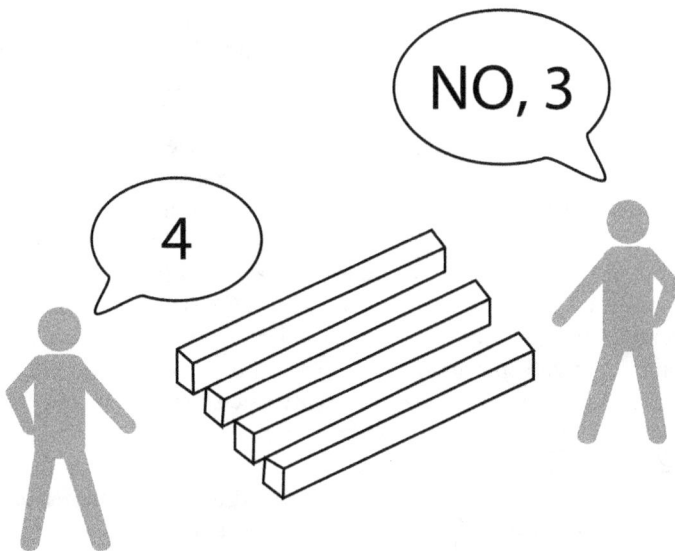

Figure 6.1 Conflicts may arise when we see reality from different angles.

However, mentalizing is not only about thoughts and imagination. Referring to Martha Nussbaum's concept, Allen (2013) described mentalizing as a form of 'emotional knowing' and points out that good mentalizing enables 'feeling clearly'. Feeling clearly, we are better able to rely on our feelings and allow them to guide us.

Mentalizing is the ability to

- See one's own and others' behaviour in relation to intentions and other mental states
- Focus and reflect on one's own and others' mental states
- Understand oneself from the outside and others from the inside
- Think and feel about thoughts and feelings
- See perceptions of reality as perceptions and interpretations of reality, not as reality itself
- Understand the concept of misunderstanding

Mentalizing, mindfulness and validation

Mentalizing is related to concepts such as psychological attitude, emotional intelligence and empathy, which relate to the ability to imagine others' emotions and motives. Empathy is a prerequisite of mentalizing, but mentalizing also involves reflection and psychological understanding. Mentalizing is associated with the ability to *validate* and with *mindfulness*, which can be defined as conscious and non-judging awareness of the present, which often, but not necessarily, pertains to one's own mental life. In a slightly tongue-in-cheek comment, Bateman (2012, p. 297) writes about mindfulness:

> We all need to be mindful in our everyday work. The psychiatrist, of both his own and his patient's mind; but then he is mentalising.

Although mentalizing and mindfulness are related in several ways, they are rooted in separate professional traditions. Mindfulness springs from Zen Buddhism and meditation and is used in the third wave of cognitive therapy (e.g., Dialectical Behaviour Therapy (DBT) and Acceptance and Commitment Therapy (ACT)), while mentalizing springs from psychoanalysis and developmental psychopathology and is used in Mentalization-Based Therapy (MBT) (cf. Chapter 12). Both are important therapeutic concepts, and it is impossible to imagine any form of psychotherapy that does not involve being mindful of one's own and the other's mental states. Moreover, both concepts involve a curious, open, non-judging and accepting attitude towards oneself and the other.

There are, however, important differences. For example, mindfulness is not limited to mental states but may also be directed at other experiences, such as breathing, walking or running, auditory experiences or the sensation of flavours. Mentalizing always relates to a social context, as it deals with awareness and understanding of social interactions between people and reflection on mental states. Although mindfulness in Buddhist literature promotes non-attachment, the capacity for both mindfulness and mentalizing relies on *secure attachment*, where security refers to the ability to explore and accept an emotional experience without rejecting it (Allen, 2013).

The capacity for mentalizing and thus communicating that one understands the other's behaviour as meaningful is also related to the ability to validate. Mentalizing means being able to understand the other's behaviour as meaningful based on mental states (such as emotions, thoughts, intentions or expectations) and, not least, to mirror the other in order to make the person feel *seen, acknowledged* and *understood* on an emotional level. Validation means communicating with and mirroring the other in a way that conveys that his or her emotions, behaviour and motives are relevant, comprehensible and meaningful in the specific situation. Invalidation, on the other hand, may occur if the mirroring is 'off' or inaccurate, which in turn may stem from poor mentalizing. Inaccurate mirroring is experienced as invalidation, which is the same as feeling non-mentalized. Thus, these key concepts have a common core, which is to understand both the other's and one's own reactions in a non-judging way and acknowledge them as meaningful in a given context. Both validation and mentalizing are sources of coherence and continuity in the self and improve relationships with others.

Mentalizing, mindfulness and validation can be interpreted as manifestations of 'sensitive responsiveness', to quote Mary Ainsworth. The mother's sensitive responsiveness is important for the development of attachment and a sense of security in the early mother–infant relationship, which in turn is necessary for the development of the mentalizing capacity and the ability to validate one's own mental states. Conversely, numerous studies have found that attachment disorders increase the risk of poor mentalizing or failure to mentalize (Bateman & Fonagy, 2004), and that non-validating parental reactions can undermine the child's ability to attribute adequate meaning to his or her mental states.

Mindfulness and mentalizing are used to treat personality disorders and self-harming behaviour in two evidence-based therapy forms, which have key differences but are also related: DBT and MBT (cf. Chapters 11 and 12).

Developing a mentalizing capacity

Mentalizing develops in an attachment relationship between infant and parents. Studies have found that mothers who used a language that dealt with mental states when they addressed their 6-month-old babies had children who were securely attached at the age of 1 year (Meins et al., 2002). Other studies show that securely attached children learn to mentalize at an earlier age than children with insecure attachment. Children learn to mentalize by taking part in mentalizing interactions, the same way they learn to speak by being spoken to (Allen, 2013).

Prior to developing an actual mentalizing capacity, the infant goes through stages where his or her perception of the relationship between reality and mental processes transition from 1) a teleological mode, where the world is understood based on its physical manifestations, via 2) psychic equivalence mode, where there is no distinction between internal and external reality, to 3) pretend mode, where the internal and the external reality co-exist side by side as two completely separate worlds.

Teleological mode

In the teleological mode, mental states only exist when they are directly manifest in concrete behaviour: 'You're only upset if you're crying' or 'You only love me if you hold me' (Fonagy et al., 2002). The infant is too young to understand that there may be a causal relationship between an emotion and the fact that someone is crying. The infant does not understand that human beings are motivated by emotions. In teleological logic, actions speak louder than words.

In that sense, the teleological mode reflects concrete thinking. Borderline patients often have a teleological perception of the world, where the focus exclusively is on manifest behaviour and, for example, again and again require lovers, close friends or relatives to produce tangible proof that they love them or care about them. The following case vignette is an example of a patient who operates in a teleological mode:

A 19-year-old woman says that she cannot feel her emotions, and therefore she is not sure how or what she feels. Cutting, however, produces a tangible sign on her body, for herself and others to see that she is in pain. In another example of concrete teleological understanding, when the same woman came to the therapist's office for her appointment one day and found that the door, which was usually open, was closed, she took this to be a sure sign that the therapist wanted to end the treatment. Initially, she was unable to conceive of any other reason why the door might be closed.

Psychic equivalence mode

During the second year of life, the child begins to sense the existence a psychological reality and understand that people act on their thoughts and feelings; at this point, however, the child still believes that what exists in his or her mind must also exist in reality. The external world is perceived as identical to the internal world. The child has not yet grasped that our perception of reality differs from reality itself.

The child's conviction that his or her own perception must be identical with conditions in the real world means that projections and impulses can give rise to idiosyncratic and scary experiences. The logic here is that when the child perceives that mum is angry, she *is* angry. In the therapy context, it can be quite exhausting for the therapist to attempt to disprove the patient's experience in the psychic equivalence mode:

PATIENT: *Why are you angry?*
THERAPIST: *I'm not angry. Why do you ask?*
PATIENT: *I can tell you're angry. Why are you denying that you're angry?*
THERAPIST: *But I'm not angry.*
PATIENT: *Yes, you are. Don't be like that. Tell me why you're angry, and why you won't admit it. I get nervous when you're angry.*

Psychic equivalence mode

• The internal reality has the same status as the external reality.
• Thoughts and feelings are perceived as real.
• Strong conviction of being right, even when that is not the case.
• Patients know what the therapist is thinking.
• Generalizations and black/white thinking, e.g., 'all men are jerks'.
• Thinking is rigid and impervious to correction by external reality or others.

The symbolization capacity is vulnerable, as the symbol and the symbolized fuse. Simply talking about anger can activate angry feelings in a person who operates in a psychic equivalence mode.

Pretend mode

Pretend mode represents the opposite of psychic equivalence mode. In pretend mode, the child perceives the internal and the external world as separate. The child's thoughts and fantasies may be unrelated to factual conditions in the real world. For example, a game where the child uses a wash basin for a ship has nothing to do with the basin that we see but revolves around the imaginary ship that the child is travelling on. In the moment, these fantasies take precedence over reality, but the child does not mix them up and has no problem keeping them apart. In pretend mode, the child is able to grasp the difference between the perception of reality and reality itself.

In psychotherapy, pretend mode may manifest as a sharp divide between words and feelings, where the conversation involves many clichés, and where insight does not lead to any changes in the real world. The conversation unfolds on a pretend level, which has no bearing on the patient's real life outside the therapy room. Often, the therapist feels shut out from the patient's internal world and experiences boredom, lack of interest and maybe irritation.

Pretend mode

• Thoughts do not build a bridge between the internal and the external reality.
• The mental world is detached from the external reality.

- The state is associated with a sense of emptiness and meaninglessness.
- Inconsequential statements that lack emotional resonance.
- Emotions often do not match the content of thoughts and speech.

The child may alternate among the three positions: sometimes dominated by a way of thinking where only actions are seen to carry meaning (teleological mode); sometimes perceiving the internal and the external world as identical (psychic equivalence mode); and sometimes perceiving the internal and the external world as completely separate (pretend mode). Around the age of 5–6 years, the child gradually begins to integrate the pre-mentalizing modes and thus becomes capable of actual mentalizing: understanding that the child's own internal experiences represent the external reality without being identical with it. The child also understands that different individuals may have different perceptions of reality due to differences in feelings and thinking. This capacity enables a new level of continuity in the child's self-perception and concept of reality.

Quality of mentalizing

Everyone has experienced fluctuations in their mentalizing capacity, and the capacity is particularly challenged in close attachment relations, where powerful feelings of anger, love, sexual desire, powerlessness, frustration, offence, hatred, guilt, shame or betrayal are easily triggered. It may seem paradoxical that on the one hand, we are stronger in close relationships, provided they feel secure and stable, and on the other hand, we are also more vulnerable in these relationships, because they often have a lower threshold for emotional activation. Often, this happens because we are more sensitive to experiences of betrayal and violation from someone we are in an attachment relationship with.

A person who generally has a poor mentalizing capacity, and who therefore finds it hard to understand others' inner states, is generally more at risk of experiencing failure to mentalize than someone with a more stable mentalizing capacity, but everyone can occasionally experience failure to mentalize.

Failure to mentalize means that one lacks a reflective understanding of what is going on inside him/herself and in others; when this happens, the person regresses to one of the pre-mentalizing modes described above:

1   *Misuse of mentalizing* occurs when only physical manifestations are seen as meaningful (the teleological level). For example, the patient cannot explain how he or she feels but can only convey it by means of self-harm or in other concrete ways. Misuse of mentalizing also involves exploiting mentalizing to further one's own goals, for example by inducing guilt, shame or anxiety as a way to control the other. Misuse of mentalizing involves an element of mentalizing but lacks the capacity for empathy (Bateman & Fonagy, 2006).

2   *Concrete understanding* corresponds to the *psychic equivalence mode*, where the internal and the external world are experienced as identical. This is the most common form of impaired mentalizing and is manifest in a lack of interest in or understanding of others' mental states. This form of failure to

mentalize often involves rigidity, prejudice and a failure to understand complexity. The person finds an explanation for a phenomenon and sticks to it as indisputable 'truth'.

3 *Pseudo-mentalizing*, where there is no connection between thought and feeling or language and experience, corresponds to *pretend mode*. The person may appear reflective and seemingly insightful with regard to his or her own as well as others' mental states yet still have a poor mentalizing capacity.

The resilience of the mentalizing capacity varies from person to person. Some people are highly reactive and are quick to lose their mentalizing capacity, while others may maintain a certain grasp, even when they are under emotional pressure, without switching to a state of alarm and reacting impulsively. It also varies how quickly we recover our capacity for mentalizing after a breakdown of the mentalizing capacity; and finally, it varies how we react when we fail to mentalize. When the inner tension rises to a certain level, we go from having flexible and reflective reactions to ourselves and the outside world and adopt a fight-or-flight position, a state of alarm where the path from impulse to action is short. Some react with self-harm, others by yelling and shouting at others, getting into fights, drinking or taking drugs, overeating or engaging in other behaviours to release their inner tension.

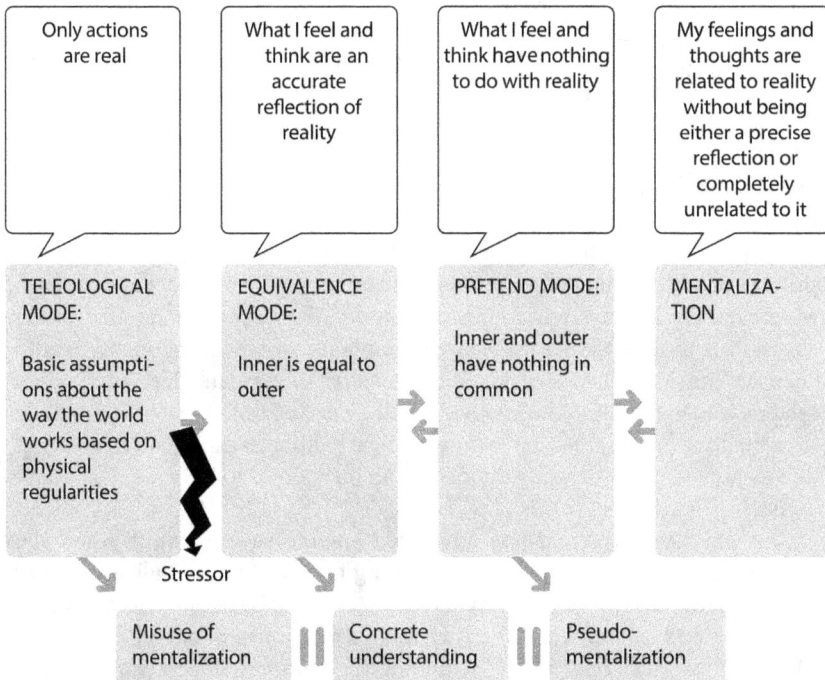

Figure 6.2 Development of mentalizing and failure to mentalize.

Source: Møhl and Kjølbye (2013).

The high level of tension that leads to a failure to mentalize triggers a shift in dominance from cortical to subcortical brain activity, which causes a collapse of automatic and controlled mentalizing in the prefrontal cortex. The more primitive fight-or-flight response simply blocks activity in the prefrontal cortex and thus shuts down the mentalizing capacity (Lieberman, 2007). When activity in the prefrontal cortex is shut down, and the subcortical structures take over, the individual loses the ability to *think* and instead responds through *action*. No one is capable of mentalizing when emotional tension runs high. Exactly when this shift occurs depends on the person's patterns of attachment and thus on early childhood experiences. Studies suggest that stress and trauma as well as the person's innate disposition influence the sensitivity and reactivity of the amygdala.

Persons with a BPD often have a hypersensitive and hyperreactive amygdala, which means that it takes comparatively less for them to experience a failure to mentalize; this in turn leads to a risk of inadequate impulse control and of self-harm. Especially when the person perceives a threat of abandonment, the attachment system is activated, and subcortical brain structures take over. This induces a state of alarm, which blocks the capacity for mentalizing. The inner working models and patterns of attachment are key in determining when and how strongly the attachment system is activated. In a person with anxious ambivalent or disorganized attachment, the attachment system becomes hyperactive even in the face of minor threats or the smallest sense of betrayal. These persons therefore have strong and often dramatic reactions aimed at re-establishing a sense of security or soothing the inner tension, for example by self-injuring.

A 23-year-old woman with BPD sought therapy because she was unable to control her self-destructive impulses, which were particularly intense when she was afraid of abandonment. This placed her in a constant state of alarm whenever she had a boyfriend. She would call him more than 50 times a day, and if he was unable to answer the phone when she rang, she would keep calling, which caused her inner tension to escalate. Her attachment system was hyperactivated; she was well aware of this reaction but unable to manage it in the situation. She was clearly able to articulate that 'I feel like a baby who has been abandoned. If no one comes to help me, I'm going to die!'

She was desperate and had attempted suicide several times when she failed to calm herself by cutting or burning herself. She was also painfully aware that her clingy behaviour was responsible for destroying her relationships. She was calmer when she was not in a relationship, but when she was single she was also desperately searching for a partner, which caused her to wind up in unhealthy relationships over and over again.

This case describes a woman with a severe attachment disorder and a hyperreactive attachment system. When her attachment system is hyperactivated, her inner tension escalates, and unless she can establish contact with her boyfriend (the attachment object), her life could be at risk due to her self-destructive impulses. A hyperactivated attachment system is unbearable, and many people hurt themselves in order to regulate their inner pain.

Individuals with anxious avoidant attachment, on the other hand, are not going to show much external reaction, because their attachment system is deactivated, but physiological signs, including their heart rate and cortisol level, indicate that they are experiencing a stress reaction. In a person with secure attachment, it takes more to trigger a reaction, and an actual failure to mentalize is less likely. This is because individuals with secure attachment have managed to internalize a good and secure inner object, which enables them to stay calm and preserve their mentalizing capacity for longer before it breaks down.

Failure of mentalizing and NSSI

Bateman and Fonagy (2004) suggest that NSSI generally reflects a reduced mentalizing capacity. Regardless which pre-mentalizing mode is dominant, NSSI may be seen as a form of concrete physical 'self-reflection', which would have unfolded on a purely mental level in a person with a more stable mentalizing capacity. According to Bateman and Fonagy (2006, p. 113), the primary purpose of NSSI 'is to maintain self-structure following sudden destabilization', which means recovering one's mentalizing capacity. NSSI is a way of managing mental states when the mentalizing capacity has been compromised, and the person is unable to make sense of his or her own as well as others' feelings and intentions.

In *pretend mode*, the mental and the physical world do not influence each other. This may explain why some individuals in the concrete situation seem to be completely unaffected by the often dramatic physical injuries they inflict on themselves. Their focus is exclusively on eliminating the psychological discomfort, and thus they have no realistic sense of what is happening on the physical level. Pretend mode can be seen as a form of dissociation, where the physical world is split off from the mental world (this is discussed in more detail later in this chapter).

In *psychic equivalence mode*, where thoughts and feelings are perceived as *real*, a feeling of, say, shame or evil cannot be regulated, soothed or modified by others. It is not immediately possible to help the person correct his or her perception; in a sense, the feeling takes on a life of its own; it grows and gains in validity, and the person is incapable of questioning whether it is real. This may lead to the use of NSSI as a form of punishment or a desperate attempt at eliminating the feeling on a physical level.

Due to the inability to sense and reflect on inner mental states, the body is used in a purely physical capacity, that is, on a *teleological* level: as a medium for representing and conveying the person's mental states. Self-injury is used as a concrete but *tacit* language for conveying one's mental state, both to oneself and to others. Fonagy and colleagues make an important point about people who self-harm:

> Not having a clear sense of themselves from within, they need to find a sense of the self through getting other people to react to them, and through treating themselves as objects, literally rather than metaphorically, because the self is experienced as a physical being without psychological meaning.
>
> (Fonagy et al., 2002, p. 406)

With this way of acting, the person affirms his or her own teleological understanding.

Finally, Bateman and Fonagy describe NSSI as an attempt at liberating the self from the alien self. In this non-mentalizing concrete understanding, 'parts of the body may be considered equivalent to specific mental states that can thus be literally physically removed' (Bateman & Fonagy, 2006, p. 27). When the alien self dominates, the person is filled with feelings of self-loathing and uselessness and may therefore opt for dramatic means, such as NSSI, as a way of achieving quick relief and alleviation of distress.

Good mentalizing

In contrast to poor mentalizing and failure to mentalize, good mentalizing involves the ability to embrace different perspectives and adopt a reflective and curious stance to oneself and others as well as a realistic awareness of one's own qualities and boundaries. It involves maintaining an open and non-judging stance towards others' behaviour, thoughts and feelings based on the notion that these will appear meaningful and understandable, given sufficient insight (Bateman & Fonagy, 2006). Good mentalizing involves being relaxed, flexible and playful, having a sense of humour and being willing to accept compromises between one's own and others' perspectives. Good mentalizing also involves the ability to forgive oneself and others.

Dissociation

Dissociation is a reaction that is triggered when the physical or emotional pain becomes overwhelming and thus intolerable for the person. It is a defence mechanism that is activated when the fight-or-flight response is not possible; such a situation overloads the nervous system and causes it to regress to a state where the usual integration of consciousness, memory, identity and perception is more or less disorganized.

In a state of dissociation, the person's consciousness is altered, reduced or fully or partially split off, sometimes making it impossible to recall a traumatic event. Dissociation is thus a way of escaping the traumatic event mentally; it also acts as a form of affect regulation, which is activated when the inner tension become dangerously high.

A female patient, who tends to dissociate, describes that as a child she was sexually abused by her father. Whenever this happened, she entered a state where she felt that she was observing herself from the outside, almost as a spectator to the assault. She could not feel anything and almost felt as if it was all happening to someone else. She was unable to avoid the attacks physically, but through dissociation she was able to remove herself mentally from the scene. In therapy, she dissociated whenever she established emotional contact with her childhood traumas, and her inner tension increased.

Dissociation may be manifest in varying degrees as either *detachment* or as *compartmentalization*.

Detachment causes a sense of disconnection from the self, an experience where the person either seems to observe him/herself from the outside (*depersonalization*) or feels separated from the external world, experiencing events as if they were happening on film (*derealization*), as described in the case above.

Compartmentalization causes psychological functions that are normally connected to be separated and unconnected, which may involve memory loss for a traumatic experience. In PTSD, where the person relives the traumatic situation in flashbacks, the experience has been split off from the ordinary (mentalizing) consciousness and is relived in a psychic equivalence mode (where mental states are perceived as being real). Flashbacks are stored in the implicit memory system, which is not accessible to language, and the nonverbal memories may take the form of sensory-perceptual images (for example a looming, shadowy Figure), sounds, smells (for example the smell of alcohol) or body sensations in the form of pain or other sensory experiences (Allen, 2013).

In the most extreme cases, certain parts of the personality are unaware of other parts, as in *Dissociative Identity Disorder* (DID). DID springs from previous experiences with extreme and prolonged assaults and abuse, where the person develops multiple self-states, each of which stores specific emotional reactions in connection with the trauma, for example aggression, anxiety, self-loathing and grief. These feelings dominate disparate self-states, so that the individual alternately appears aggressive, anxious, self-destructive or depressive. To survive mentally, the person needs to keep the disparate and incompatible emotions disconnected and separate by means of dissociation. Some of these unintegrated emotions may emerge as projections, giving the impression that others incarnate the respective emotions.

A woman with easily triggered dissociative reactions was sometimes able to see or, rather, sense her grandfather, who had abused her sexually when she was a child. She could sense his presence in the room and see him as a shadowy Figure. She was erroneously diagnosed with schizophrenia, because the doctor interpreted her hallucination as a manifestation of a schizophrenic delusion, not as a sign of dissociation.

Dissociative phenomena exist to varying degrees, ranging from the completely normal, for example driving on a familiar route while allowing one's attention to wander to a radio broadcast (being in two places at once) over daydreaming to the pathological level of having more or less clearly compartmentalized personality elements. Regardless how trivial or severe the dissociation is, it always serves an *adaptive* function, helping the person adapt to and deal with reality here and now. In the acute stage, for example in connection with sexual abuse, dissociation protects the child from confronting overwhelming psychological and physical pain, and in its trivial, everyday form, doing two things at once (for example driving a car while listening to the radio) can be an efficient and rational way of dealing with chores.

Although dissociation during a traumatic event may offer temporary relief, it comes at a cost, in part because the traumatic experiences are not integrated in the conscious mind and thus are not accessible for processing. This leads to an impaired capacity for mentalizing as well as a sense of unreality, numbness, emptiness or even semi-psychotic symptoms, where the person, for example, senses a presence (cf. the case above). Another problem is that the dissociative defence is triggered with growing ease once it has been activated. In some persons, dissociation can become an almost constant state, which leads to severe problems with maintaining a grip on reality and, not least, maintaining contact with others, who find the dissociating person distant and trance-like (cf. the case of Louise in the Introduction, pp. 13–15 f).

Dissociation and self-injury

Many studies have concluded that dissociation is common in connection with NSSI. The chronological link between dissociation and NSSI is complex, however, as some patients use NSSI to *escape* a dissociative state, while others use NSSI to escape reality and *enter* a dissociative state. Both are used to preserve the sense of a coherent self and identity under overwhelming emotional pressure. In this sense, the use of NSSI as means of affect regulation and a way of regulating the dissociative defence aims to prevent the experience of fragmentation and a loss of self.

Favazza points out that cutting 'is the most effective way of breaking through the paralyzing spell of dissociation' and 'a morbid act of self-help . . . converting chaos to calm, powerlessness to control' (cited in Strong, 1998, p. 43). With this statement, Favazza argues that cutting can both recreate the sense of connectedness to the self and the environment and help focus the person and thus end the experience of disintegration and fragmentation.

Levenkron (1998) distinguishes between *non-dissociative cutting*, where the person tries to escape a dissociative state by means of NSSI, and *dissociative cutting*, where the person seeks to create a distance to him/herself and the environment through NSSI.

Examples of *dissociative cutting* are seen in some of the individuals who use NSSI as a means of affect regulation and thus manage to *distance* themselves from a painful emotion or situation. They use NSSI to *escape* reality. Some individuals who engage in NSSI enter a trance-like state where they cannot sense themselves or their surroundings, and some even have amnesia with regard to the act of NSSI. More profound forms of dissociation during the self-injuring act can be dangerous because it puts the individual into a trance-like state where he or she does not feel any pain and therefore cannot control how deep the cuts are.

A woman had sometimes found herself 'coming to' while she was cutting and found herself bleeding profusely without having any recollection of the actual act. She could tell that she had prepared for the cutting, as she had bandages and disinfectant ready, as usual. Normally, when she cut herself without experiencing amnesia, she would enter a trance-like state where she felt as if she were cutting a stranger's arm. In those situations, she could still recall what happened but sometimes felt as if she were watching a scene from a film.

Non-dissociative cutting refers to NSSI as a means of ending the dissociative process. Being in a dissociative state is often described as a feeling of being inside a *bell jar*, without any real contact with the external world or oneself. Some experience a prolonged sense of numbness where they feel alienated from their own body and have the feeling that they are dissolving: a terrifying experience.

Another example of painful dissociation is flashbacks, where traumatic experiences are replayed over and over again, while the person is powerless to control the experience. To escape these distressing states, some use NSSI as a way of reconnecting with themselves and the external world, as this may recreate the sense of integration and coherence.

The biosocial theory and the impact of an invalidating childhood environment

Marsha Linehan (1993) has developed a theory about the development of BPD, which in her assessment is primarily associated with emotional dysregulation. Emotional dysregulation involves a severely elevated risk of developing pathological forms of affect regulation such as NSSI. In her *biosocial theory*, Linehan argues that emotional dysregulation develops and is maintained by both biological and psychosocial factors. In biological terms, emotionally dysregulated individuals have a higher vulnerability, conditioned by prenatal or early influences, which leads to heightened sensitivity and more intense and prolonged reactions to distressing stimuli. When a person with this kind of vulnerability grows up in an invalidating environment, he or she will have a severely elevated risk of developing emotional dysregulation and a borderline personality disorder (Musser et al., 2018).

According to Linehan (1993), 'an invalidating environment is one in which communication of private experiences is met by erratic, inappropriate, and extreme responses', an environment in which inner experiences are dismissed or punished rather than being validated. In these environments, 'the experience of painful emotions, as well as the factors that to the emotional person seem causally related to the emotional distress, are disregarded. The individual's interpretations of her own behavior . . . are dismissed' (p. 49).

Someone who is consistently met with degrading, inappropriate, erratic or extreme reactions will fail to develop a sense of being appropriately affirmed or mirrored. Unable to recognize him/herself in others' reactions, the person does not learn to trust his or her own feelings and is therefore incapable of expressing or regulating them appropriately. In other words, an invalidating environment is characterized by *incongruent* mirroring (cf. p. 106 f).

An invalidating environment is not necessarily brutal or insensitive, and many parents try to help by offering advice, trivializing the child's experiences as a way of comforting the child or distracting the child's attention away from his or her emotional reactions. Although this may be done with the best intentions, it often reflects the parents' inability to contain and mirror the child's emotional reactions.

If the child is consistently met with reaction such as 'there's no reason get so upset about that' or 'stop crying now; pull yourself together. You're too big to cry about that' or 'go to your room. Stay there until you're done carrying on like that', he or she does not learn to validate his or her own feelings and therefore perceives them as wrong, inappropriate, unreasonable, embarrassing or shameful. As an adult, the person will continue to *judge* him/herself for having the 'wrong' feelings: 'It's unreasonable of me to get so upset because he didn't come to see me, as he had promised!' The person comes to distrust his or her own feelings and interpretations of a given situation and instead has to rely on *others*' assessments and feelings.

Invalidation can take many different forms, but the essence is that the child is told, more or less explicitly, that his or her private emotions are not legitimate, do not make any sense or are not worth paying attention to. Most, if not all, of us will have been invalidated at some point in our lives. It occurs in any relationship, but it is only when the invalidation becomes the rule rather than the exception that things get really difficult for the person. The following example illustrates how the patient's mother, probably with good intentions, invalidates the patient so profoundly that she disengages from the dialogue.

Both parents were present during an uptake interview with a 16-year-old girl with three attempted suicides, numerous NSSI incidents where she inflicted deep cuts to various parts of her body and severe anorexia, which had led to two cases of compulsory hospitalization with forced tube-feeding. They were, naturally, very concerned for their daughter's health and repeatedly interrupted the psychologist, who was trying to connect with the girl. At one point, the daughter said, with a meek voice, that she cuts in order to punish herself, and the mother cut her off, saying, 'No, that's not true. She does it whenever she has gained 200 grams'. Understandably, the girl reacted by shutting up completely and detaching from the dialogue after this invalidating comment from her mother. It was only when the parents were asked to go for a walk, and the psychologist was alone with the young woman, that it gradually became possible to establish a conversation, during which the psychologist offered consistent validation in the interaction.

Three types of emotionally invalidating families

- *The chaotic family*, where children are not heard and seen, because the parents are too absorbed in their own problems. The parents' reactions to the child are unpredictable and inconsistent.
- *The obsessively perfect family*, where the parents cannot tolerate negative emotional responses from the child, such as anger, jealousy, sadness or other negative states.
- *The performance-oriented family*, which puts a high priority on achievements and controlling emotions at the cost of expressing and acknowledging emotions (Linehan, 1993).

Someone who has been raised in an invalidating environment will often express his or her emotions in a roundabout way, for example by displaying shame or anxiety in the form of aggression. This increases the risk of encountering invalidating reactions from others, who respond to the aggression (the secondary emotion) rather than the underlying shame or anxiety (the primary emotion). It also places the person at great risk of developing a maladaptive form of affect regulation, for example NSSI, overeating or substance abuse, which may offer short-term relief, but which only exacerbate the problem in the long term. A child who has grown up in an invalidating environment risks being caught up in a vicious circle, where he or she remains extremely sensitive to invalidating reactions from others, also as an adult.

In a phone conversation, Eva learned that her family would be going on holiday together while she was in hospital. This made her furious, and she began to yell at her dad on the phone. His response was that her reaction was ludicrous, as they were only going to be gone for a week. That made her even more distressed and angry. After the phone call, she reacted by breaking a glass and yelling and screaming at the hospital staff when they wanted to help her. It was only the following day in a conversation with her therapist that she was able to express that she felt abandoned and all alone in the world, and that her dad's failure to acknowledge her feelings had only added to the pain.

A sensitive child who is raised in an invalidating family is going to grow up to 1) have difficulty sensing and understanding his or her feelings accurately, 2) lack adequate mechanisms for affect regulation, thus often being emotionally dysregulated in situations where he or she does not feel validated, and 3) tend to invalidate him/herself. The vulnerability to invalidation can become very pronounced as even a minor sense of invalidation can reactivate a childhood pattern of invalidation, which happens outside the conscious level. Therefore, a person with emotional dysregulation is often very quick to 'fly off the handle', reacting strongly to invalidation or to the sense of not being seen, met, acknowledged or respected. Responding with strong and frequently 'misdirected' reactions makes it even more difficult for others to validate the person's feelings.

A patient said that her mother had found out that she was cutting. The mother had become 'really angry', which had made the patient furious. By carrying out a chain analysis and reflecting on the situation with her therapist, the patient realized that the mother had probably reacted the way she did because she was scared and concerned, which the mother confirmed when the patient later discussed the incident with her.

Families characterized by inadequate validation often have a high degree of direct or latent conflict. The lack of validation creates a tense, anxious and aggressive atmosphere charged with feelings of shame and a lack of mutual trust. Consequently, an experience of invalidation can trigger an intense reaction.

Beth, a 13-year-old girl, comes home from school crying, goes straight to her room, slamming the door behind her. Worried, her mother goes up to talk to her. Initially, Beth refuses to talk to her mother but eventually tells her that she was teased by some of the girls in her class. Beth's mother responds by saying, 'they probably don't mean anything by it' and encourages Beth to forget about the incident. She says this to calm her daughter down, but it has quite the opposite effect on Beth. She is furious with her mother and calls her 'a stupid cow'. The mother gets angry and blames

Beth, saying she is 'nothing but trouble'. The outcome is that Beth isolates herself in her room, refuses to come down for dinner and also refuses to open her door when her parents want to come in and say goodnight. She eventually calms down late in the evening by cutting.

Beth's mother did her best, acting on good intentions, which was to try to calm her daughter down by trivializing her experience. That had the opposite effect, however, because Beth did not feel heard, seen and understood – validated. Eventually, Beth's mother got angry with Beth, because she reacted to her aggression without connecting with her distress and her fear of being excluded from the girls' group. In most cases, aggression generates aggression. Beth's experiences of emotional invalidation triggered an intense reaction and instantly made her see red. The outcome of the specific incident is that she withdraws from her parents in order to be left alone and perhaps also as a way of punishing them. Beth and her mother both feel invalidated, and it is easy to imagine them both feeling increasingly at a loss for what to do, which only serves to further increase the emotional tension in a self-fuelling snowball effect.

If Beth's mother had simply commented on Beth's state, for example by saying, 'I understand how that would make you upset', the situation would probably have taken a different course, because Beth would have felt validated: met and acknowledged in the emotion that is filling her up. That may sound simple, but it is often hard to do, in part because Beth's mother also feels invalidated, as her good intentions meet with rejection.

As mentioned earlier, someone who has grown up in an invalidating environment is usually very sensitive to invalidating reactions – a sensitivity that may be lifelong. Invalidation during childhood leaves emotional impressions that are stored in procedural memory and in the limbic system (the amygdala). These impressions may be reactivated by certain sensations or moods, which trigger powerful impulsive reactions that can result in NSSI. Therefore, a validating and empathic connection is an absolute condition for establishing a therapeutic alliance with a patient who is sensitive to invalidating reactions.

7 From meaning to function

Self-injuring behaviour carries different meanings for different people in different situations, which they will be able to articulate more or less clearly.

The desire to uncover *the meaning* of a particular behaviour is reflected in the question, 'Why *are you cutting yourself?*' Often, however, it would be more constructive to ask, '*What do you* achieve *by cutting yourself?*' The latter question focuses on the *function* self-injury fulfils for the individual. The key is to discern '*why this* particular *behavior, at this* particular *time, to serve this* particular *function, for this* particular *patient*', to quote Suyemoto's classic article from 1998 (Suyemoto, 1998, p. 537). This implies that we cannot speak generally about the meaning or function of NSSI, as it will vary from person to person and over time.

A *functional* analysis of NSSI is aimed at identifying the factors that motivate, intensify and perpetuate self-injuring behaviour. The attempt is to understand the behaviour based on what went *before* the incident (for example an intensification of painful psychological tension) and what follows *after* the incident (consequences). If a person experiences a drop in the intensity of negative emotions immediately after self-injuring, either as a result of automatic internal psychological or physiological processes or because others' response to the act serves to soothe the negative feeling, it makes sense for the person to repeat the behaviour. NSSI then serves a positive function for the person, and the use of NSSI becomes self-reinforcing.

A functional model of NSSI

In light of the perspective outlined above, where the emphasis is on the function and purpose of NSSI and on modern behavioural therapy, Nock and Prinstein (2004) have developed a functional model for understanding what the person gains by NSSI and what reinforces and perpetuates the behaviour (the Four-Function Model).

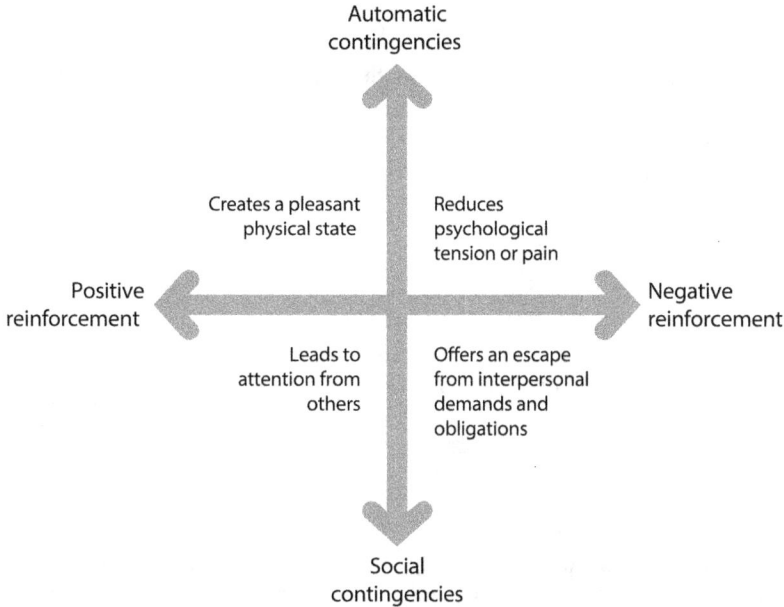

Figure 7.1 The Four-Function Model.

Source: Adapted from Nock and Prinstein (2004).

The model illustrates how NSSI can be analysed based on two dimensions: whether NSSI is followed by consequences that are the automatic result of psychological or physiological processes in the individual (*automatic* reinforcement), or whether it is reinforced by social interactions with others (*social* reinforcement). Moreover, the model operates with a reinforcement of the behaviour that is either *positive* (positive reinforcement: the behaviour has favourable consequences) or *negative* (negative reinforcement: the behaviour is followed by the *removal* and thus the *avoidance* of an aversive stimulus).

In *automatic-negative reinforcement*, NSSI eliminates or reduces the aversive feeling, which results in a reduction of psychological pain. This is the function that is most commonly mentioned by both theorists and people who engage in NSSI: 'to stop bad feelings' (Nock & Prinstein, 2004, p. 885). NSSI reduces the inner pain, whether it manifest as stress, anger, anxiety, diffuse tension or flashbacks, for example reliving sexual abuse over and over again, where the positive reinforcement of NSSI is that it puts an end to the painful flashbacks. The affect-regulation function is driven by automatic-negative reinforcement.

Automatic-positive reinforcement refers to a situation where NSSI produces a positive feeling, for example because the person feels a 'rush', feels lighter or feels more in touch with his/her own body. Often, NSSI begins with automatic-negative reinforcement, where the person self-injures in order to escape an inner sense of discomfort, but continues due to automatic-positive reinforcement, because the person experiences a form of inner pleasure as a result of the self-injuring behaviour.

> During her therapy course, Andrea was able to stop NSSI, which involved cutting. After going a full month without cutting, she celebrated her achievement by cutting herself. 'It gives me so much pleasure that I simply have to do it again, and it seemed a nice reward', she explained.

Unlike the processes that unfold *automatically* and leave the individual feeling instantly better after NSSI, either because NSSI in itself produces a positive feeling or because it removes a negative feeling, some processes have a *social* component, because the individual influences his or her surroundings in a way that has a positive outcome. In *social-positive reinforcement*, the self-injuring person receives attention or care from his or her surroundings or is able to 'punish others' by NSSI. NSSI itself may be unpleasant, because it involves physical pain, but the benefits and reinforcement of the self-injuring behaviour lie in the reaction it produces in others.

> 'Sometimes I use NSSI to let my mother know how bad I feel. When she sees the cuts on my arms, she's there for me, on a different level. Once, we stayed up most of the night talking, because she saw that I had cut myself', says a 19-year-old woman who lives alternately with her mother and her father, and who feels quite lonely.
>
> While she was hospitalized in a psychiatric ward, a 23-year-old woman had cut herself during a group session by clutching a piece of broken glass in her hand. Afterwards, she said that she needed someone to listen to her and be with her. 'It's the only way to get any help in this f***ing ward!' In fact, she did receive a great deal of attention from the other patients in the group, from healthcare workers who checked on her every 15 minutes, from a nurse who bandaged her hand, from a doctor who had to assess her condition and from the ward's psychologist, who came to see her outside their normally scheduled talks.
>
> A 20-year-old man who regularly burned himself with cigarettes often did so to punish his girlfriend and to let her know how he felt about the way she was treating him. 'It's not a cry for help', he emphasized. 'But I want her to know that she's treating me like sh*t!'

Somewhat simplistically put, actions speak louder than words, and when a person performs NSSI in order to communicate something to others, it will produce a reaction, although it is not always the reaction that the self-injuring person had anticipated (Nock, 2008).

> In order to attract her parents' attention and in the hope that they might talk to her and care for her, 16-year-old Meredith made sure that her self-inflicted cuts were visible to her parents. Instead, they reacted with anger, insisting that she 'stop this nonsense' immediately, and threatened to place her in an institution. Meredith achieved exactly the opposite response to her self-injury that she had been hoping for.

One of the costs of social-positive reinforcement is that it can put quite a strain on the person's relationships with others. People who are close to individuals who self-injure often tell how stressful they find it to have to contain the self-injuring behaviour, and say that it leaves them feeling anxious, overwhelmed and angry. As one family member said about her severely self-injuring daughter: 'In order to protect myself, I have to keep my distance and leave her be. There's nothing I can do, anyway. And I just wind up hating her'.

The fourth and last category is *social-negative reinforcement*, where the person uses NSSI as a way of avoiding or escaping social demands or obligations.

> Linda is a 21-year-old woman who has been subjected to repeated sexual abuse, both as a child and later as an adult. When she went out with her friends, she would sometimes cut herself in different parts of her body as a way of 'putting men off'. She Figured men would leave her alone if they saw her injuries.

The Four-Function Model (Figure 7.1) can be used to analyse what the individual achieves by NSSI, which in turn makes it easier to help the person develop skills that he or she can use to achieve the same benefit in a healthier or less costly way. If the self-injuring behaviour is motivated by *automatic-negative reinforcement*, the person needs to learn about methods for regulating his or her negative feelings in a way that is effective and, in the long run, less destructive than NSSI (for example distraction exercises such as playing computer games, going for a run or taking a hot bath or shower).

If the self-injuring behaviour is motivated by *automatic-positive reinforcement*, where the person uses NSSI in order to feel his/her own body or achieve positive feelings, he or she needs to learn ways of achieving this positive state in different ways (e.g., mindfulness exercises, listening to music, taking a hot bath or shower or doing something else that produces a pleasant bodily sensation).

If the self-injuring behaviour is motivated by *social-positive reinforcement*, where the person performs NSSI as a way of getting attention and achieving secondary gains from his or her social environment, the key is for the person to acquire skills that make it possible to achieve the same benefits in a way that is less destructive and put less of a strain on those close to the person (for example by improving the person's relational skills or mentalizing capacity).

If the self-injuring behaviour is motivated by *social-negative reinforcement*, where the person uses NSSI to avoid something unpleasant, he or she needs to develop skills that make it easier to draw boundaries or to say no.

It is no simple task, however, to change the way one manages one's life and personal challenges, and it is rarely sufficient simply to acquire the relevant skills. The point is, however, that if the person can achieve the same benefit in an alternative and less self-destructive way, it will be easier to give up NSSI. It can be difficult to modify the coping strategies one has developed, however, especially if they seem effective. Every time the person experiences a positive effect of his or her NSSI, that experience will serve to perpetuate and reinforce the use of NSSI as a coping strategy. The problem is that the self-injuring behaviour may offer instant relief while exacerbating the problem in the long term. The use of NSSI as a coping strategy thus becomes part of the problem and further contributes to the person's vulnerability.

Reactions that perpetuate self-injury

- *Reinforcers*: consequences that increase the use of self-injury.
- *Positive reinforcement*: increases the frequency of self-injury by providing a reward (for example a good bodily sensation, a 'rush' or positive attention from others).
- *Negative reinforcement*: increases the frequency of self-injury by removing an aversive state or unpleasant feeling (for example by dampening or eliminating psychological pain). Negative reinforcement offers relief.

Functions of NSSI

People engage in NSSI because it makes them feel better. Most people will find the idea of hurting oneself to feel better counterintuitive, but it is important to remember that, like everyone else, people who practice NSSI do the best they can to have a good life. They hurt themselves because the practice is functional and serves a purpose for them, but also because they lack better skills for, for example, regulating their emotions, communicating with others or expressing themselves.

Many studies have examined the functions of NSSI and identified numerous motives and functions (for a review see Taylor et al., 2018). In a review, Klonsky (2007) examined the empirical research into the functions of NSSI. The literature includes self-reports of reasons for NSSI, descriptions of the phenomenology of NSSI and laboratory studies of the effects of NSSI proxies on affect and physiological arousal.

The review identified seven functions, which were examined in the 18 studies included in the review.

1   The *affect-regulation model* of NSSI suggests that NSSI is a strategy to manage or regulate emotions (decrease negative emotions and increase positive emotions). The studies found a strong support for the affect-regulation model.

2   The *self-punishment model* suggests that NSSI is an expression of anger or derogation towards oneself or a way to penalize oneself. The studies also find strong support for the self-punishment model but more modest support for the following models.

3   The *anti-dissociation model* characterizes NSSI as a response to periods of dissociation or depersonalization (e.g., feelings of not being real or feeling as if one is watching oneself in a film).

4   The *anti-suicide model* views NSSI as a coping mechanism for resisting urges to attempt suicide.

5   The *interpersonal-influence model* stipulates that NSSI is used to influence or manipulate people in the self-injurer's environment.

6   The *interpersonal-boundaries model* holds that NSSI is a way to affirm the boundaries of the self.

7   The *sensation-seeking model* regards NSSI as a means for generating excitement or exhilaration (getting a kick).

The general pattern of findings across the seven functions tended to remain consistent, across sample types (e.g., non-clinical versus clinical versus forensic, adult versus adolescent, outpatient versus inpatient, women versus men) (Klonsky, 2007).

In addition to the above-mentioned functions, it is my experience that self-injury may also be a means of self-care:

Ricky had recently been abandoned by his boyfriend, and when he thought of him, he would often be overwhelmed by painful emotions of loss, loneliness or self-loathing. In order to manage the intense emotions and to be able to be within his own skin, he would take a lit cigarette to his own arm or the soles of his feet. Afterwards he would go to bed, tucked up under the blankets, occasionally bringing a plate of chocolate because he felt that he deserved a treat after all the pain he had been going through. However, the chocolate was not enough in itself. It was only after punishing himself by self-injuring that he would allow himself a treat.

In a systematic review of literature reporting first-hand accounts for the reasons for self-injury than intent to die including 152 studies (113 questionnaire-based and 39 interview-based), the authors (Edmondson et al., 2016) found the following main reasons for NSSI, ranked according to frequency. The quotations in the text are from different studies in the systematic review:

Managing distress/affect regulation

Ninety-three per cent of the questionnaire-based studies identified items such as 'to get relief from a terrible state of mind'. Similarly, 92% of the qualitative studies endorsed this motivation, described as 'doing this relieved the emotional pain'. A common notion related to this theme was the idea of preferring to deal with physical pain over emotional pain: 'I wanted to take the pain away from my heart and put it elsewhere'.

Exerting interpersonal influence

Eighty-seven per cent of the questionnaire-based studies found evidence of interpersonal influence, including 'to seek help from someone'. Fifty-six per cent of the qualitative studies found similar evidence: 'Doing this [self-injure] I found . . . I received the warmth, love and attention I had been looking for'.

Punishment

Sixty-three per cent of the quantitative studies found evidence to support the idea of self-injury as punishment, for example, 'I wanted to punish myself', but occasionally also as a way of punishing others (look what you made me do) or inviting criticism or punishment from others. Fifty-one per cent of the qualitative studies described such reasons:

> Eve punishes herself by cutting, over and over again, when she feels that she has done something wrong. Her self-assessment is generally very negative and associated with feelings of shame. Her motivation for punishing herself might be, for example, that she does not feel she is entitled to receive praise from her therapist or to enjoy a visit from a friend while in hospital.

Dissociation

Forty-eight per cent of the quantitative studies supported a link between self-injury and dissociative experiences. This included inducing a dissociative state. For example: 'produce a feeling of numbness when my feelings are too strong'.

The authors allocated these reasons here rather than categorizing them as affect regulation because they entailed an active pursuit of numbness rather than a containment of other unpleasant emotions. Under this theme, the authors also included acts aimed at terminating a dissociative state in statements such as 'feeling generation'. Similarly, 38% of the qualitative studies described inducing a dissociative state, for example: 'you feel a lot but then you don't feel anything'. Under this theme (dissociation), the authors also included acts aimed at terminating a dissociative state in statements such as 'I feel numb – physically and emotionally. I can't feel my own skin. [after self-harming] I can physically feel again. My senses come back. I get a surge of energy and regain sensation'.

Sensation-seeking

Self-injury as a way to generate excitement was identified in 20% of the quantitative studies – 'to feel more alive' – and in 12% of the qualitative studies: 'It felt nice I quite liked it, adrenaline and that. Since I've been on [the unit], I just do it for the adrenaline. You can get addicted to it'.

Averting suicide

In 15% of the quantitative studies, respondents reported self-injury as a way of dealing with the risk of suicide: 'to stop myself from killing myself'. The same was reported by 7% of the qualitative studies: 'if I don't cut for a long time I end up overdosing'.

Maintaining or exploring boundaries

Eight per cent of the studies reported evidence to support a boundary-defining function in statements such as 'to create a symbolic boundary between myself and others'. Five per cent of the qualitative studies reported such reasons: 'When the emotions are too much it feels as though my body shuts down like I couldn't tell where the edges of my body were . . . self-harming kinda defined the edges of my body'.

Expressing and coping with sexuality

Self-injury to serve a sexual function was the least endorsed reason in the quantitative literature. Six per cent of the studies found evidence to support this in statements such as 'to provide a sense of relief that feels much like sexual release'. Not all statements suggested pleasure: responding to sexual identity problems, 'coping with sexuality' seemed closer to affect regulation. Only one qualitative study (2.5%) found self-injury to serve a sexual function. The study reported how patients likened cutting to sexual experiences and described a sense of release as blood flowed from the cut.

Many studies reported at least one reason for self-injury that did not fit into the above-mentioned categories. The additional reasons for self-injury could be summarized as either 1) *self-injury as a positive experience* or 2) *self-injury as a means of defining self.*

Self-injury as a positive experience

Twenty-one per cent of the studies report a form of gratification that was not overtly sexual. The authors felt that these were describing something different to sensation-seeking, as the feeling was more comforting than excitement-inducing. Many questionnaires include response categories that describe a sense of pleasure from the act of self-injury such as 'can be enjoyable or comforting'.

Some of the statements also included discussion of the pleasurable feelings, for example 'I like the blood, the blood itself, the appearance of the blood was a lot of the satisfaction'.

In 10% of the studies exploring reasons of self-injury for young people, self-injury was sometimes described as 'experimental': 'when I started secondary school, my puberty was beginning. At that time I cut myself for the first time. It was just an experiment'.

In 14% of the studies, self-injury was described as protection of self or others: 'I've been cutting myself so that if someone does try anything they'll see my body and think what a freak, she's disgusting, she's ugly'.

Self-injury as protection of others, for example from consequences of the respondent's anger, was evident in statements such as 'I banged my head and I'd scream. . . . I do it because I don't want to hurt somebody else and I have to get rid of it'.

Self-injury as defining the self

A sub-theme of validation was identified in 21% of the studies in which self-injury could be a way of demonstrating strength or toughness: 'I feel powerful that I am immune to being hurt by it [the cutting]'.

A sense of self-validation was also evident in comparison with others: 'You know, other people are afraid of doing that . . . They can't imagine how or why you would do that, and . . . in an arrogant sense it puts me above them'.

In 13% of the studies, self-injury was used to achieve a sense of belonging 'to feel more part of a group' or 'to not feel like an outsider'. In another 13% of the studies, self-injury was described as a way 'of communicating the pain within', and in 3% of the studies writing on the skin was described as a reminder of a special experiences 'to create physical reminders of important events'.

In 27% of the studies, self-injury was found to achieve a sense of personal mastery or of being in control: 'I self-injure for a feeling of control, I cut to make myself feel I still have the power to handle the situation' (Edmondson et al., 2016, p. 113).

It can be problematic, however, to examine what feelings make an individual perform NSSI, because many have only a vague sense of the psychological processes unfolding inside them and in their interactions with others. Many people who engage in NSSI may have difficulty distinguishing between different feelings such as anger, self-loathing, anxiety, depression, stress, loneliness, guilt etc. and may perceive these feelings as a diffuse inner tension that is almost physically unbearable and requires immediate release. They cannot confidently distinguish one feeling from another, and when the emotional intensity becomes overwhelming and seems unbearable, they react with NSSI to regulate the inner tension. Studies indicate significantly higher levels of alexithymia in people who engage in NSSI compared with people who do not (Norman & Borril, 2015).

Alexithymia means 'absence of words for emotions' and refers to an impaired ability to identify, describe and communicate one's own feelings, which in turn reflects difficulties with affective self-regulation (Gatta et al., 2016). Alexithymia occurs more frequently in people who self-injure than in the general population. Alexithymic features, such as difficulty in identifying and describing feelings, are associated with poor attachment styles and emotional trauma, which impair the capacity to mentalize and regulate affect. Additionally, emotion regulation has been found to be the most commonly identified function associated with NSSI in adolescents as they attempt to modulate strong emotions (Cerutti et al., 2018).

Model of perpetuating self-injuring behaviour

Above, we have seen how NSSI can serve as a sort of coping strategy or a form of self-medication to achieve an instant reduction of difficult, negative feelings, activate a positive feeling or influence one's relationship with others. The model

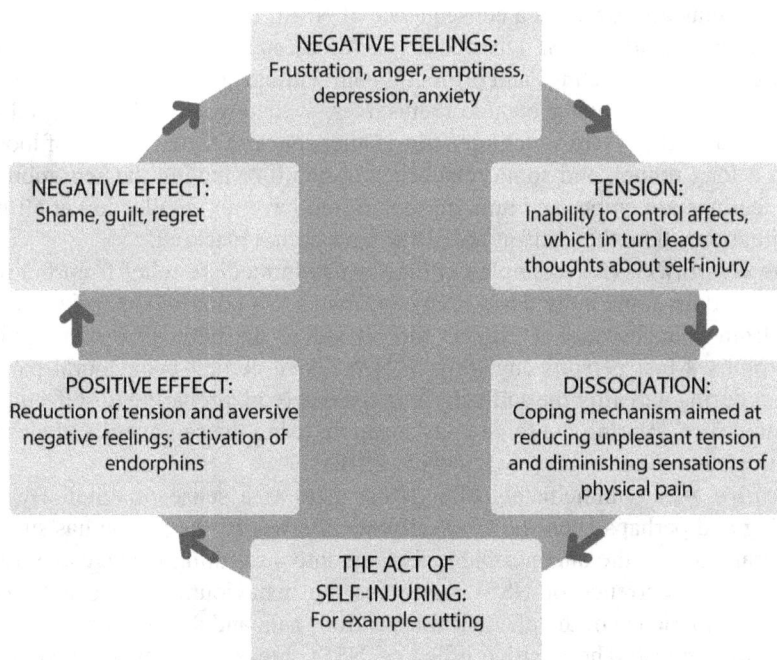

Figure 7.2 Model for perpetuating NSSI.

Source: Adapted from Møhl (2015).

below illustrates how *automatic reinforcement* can perpetuate self-injuring behaviour, because the individual will be naturally inclined to continue using NSSI if it appears to work. The model further illustrates how NSSI can become a self-reinforcing process that leads to both psychological and physiological addiction: *psychological addiction,* because NSSI becomes the dominant coping strategy, which leads to a growing deterioration of the individual's ability to cope constructively with problems, and *physiological addiction,* because in some persons, NSSI (especially cutting) activates endorphins, which provide a pleasant sense of relief or even a 'rush' or a kick (auto addiction). The model is cyclical, but the process often begins with the negative feelings that trigger the complex cycle of NSSI.

Negative feelings: The urge to NSSI often begins with negative or aversive feelings. Some authors break these negative feelings down into three categories: 1) anger directed at oneself and others, frustration and bitterness; 2) a sense of alienation from oneself, isolation, loneliness and emptiness; and 3) depression, melancholy or a sense of being disgusting or 'wrong'.

Tension: The negative feelings become overwhelming, and the person considers NSSI, for example cutting, as a way of escaping the pain (affect regulation) (*automatic-negative reinforcement*). The person may continue to the next stage impulsively, or he or she may have made preparations, getting plasters, disinfectant and bandages ready while the tension builds.

Dissociation: This state occurs as a direct consequence of the overwhelming and uncontrollable feelings that are a result of growing inner tension, but dissociation may also occur as a consequence of NSSI. Dissociation may thus occur both before and after NSSI. Dissociation is the defence that enables the person to experience intense feelings and profound pain without 'falling apart'. Some have the sensation of standing outside themselves, watching everything unfold at a distance, as if they were watching a film. Others have related a feeling of looking down a long tunnel, and some relate feeling numb or having the sensation that their feelings are empty and unimportant. Some have no recollection at all from the situation where they self-injure. They have a total blackout.

The act of NSSI (for example cutting) brings immediate relief from the inner tension and for some individuals even contributes to a sense of euphoria and freedom from pain, because it triggers the release of the body's own 'morphine': endorphins. Most persons engaging in NSSI have certain behavioural patterns before, during and after the self-injurious episode (e.g., preparing to self-injure in the same way, injuring the same body location, using the same tool and cleaning the injury in the same way) (Stacy et al., 2018).

Positive effect: immediately after NSSI there is a sense of relief. By self-injuring and perhaps even showing self-care afterwards, the person has successfully transformed the uncontrollable feelings into something manageable. Every subsequent occurrence of NSSI reinforces the behaviour, because it brings a renewed experience of the pleasant release from pain and discomfort.

Negative effect: The positive effect of NSSI, however, is short-lived. When the endorphin rush fades, and the person realizes the consequences of NSSI, the negative feelings rush in: 'Oh, no. Not again!' followed by shame, guilt, regret and self-loathing. In addition, all the negative feelings that were present prior to NSSI have not gone away but are now returning with a vengeance. Consequently, the person may self-injure again, reactivating the cycle.

Over time, it will take less and less to set off the self-injuring process. Even minor frustrations will activate the negative thoughts that trigger the urge to regulate the inner tension, use NSSI to communicate, punish oneself or otherwise manage painful affects. The person who engages in NSSI is vulnerable at every step of the cycle, and the self-reinforcing process develops very quickly; as a result, the person gradually loses his or her capacity to apply more constructive coping mechanisms. The ability to contain and deal with rejection, for example, without activating the negative thoughts that lead to the almost automatic desire to self-injury, continues to diminish. It is as if the person barely has time to grasp the notion that 'Nobody likes me' or 'I'm useless' before he or she feels an irresistible and almost physical urge to NSSI.

It is not uncommon for NSSI to coincide with the person drinking alcohol, getting insufficient sleep, not eating enough, maybe failing to take prescription medicine or being subjected to stressors that weaken the person's defence against the self-destructive impulses. The process gains momentum very easily, and the NSSI may run its course and result in actual addiction.

Tina felt that she had to cut herself to calm down at night – even when she wasn't 'wound up', as she put it. Without cutting, she often had an unpleasant feeling of restlessness that might escalate into actual anxiety. Cutting quickly gave her a feeling of calm and relaxation that enabled her to lie down and fall asleep. In therapy, she learned to use a therapeutic ball blanket instead of cutting to calm down.

8   Pathophysiology and neurobiological perspectives on self-injury

Despite a fair amount of research, the scientific understanding of the neurobiological basis of NSSI still rests on a fairly sparse amount of data. NSSI is a non-specific phenomenon within a spectrum of disorders ranging from major depression or BPD to no psychiatric disorder, and due to the complexity and diversity of the function and dynamic background of NSSI, it is not possible to propose a general model that captures the full spectrum of NSSI.

The infant's brain is designed to be moulded by the environment the child encounters. Caldji et al. (1998) suggest that 'maternal care during infancy serves to "program" behavioral responses to stress in the offspring'. Thus, early interactions with the mother/caregiver play a crucial role for a person's capacity and methods for stress management later in life and thus for the risk of engaging in NSSI.

According to Brown and Plener (2017), findings from neurobiological studies of NSSI point to abnormalities on the HPA axis, the endogenous opioid system, and in the neural processing of emotionally, socially or physically adverse stimuli (for a review of the neurobiology of NSSI, see Schreiner et al., 2015).

The role of neurotransmitters in NSSI

In the search for biological causes of NSSI, researchers have focused on some of the most prominent behavioural features of persons who practice NSSI: impulsivity, vulnerability, (self-directed) aggression, increased occurrence of and reduced capacity for regulating negative emotions and addiction to self-injury behaviour. The main neurotransmitters influencing these features are *adrenalin*, *noradrenalin* and *cortisol*, which are part of the hypothalamic–pituitary–adrenal (HPA) axis and act as stress hormones that put the body on 'high alert'; *serotonin*, which regulates impulsivity, aggression, mood, sleep and appetite, among other features; *dopamine*, which produces a sensation of pleasure; and *endogenous opioids*, sometimes referred to as 'the body's own morphine', which affects pain perception and arousal, among other processes. In addition to these specific neurotransmitters, it is also important to consider the respective circuits they affect, in particular the HPA axis, the limbic system, the prefrontal cortex and the serotonergic system.

Neurotransmitters mediate communication between neurons in the brain and between the brain and peripheral nerves, muscles and glands throughout the body. Both the brain and the peripheral nervous system are made up of neurons. A neuron consists of a cell body and two types of projections: axons, which transmit signals from the cell body to other cells, and dendrites, which receive incoming signals from other neurons. Signals are transmitted between the neurons by means of electric impulses and chemical substances called neurotransmitters. When a signal passes through a neuron, the tip of the axon releases a specific neurotransmitter, which is released into the tiny gap between axon and dendrite called a synapse. The dendrite contains specific receptors that capture the neurotransmitter, which in turn triggers a new signal in the next neuron in the chain, and so on. Eventually, the signal is transmitted to a specialized cell where it triggers a specific reaction, for example a muscle contraction or the release of a substance from a gland. Specific disorders in the metabolism of these neurotransmitters influence the person's psychological functioning, among other things, and may thus also affect the risk of NSSI.

Adrenalin, noradrenalin and cortisol

Intensely stressful experiences during childhood may have a permanent influence on stress responses and stress management later in life. Exposure to stress activates two interlinked systems: the *autonomic nervous system* (ANS) and the *hypothalamic–pituitary–adrenal (HPA) axis*.

The ANS releases the hormones adrenalin and noradrenalin, known as catecholamines, which activate the sympathetic part of the ANS, putting the body on alert and mobilizing energy for either flight or fight. In the short term, this is a vitally important function that has helped secure our survival as a species. However, a constantly elevated adrenalin level, due to persistent stress or a dysfunctional stress response, affects concentration and memory and disrupts the sleep pattern, something that is commonly found among individuals who self-injure, particularly among women (Walrath, 2017), and which renders the person vulnerable and leads to an increased risk of depression and anxiety (Hammen, 2018).

The other systemic stress response is the release of cortisol, from the adrenal cortex under influence from the HPA axis. The HPA axis is a complicated feedback system of inhibiting and activating functions that are similarly involved in mobilizing energy to prepare the body to deal with stress. The amygdala, which is part of the limbic system and involved in the processing of sensations and emotions, has an *activating* effect on the HPA axis, while the hippocampus has an *inhibitory* effect and thus tones down the stress response.

In evolutionary terms, the amygdala is an old brain structure. Among its functions is drawing on sensory input to scan our environment for situations or objects that pose a potential threat, but the amygdala is also the seat of our emotional memories. The amygdala is active from birth. Long before we develop language and consciousness, the amygdala is able to store reactions of anxiety and anger from interactions with the caregiver. These preverbal memories may be reactivated impulsively in interpersonal interactions, flooding the person with emotions that he or she is unable to understand or regulate. The amygdala is particularly sensitive to *kindling*, a process where neurological circuits that have been stimulated repeatedly eventually become self-activating, putting the body on alert, even *without* an external stimulus. This is important for understanding why many who self-injure are in a constant state of alert and unable to relax. Moreover, there are more neural pathways running from the amygdala to the affect-regulating part of the brain, the prefrontal cortex, than in the opposite direction. Hence, the preverbal memories that activate the amygdala are more effective than the conscious, rational reflections in the more mature part of the brain. This explains how our emotions can sometimes overpower us, in particular when we are tired or otherwise vulnerable. Through the pathways running from the prefrontal cortex to the amygdala, thoughts and worries may activate the amygdala and thus maintain our physiological state of alert – thus, metaphorically speaking, our thoughts can fan the flames of our emotions.

Studies suggest that persons with emotional dysregulation and NSSI have a more sensitive and active amygdala response, which offers a physiological explanation of their tendency to be more impulsive, sensitive, reactive and tense (Chamberlain et al., 2017).

The low road and the high road

The limbic system, including the amygdala, is part of a complex network, which also includes the thalamus, the prefrontal cortex and the hippocampus, among other structures, the latter having important functions in connection with impulse control and the regulation of emotions (including aggression) and our explicit memory. The thalamus receives sensory impulses from the whole body, thus monitoring the external environment. LeDoux (1996) has described the parallel processing that takes place, as the thalamus simultaneously transmits impulses directly to the amygdala ('the low road') and to the prefrontal cortex ('the high road').

The direct impulses to the amygdala transmit a message to the hypothalamus, which releases the hormone CRF (corticotropin-releasing factor); this triggers the release of ACHT (adrenocorticotropic hormone) from the pituitary gland, which in turn releases cortisol, among other substances; this activates the autonomic nervous system, putting the body into a state of alarm. This chain reaction is reflexive and occurs almost instantaneously and outside our conscious awareness. In a parallel chain, impulses are transmitted to the prefrontal cortex, where the incoming information is compared with memories of previous experiences (stored in the hippocampus). This conscious analysis takes longer and is also more nuanced than the rapid scan conducted by the amygdala. That is why our emotional response to a threat is quicker than our cognitive assessment. The prefrontal cortex is involved in the complex process of mentalizing, that is, analysing both our own and others' emotional states.

The presence of the two parallel circuits or ways of processing input from the thalamus helps to explain why some people react emotionally by panicking in situations where a more thorough assessment would show that there is no real threat (LeDoux, 1996).

In addition to the difference in pace, the two modes of processing also result in two different kinds of memories. As mentioned above, the amygdala is involved in processing physical, emotional stimuli and operates on a nonverbal basis. Thus, the resulting memories are not conscious but stored in our implicit memory. The prefrontal cortex and the hippocampus are capable of comparing the current situation to stored knowledge (experiences) and thus of putting the situation into context. This makes it possible to conduct a conscious analysis that can be accessed later from the explicit memory system.

Many who self-injure have a hyperactive amygdala, which causes intense, impulsive and rash reactions in situations that bear some superficial resemblance to previous traumatic experiences. These persons often react to moods and vague sensations. For example, many people with BPD have an unconscious memory of their insecure attachment to their caregiver during infancy that causes them, even as adults, to react with an intense activation of the attachment system and go into a state of alarm in face of minor perceived slights or rejections. LeDoux uses the term *precognitive emotions*, while Bateman and Fonagy speak of *unmentalized affects* which lead to a breakdown of the mentalizing capacity and, often, NSSI.

> A 20-year-old woman says that she becomes desperate if her boyfriend does not answer the phone when she rings. Although she knows that he may have valid and legitimate reasons for not answering, she often rings over and over again and eventually cuts herself to calm down. Intellectually, she knows that she is exacerbating her condition by calling him constantly, but she cannot help herself. She needs to be in contact with him, and when she succeeds in reaching him she calms down instantly, regardless how agitated she had been. She is painfully aware how vulnerable she is to the sense of rejection and separation.

Among other consequences, amygdala hyperreactivity blocks the functioning of the hippocampus, and the individual momentarily loses his or her composure and capacity for rational thinking and mentalizing. Only after the intense activation of the amygdala has decreased, and with it the level of arousal, can the person regain his or her capacity for mentalizing and reflection. Reflections such as 'I should have done X or said Y' may occur, but the person is unable to learn from these experiences as long as his or her system is in a state of alarm. No one can think clearly while they are overwhelmed by emotions.

Some researchers have suggested that emotionally dysregulated persons with NSSI may have a 'dual' brain disorder: an hyperreactive amygdala *and* a reduced activation of the prefrontal cortex, which may explain the impulsivity and constant state of stress seen in many individuals with emotional dysregulation. The prefrontal cortex plays a crucial role in mentalizing, and reduced activity in this region combined with increased activity in the amygdala may offer a neuropsychological explanation of the unstable mentalizing capacity in emotionally dysregulated individuals.

LeDoux's theories also help to explain why the person may be unaware what causes the urge to self-injure, as the trigger may be an external stimulus that is merely reminiscent of a threat, which activates the anxiety reaction via 'the low road'. Studies have found that BPD patients with a hypersensitive amygdala tend to interpret neutral facial expressions as negative. Persons with expressionless faces are perceived as threatening and unreliable, which may suggest that the amygdala is involved in excessive vigilance. Perhaps the amygdala reacts because the expressionless face reactivates memories of the mother's unresponsiveness during infancy. It is extremely distressing for infants to fail receive an empathic and reactive response (as illustrated in film sequences from Ed Tronick's Still Face experiment, e.g., www.youtube.com/watch?v=apzXGEbZht0).

From an evolutionary perspective, the simultaneous processing in the amygdala and in the cortex offers an advantage, as an impulsive 'low-road' reaction may be vital in a life-or-death situation, where a more detailed 'high-road' assessment would take too long. The conscious registration of a threat does not occur until the impulse from the thalamus is processed in the prefrontal cortex and hippocampus. Thus, the benefit of the 'low road' is the ability to act quickly and avoid immediate danger; however, the cost is a tendency to overreact, so that even obscure signs of danger activate the emotional reactions (anxiety).

Amygdala hyperreactivity may be a predisposing factor for the development of NSSI as a coping strategy because it limits the development of alternative, less burdensome coping strategies.

Endogenous opioids

Studies of the endogenous opioid system (EOS) seem to shed light on both the aetiology and maintenance of NSSI. Endogenous opioids are a range of substances similar to morphine that the human body produces naturally in connection with pain or intense physical activity. Endogenous opioids include *enkephalins*, *beta-endorphins*, *endomorphins* and *dynorphins*, which are important in regulating pain perception, produce a sense of inner calm and can lead to a pleasant, euphoric state and thus also influence affect regulation. Endogenous opioids help explain why NSSI can have an instantly calming effect (Nixon et al., 2002).

There are two hypotheses about the link between NSSI and endogenous opioids, which Yates (2004) calls, respectively, the *pain hypothesis* and the *addiction hypothesis*.

Studies have found that individuals who engage in NSSI have a lower level of endogenous opioids, which affects their sense of pain and likelihood of experiencing negative feelings, such as dysphoria or dissociation (Bresin & Gordon, 2013). The low level of endogenous opioids may either be innate or result from chronic and severe trauma and stress in childhood due to abuse or neglect. Traumatic childhood experiences lead to an altered stress response pattern in adulthood, and individuals who self-injure are generally found to have a heightened stress response and thus require an increased level of endogenous opioids to regulate the inner tension. This makes them vulnerable to other methods of increasing the level of endogenous opioids e.g., NSSI.

The addiction hypothesis centres on the release of endogenous opioids, suggesting that they not only reduce the negative feelings and stress response but also create a pleasant, even euphoric, state (providing a rush or a kick) (positive automatic reinforcement). With repeated incidents of NSSI, the release of endogenous opioids can lead to physiological dependency, which may be no less intense than addiction to morphine or heroin. This is referred to as *auto addiction*, addiction to endogenous substances.

Auto addiction can meet all the classic criteria for addiction, including craving, loss of control, withdrawal symptoms, the development of tolerance, a dominant role with regard to priorities and time spent and continued use despite awareness of damaging effect. Auto addiction is described specifically in connection with cutting, where the person may develop an extremely powerful urge to cut him/ herself (*craving*), and often the person's thoughts persistently turn to the possibilities of giving in to the urge. The impulse pressure grows until the person *loses control*, gives in to the urge and then feels immediate relief. The person's psychological state changes during the time leading up to, during and after the act of self-injury, and in order to achieve the 'high' the person often ignores the long-term consequences and other people's reactions. NSSI also involves *growing tolerance*, meaning that it gradually takes more and more for the person to achieve the desired effect of the NSSI. If the behaviour is given up abruptly, the person may develop *withdrawal symptoms* in the form of restlessness, nausea, hot flashes and anxiety; there is also a significant relapse risk, stemming from both the psychological and the physiological function of NSSI. In a study of hospitalized adolescent patients, Nixon et al. (2002) found that 98% of the patients performed NSSI in a pattern consistent with addictive behaviour. Rubæk & Møhl (2016) found a similar pattern among adult self-harming inpatients; 88% of these patients had a pattern of self-injury that matched ICD-10 criteria for a dependency syndrome.

A 24-year-old woman with BPD had developed a strong addiction to cutting. She explained that she cut herself on an almost daily basis, and that she had to 'finish' cutting before she was able to calm down and relax. To 'finish' cutting meant that she had to cut deep enough and long enough to experience the satisfaction she was craving. The staff in the assisted living facility for psychiatric patients had tried to intervene and stop her cutting, which could be very extensive. On more than one occasion her blood loss was so severe that she had to go to hospital to receive a transfusion. If they caught her in the act and tried to stop her, she would continue as soon as she saw the opportunity. When she was prevented from 'finishing', her craving intensified, and she became desperate to cut again. Only 'finishing' enabled her to relax.

It is, however, debated whether cutting and other forms of NSSI result in actual physiological addiction or whether it is merely an *addiction-like* condition. Sometimes NSSI, particularly cutting, can be 'habitual', and the escape from negative feelings can create a recurring need for NSSI that resembles addiction without actually meeting the criteria.

Victor et al. (2012) studied craving and addiction in connection with NSSI and drug abuse. They found that the level of craving associated with NSSI is generally lower than in drug abuse, and that craving mainly occurs when the self-injuring person is under the influence of negative emotions. Thus, they conclude that addiction to NSSI has more to do with the positive psychological outcome of affect regulation than with the activation of endorphins.

Finally the pain offset theory should be mentioned. Due to a neural overlap, especially in anterior cingulate cortex and anterior insula, the brain does not clearly distinguish between physical and emotional pain. The pain offset theory suggests that the relief from physical pain that follows NSSI essentially tricks the brain into perceiving relief of emotional pain, too (Franklin et al., 2013).

Serotonin

The biggest concentration of serotonin in the brain is found in the raphe nuclei in the brainstem, which have links to large parts of the brain, in particular to the hypothalamus, which is key in regulating impulsivity and aggression. Serotonin also influences certain basic physiological functions, such as appetite, sleep, sexuality, mood and sleep patterns. Studies have found a connection between reduced serotonin levels and increased impulsivity, aggression, suicide attempts and NSSI (e.g., Hankin & Abela, 2011).

Generally, reduced serotonin levels seem to be associated with an increased risk of impulsive aggression against both self and others, in part because amygdala activity is balanced by serotonin. Patients with depression, anxiety and OCD have been found to have reduced serotonin levels, and treatment with SSRI (selective serotonin reuptake inhibitors), which increases serotonin levels in the synapses, does diminish symptoms of these conditions as well as aggression and NSSI. Probably, SSRIs reduce the risk of NSSI by inhibiting impulsivity and aggression and by reducing anxiety and depression, which can be among the underlying causes of NSSI. Serotonergic dysregulation may also be the basis of comorbidity between NSSI and other impulse control disorders, such as substance abuse, addictive gambling, bulimia and overeating, internet dependency and compulsive shopping. However, further studies are needed to shed light on the correlation between serotonin and NSSI.

Other neurotransmitters

A small number of studies suggest a link between NSSI and reduced dopamine levels. The studies in questions have mainly involved patients with developmental disorders and Lesch-Nyhan syndrome, disorders that lead to reduced dopamine levels in the basal ganglia, which is believed to be associated with the stereo-typical form of NSSI displayed by some people in these groups (Turner & Lewis, 2002). Although there is no firm documentation of a link between dopamine and NSSI, neuroleptic drugs (dopamine antagonists) are widely used to treat NSSI. However, it remains a question whether it is the self-injury behaviour per se or rather the underlying dynamic leading to self-injury that responds to dopamine antagonists (Sandman, 2009).

As mentioned in the introduction to this chapter, it is not possible to design a simple model that captures all the biological factors involved in NSSI, because self-injury is a complex phenomenon. NSSI may be driven by a wide range of motives, including seeking distraction from psychological pain, stopping flash-backs and escaping a dissociative state or expressing inner suffering and distress to others. It seems likely that different subgroups will have different psychochem-ical profiles, an issue that needs to be further explored and documented.

9   Assessment of patients with non-suicidal self-injury

Even for experienced clinicians, self-injury is a very provoking and difficult issue to deal with (Lindgren et al., 2018). For most clinicians, self-injury activates strong emotions, which may cloud their clinical understanding and thus have a destructive impact on the treatment. NSSI is often a secretive behaviour conducted in isolation, and for many patients it is associated with shame, embarrassment and guilt. Many patients do not tell the clinician that they self-injure because they fear being labelled as BPD, suicidal, manipulative or attention-seeking. Sometimes the clinician accidently discovers signs of NSSI. One example is the general practitioner who needed to check a young woman's blood pressure in connection with prescribing birth control pills: when the doctor pulled up the woman's sleeve, he noticed multiple scars on her upper arm which apparently originated from self-cutting. The woman had been his patient for years but had never brought up the issue of her self-injury.

Most patients are quite sensitive to clinician's reaction to their NSSI, and one of the most frequent reasons for not reaching out for help with NSSI is the fear of judgement or condemnation. Often, the patient's family and friends find the behaviour incomprehensible and respond with a mix of fear, anger, condemnation, blame and reproach.

Hence, it is essential for the clinician to meet the patient with a non-judging, positive, authentic attitude that builds trust from the outset (during the assessment phase). Unfortunately, that is not always the case, at least as the patient perceives it. To ensure that patients with self-injury receive appropriate, caring treatment, the British National Institute for Health and Care Excellence (NICE) in 2013 released a comprehensive guideline for the care and treatment of patients who self-injure. The purpose of the guideline is to ensure that

> everyone who uses healthcare services should be treated with compassion, respect and dignity. For people who have self-harmed, however, staff attitudes are often reported as contributing to poor experiences of care. Punitive or judgemental staff attitudes can be distressing for people who have self-harmed and may lead to further self-harm or avoidance of medical attention.

Staff treating patients who inflict injury on themselves, for example by cutting, may find the behaviour completely baffling and contradictory to a standard perception of illness as something that is beyond the person's influence. Under-standing NSSI requires the professional to revise the traditional biomedical con-cept of illness and acknowledge that persons who practice NSSI are not in control of their behaviour in a traditional sense. They are driven by an inner urge, which means that NSSI may be their best option here and now, despite the detrimen-tal long-term consequences. For mental health professionals, it can be a chal-lenge to relate to patients whose behaviour seems counterintuitive to most people. Hence, they may respond to the patient in a way that leads to further self-injury, as addressed in the NICE guidelines.

Clinicians who have limited experience with treating self-injuring patients may mistake NSSI for a suicidal act, a misinterpretation that often makes the patient feel worse and emotionally isolated. Other clinicians may react with fear, confu-sion, powerlessness, suspicion and disgust and thus display a dismissive attitude towards the self-injuring patient. The latter is especially likely if the clinician believes that the patient could simply stop self-injuring if he or she wanted to. Cli-nicians who view the self-injury as being outside the patient's control often have a more understanding and positive attitude towards the patient (Taylor & Hawton, 2009). Finally, some clinicians ignore it (Robinson et al., 2016) or devote great attention to the self-injury behaviour, sometimes based on phantasies of 'saving' the patient; however, that risks reinforcing the behaviour because the patient feels 'rewarded' by the clinician's interest in the NSSI.

If the patient fails to improve or has frequent relapses, the risk of failure can seem overwhelming, and some clinicians react with symptoms of fatigue and burnout as well as irritation, anger and even hate, as described by D. W. Winnicott in the classic article 'Hate in the Counter-Transference' (Winnicott, 1949).

Therapeutic contact with the self-injuring patient

The first meeting between the self-injuring patient and the clinician is crucial for the treatment outcome. Studies show that patients find healthcare profession-als' stance or attitude towards them essential for their ability to benefit from the treatment (Lindgren et al., 2018). In addition to what Caroline Kettlewell calls 'respectful curiosity' in her autobiography *Skin Game* (Kettlewell, 1999), the ther-apist should seek to establish a contact with the patient that is driven and framed by the following qualities:

1   *Being non-judgemental.* The patient is doing the best he or she can but has to learn to do something better, to borrow a phrase from DBT. No patient profits from the clinician acting with condemnation or reproach; in fact, the research consistently shows that a negative or judgemental attitude increases the patient's feelings of shame, guilt and being wrong, which increases the risk of NSSI.
2   *Responding with a calm, low-key, dispassionate demeanour,* meaning avoid-ing showing excessive interest or attention to NSSI, as this might inadvert-ently reinforce the behaviour (Walsh, 2006).

3 *Validation and understanding.* From the initial contact, it is important to validate the patient's feelings and use of NSSI, which is not the same as accepting or approving of the behaviour. Validation means communicating that one understands and empathizes with the patient's need for NSSI under the specific circumstances. No one self-injures without reason. Validation is the oil that makes the treatment run smoothly. One purpose of the treatment is to apply less destructive skills and thus find a more adaptive response. Insight into the underlying dynamics usually makes it easier to address the behaviour.

Fiona was 20 years old when she first came into contact with a psychologist due to NSSI. She cut her arms and legs when she was distressed and under pressure. During the first psychotherapy sessions, it became clear that Fiona cut herself when she came into contact with a feeling of abandonment. Until then she had been unaware that the inner turmoil and the 'toxic feeling', as she called it, were associated with a specific condition. She had cut herself late one night after being out on the town with her friends when she discovered that they had moved on to a different bar, without Fiona noticing it because she had been engrossed in conversation with a young man. She was overwhelmed by the 'toxic feeling' and went home to cut herself in order to regulate a 'certain kind of emotional pain' which she recognized from earlier in her life, although she was unable to identify it or put a name on it.

Fiona had spent her early childhood with both her parents and two elder siblings, living in an economically secure household. However, she had experiences of abandonment that were traumatic for a sensitive child. As a baby she was hospitalized in an isolation ward, where her parents were not allowed to touch her; she was looked after by her grandparents on occasions when her parents were travelling abroad; she recalls an intense feeling of abandonment in connection with being dropped off in kindergarten. When she was 6 years old, her parents were divorced, which led to a 'constant sense of inner turmoil and of missing' the parent who was not around. During the therapy, she soon developed an insight into the background of her easily triggered sense of abandonment, which she was only able to manage by cutting herself. It thus made sense for her to do whatever she can to avoid getting into contact with the overwhelmingly painful and unbearable feelings. Fiona found it very helpful when the therapist expressed his understanding for her need to cut herself. This validation of her feelings undoubtedly contributed to a rapid development of a positive therapeutic alliance.

---

4 *Hope and motivation.* For many patients, self-injury has been an important coping strategy, and it may seem frightening to consider trying to eliminate this option for immediate relief. The patient needs to hear that there are other

ways to manage stress and problems than NSSI, and that many have suc-
ceeded in giving up NSSI, although it may take time and hard work.

5 *Respect for the patient's autonomy.* There is no point in demanding that the
patient give up NSSI immediately, unless of course it is life-threatening.
Respect for the patient's autonomy includes not imposing any ultimatums. It
would undermine the therapy process and ultimately be harmful to the patient
if the clinician allows his or her own agenda to guide the course of therapy.

6 *Containment and mentalizing.* It is important to adopt a stance of interest,
containment and humble curiosity rather than taking *action*. The patients'
actions tend to make the therapist want to *act*, which is rarely constructive
(except in an emergency situation). Containing and mentalizing the patient is
often the best approach, also in the initial contact. Even when the therapist
feels a pressure to act, it is important to bear in mind that most patients have
lived with their NSSI for a long time before seeking help; hence, it is more
important to secure the therapeutic alliance than to stop the self-injury here
and now.

7 *Psychoeducation.* The patient should have as much knowledge as possible
about his or her problems. The therapist can provide the patient with information material and talk with the patient about the quality of the information that
is available online, where some websites actually reinforce the self-injury
behaviour via 'social contagion' and by legitimizing self-injury.

8 *Engaging the patient in the treatment.* The clinician should aim to engage the
patient as an active participant in the treatment. It is important for the treatment alliance that the clinician remains aware of the patient's resources and
considers the patient an expert in his or her own life. A mutually respectful
relationship and exchange between patient and clinician can be achieved in a
variety of ways. The clinician has knowledge about the treatment of NSSI that
can be helpful to the patient, while the patient, on the other hand, has valuable
first-hand knowledge and experiences with NSSI that the therapist can learn
from as well as important resources and contributions to make to the dialogue.

A 21-year-old woman who was referred to a psychologist because she had
begun to cut herself was very pleased to be offered some literature on the
subject. When she came in for the next session, the article she had been
handed was full of notes and underlined passages, which led to a productive conversation where therapist and patient were on equal terms, each in a
position to expand the other's understanding of self-injury.

In long-term therapeutic relationships it can sometimes be a challenge to preserve
what might be called 'therapeutic licence' or latitude in relation to the patient.
Thus, the therapist may experience emotional pressure to act in a way that may
not be optimal from a therapeutic point of view. For example, the therapist may

feel personally responsible for preventing the patient from self-injuring and hence adopt a more cautious and less confrontational style than he or she would normally choose. The treatment of patients with NSSI can involve a complicated therapeutic relationship, like the treatment of traumatized patients with BPD who unconsciously re-enact their original trauma by installing a victim/abuser dynamic in the relationship with the therapist (Gabbard & Wilkinson, 1994).

Many patients with NSSI have problems describing and understanding their emotions (alexithymia). Often, they are unable to identify the connection between a particular emotion and NSSI, as was the case for Fiona in the case above. They describe an almost physical, vague inner sense of tension and a bodily and physical urge to self-injure. Sometimes it may be difficult for the clinician to understand the psychological motives or functions of NSSI. The patient is often unable to explain or describe the motivation to the clinician. When the clinician finds it difficult to understand what is going on with the patient he or she will typically opt for *action* – doing something to help the patient. This may involve prescribing medication, having the patient hospitalized or making changes in the patient's environment. This may reinforce the patient's use of NSSI as a means of strengthening or maintaining a sense of control. Actions lead to actions. The patient and the clinician easily develop what might be called a 'tacit dialogue' (cf. p. 234). Thus, a key challenge in the treatment may be to replace actions with words and concepts, enabling the patient to put his or her inner pain into words instead of acting it out.

In relation to suicide, NSSI is both a short-term protective factor and a long-term risk factor. That makes it important to develop a clear contingency plan, spelling out, for example, how the patient can use the emergency clinic in case of suicidal ideation or other emergency situations. For young patients with NSSI, such a safety plan may also specify the circumstances under which the clinician is allowed to contact the patient's parents to inform them about the patient's condition.

Some people with NSSI may find it difficult to accept help and care and hence react by distancing themselves from the therapist when they need help. Some patients may even react by self-injuring after an empathic, caring conversation because they feel unworthy of receiving 'something good' and are therefore overwhelmed by feelings of shame and guilt. This reaction stems from the negative self-perception and self-loathing that are widespread among patients with NSSI.

The following vignette illustrates how a patient may need to control the relationship, even to the extent of attacking the relationship aggressively when he feels let down or at risk of being abandoned. The patient needs the therapist's help but simultaneously needs to defend himself against the closeness of the relationship, which reactivates the patient's disorganized attachment disorder.

A 37-year-old man who engages in multiple forms of NSSI (cutting, burning and sticking needles under his skin) and had a very turbulent childhood characterized by neglect and sexual abuse appeared aggressive and devaluing in therapy. Even though he stated that he was not benefiting from the therapy, he never missed a session, often showing up 10–15 minutes early and waiting outside the office. His aggressive, devaluing attitude was especially pronounced when the session was drawing to a close, and on several occasions it was difficult to get him out the door when the time was up. When the therapist told the patient that he would be going away for a month, the patient was very upset and angry. Later, when the relationship had become more secure, and the therapeutic alliance was stronger, he explained that in his desperation and powerless rage he had considered complaining to the consultant doctor that the psychologist was going to be away for so long.

From the initial stage of the treatment, it is important to adopt an engaged, containing and validating attitude that signals an alternative to the relationships the patient experienced growing up with, which will often have involved invalidation, shame, hostility or perhaps even neglect or abuse (cf. Chapter 6). The corrective emotional experience in the therapeutic relationship is an important aspect of the therapy.

Assessing patients with self-injury

As mentioned above, NSSI is a non-specific or transdiagnostic symptom, and it is not in itself an indicator of a specific personality structure or a certain personal style. There is no such thing as an 'NSSI personality'. NSSI has different functions for different people, and in assessing NSSI it is important to adopt an open-minded, 'naive', not-knowing stance and a respectful curiosity to make it possible for the patient to reveal his or her own story about living with NSSI.

The assessment of a patient with NSSI depends on a number of conditions, including time constraints, the clinician's relationship with the patient (whether he or she is, for example, the general practitioner, an emergency room doctor or nurse, a student counsellor, a psychologist or a psychiatrist working with psychotherapy) and the specific treatment context. Thus, assessment in an emergency room setting where the patient presents to have a wound assessed and treated is quite different from assessment in connection with planning a psychotherapy course.

The assessment of patients for NSSI can be conducted in a formal way, with questionnaires and set protocols for administration and scoring, or more informally, in a semi-structured face-to-face interview. The latter provides more nuanced information about the patient's personality and behaviour in the clinical situation. A face-to-face interview allows the clinician to adapt to the dynamics of the communication and focus on relevant areas as they come up. Specifically, it lets the clinician observe the patient's nonverbal behaviour and thus provides an impression of how the patient feels about discussing NSSI.

In an interesting study, Brown et al. (2009) found that nonverbal shame behaviour among women with BPD predicted subsequent NSSI and suicidal behaviour. Nonverbal shame behaviour (moving their gaze or head down) was assessed by an observer while the women talked about past NSSI episodes. Shame is generally linked to a negative self-attitude and self-hatred (Mahtani et al., 2018) Self-injurers reports much higher overall shame than people without NSSI (Hack & Martin, 2018), and shame can lead to NSSI as a means of self-punishment. Hence, it is important to be sensitive to shame behaviour in the assessment interview.

A thorough and careful assessment of the patient must involve both formal and informal methods.

The semi-structured clinical interview is the most common way of assessing patients. Some semi-structured interviews use acronyms to help clinicians remember to address specific areas in the assessment interview (cf. pp. 167–169). Certain areas should always be included in the assessment of NSSI, but the relative emphasis depends on the patient, setting and time constraints.

Relevant areas to consider in the assessment of NSSI are described in the following.

The form and history of self-injury

Most assessments begin with an evaluation of the form of self-injury. It is important to get detailed information the specifics of the NSSI behaviour. This includes NSSI *methods* (for example cutting, burning or hitting), *frequency* now and earlier (When was the latest incident? What happened?), the extent of *physical injury* in a typical NSSI incident, the most recent incident, the most severe incident, how often the person has needed *medical attention* (for example visits to his or her own general practitioner or the emergency room), *age* of onset, development since then, periods of increased intensity or absence of NSSI, any increase in tolerance (whether more severe behaviour is required to achieve the same effect), *attempts to give up* NSSI, *localization* of the injuries (arms, legs, torso, face, genitals, chest), *how many* injuries the patient inflicts in a typical incident and what *instruments* he or she has used (for example, razor blade, knife, scissors, shard(s) of glass, scalpel). With regard to the latter, some patients use the same instrument over and over again, while others use whatever is at hand. In the former case, the treatment would obviously focus on encouraging the patient not to keep, for example, razor blades around at home.

The assessment should address how many different methods the person uses for NSSI, and whether the methods have changed over time. Eighty per cent of people performing NSSI use more than one method (two or three methods is common). Some use up to 11 different methods (Wester et al., 2016). The greater the number of methods, the greater the risk of suicidal behaviour.

It is also relevant to address whether the person takes *drugs* or drinks *alcohol* before the act of NSSI. Does NSSI occur while the person is in a dissociative state? Being in a dissociative state or under the influence of drugs or alcohol diminishes the person's inhibition and control and increases the risk of unintended severe damage. Does the person use other forms of self-harming behaviour (for example, an eating disorder, high-risk behaviour, self-destructive sexual encounters) (Zetterqvist et al., 2018)?

It is also important to assess the intensity and frequency of the *urge* to self-injure. This could be done by asking the person to rate the urge on a scale from zero to ten in order to provide an impression of the intensity. Has the person ever managed to resist the urge? How long is the typical interval between the urge and the eventual act? Some patients act on the urge immediately, while others are able to delay the act for hours. This may reflect their degree of inner control, but it may also depend on external circumstances, for example an opportunity to be alone. The longer it takes from when the urge occurs to the act, the better the chance that the person will be able to use strategies or skills to prevent it altogether (Klonsky & Glenn, 2008).

Assessing the physical consequences of self-injury

It is debated whether psychotherapists working with someone who self-injures should ask to see the person's wounds or scars. There can be both pros and cons. In an emergency room, the study of physical injuries is an important aspect of the assessment, and in some cases the physical examination and treatment may have to take priority over the psychosocial treatment. For a therapist in a psychiatric ward, for example, it may be appropriate to refer the person for a physical examination by a nurse or a doctor. However, if the NSSI affects a part of the body where an inspection would not violate the patient's modesty (for example, if the patient cuts his or her arm), it may be helpful to inspect the injuries. Many persons perceive it as shameful, and hence unpleasant, to show their wounds or other injuries. However, the experience of showing the therapist the injuries without being met with contempt or condemnation may have a destigmatizing effect and help to strengthen the alliance. On the other hand, it is also important to avoid giving the patient too much attention and care based on the injuries, as that may serve as a secondary gain and thus reinforce the behaviour.

> During supervision of a younger colleague it emerged that the patient presented her wounds as an almost ritualized part of every session. The therapist clearly revealed her care and concern for the patient, and it is not unthinkable that the 'ritual' gave the patient a secondary gain and thus an additional motive for self-injuring.

Context

Examining the contextual factors is an important element of the assessment. Klonsky and Weinberg (2009) distinguish between *social, cognitive, emotional* and *biological* context aspects.

Social factors refer to events in the person's surroundings that precede, accompany or follow after an act of NSSI. Events involving family, friends or other significant persons at school or at work may provide important insights in the evaluation of what precipitates or maintains NSSI. For example, NSSI may occur in response to an interpersonal conflict or to stressors related to exams, papers or other academic requirements. Exposure to cyberbullying or pro-NSSI websites can also trigger NSSI (Brown et al., 2018a). The therapist should strive to develop a clear picture of the social circumstances surrounding NSSI. Does the person self-injure alone or together with others? Does the behaviour repeatedly occur in the same location (for example in the school lavatory)? Who knows about it? At what time of the day does it happen? Do classmates or peers also self-injure? Schools and subcultures can cause NSSI to spread, and it make it an identity marker for 'dark, sinister and morbid' subcultures such as Goths and Emos (Young et al., 2014). Social contagion is a particularly pertinent issue for young people.

Cognitive factors refer to thoughts and ideas that the person may have had before, during or after the act of self-injury. Thoughts can be important for understanding both how NSSI began, and how it is maintained. The following are examples of thoughts that may be associated with self-injury behaviour:

'I self-injure because I deserve it' 'I self-injure because it takes my mind off my problems, and I feel better afterwards'. 'No one's going to help me. I am on my own, so I may as well cut myself'. 'If my boyfriend sees that I've cut myself, he will realize how much he's hurt me'.

Ruminating on negative thoughts and feelings, where the person, so to speak, mentally sinks into a black hole, may exacerbate the emotional state and thus increase the risk of NSSI. A positive attitude towards NSSI is another risk factor for future NSSI.

It is important to clarify the *emotional factors* that influence the person before, during and after NSSI. Intense negative emotions may activate NSSI, which is followed by momentary relief or other positive emotion. Studies have also found that the persons who use NSSI most frequently are the ones who achieve the biggest relief or the most positive effect from it (Klonsky, 2009). The most frequent motive for NSSI is affect regulation, and the most common affects to trigger and thus precede NSSI are shame, guilt, anger directed at oneself or others, stress, depression/sadness, feelings of emptiness, hopelessness, anxiety (especially fear of abandonment) and feelings of loneliness. During the act some experience a kick that probably stems from the activation of endorphins, which means that some may need to 'finish cutting' without being interrupted. After the act, the dominant feelings are usually relief, calm and the aforementioned kick, but many find that their feelings of shame and guilt are exacerbated after NSSI (Mahtani et al., 2018).

Biological factors. Alcohol and illegal drugs can increase the risk of NSSI because they reduce inhibitions, increase impulsivity and dampen the perception of pain. The latter has been described as a risk factor for more severe physical damage (Klonsky & Weinberg, 2009), which may occur because the person does not feel the pain and thus cuts deeper to achieve the sensation he or she normally gets from NSSI. Stress, fatigue, disease, PMS and sleep disorder are factors that increase the vulnerability to being overwhelmed by negative emotions and impulse breakthroughs followed by self-injury.

Functions of NSSI

It is important to assess what function NSSI serves for the person, also referred to as the motives or reasons for self-injuring. The function of NSSI may vary across situations, and it is thus important to be specific and help the patient verbalize his or her reasons for performing NSSI. As mentioned above, it is not always easy to get a clear description of specific emotions or reactions, because many self-injuring patients suffer from alexithymia (inability to name emotions), a reduced mentalizing capacity and, in some cases, dissociation, which compromises the ability to differentiate between emotions.

In case of dissociation, the patient may have total or partial amnesia, but usually there will be a vague sensation without specifics. Finally, some only recall the secondary emotion (for example, anger) and not the primary one (for example, separation anxiety). Many patients will mention that they have self-injured due to an almost physical, vague inner sense of tension that makes it impossible for them to differentiate one emotion from another. However, it is important to get as precise an understanding as image possible of the motivating feelings, because they are important for the case conceptualization and the treatment plan.

If we look at the specific emotions, as mentioned in Chapter 8, *affect regulation* is the most commonly stated motive for self-injury. 'To get rid of intolerable emotions' or 'I calm down' (Klonsky, 2009). Other motives are *self-punishment* or aggression directed at the self – 'I do it because I deserve to be punished' – or to *put an end to dissociation* in the form of flashbacks – 'When I have flashbacks of the sexual abuse, cutting is the best thing I can do. Then it stops' – or that the dissociative defence causes a sense of unreality or being drugged. Especially among younger people, NSSI can be used as a way of strengthening the bond with others in a subculture or in relation to a close friend, where self-injury is a shared feature. Most people have multiple reasons for performing NSSI, and insight into the person's motives helps the clinician develop a better treatment plan (see the Four-Function Model on p. 131).

One of the general tasks in connection with assessing NSSI is the assessment of suicidal intent and the risk of suicide. Although NSSI and self-injury with suicidal intent are two different things, it is important to remember that NSSI is in itself an important risk factor for both suicide and attempted suicide. Uncovering suicidal ideation and intent in connection with NSSI should have a high priority in any assessment of NSSI, as should those aspects of NSSI that are known to be correlated with an increased risk of suicide attempts: many different methods, a long history of NSSI and a lack of pain perception in connection with self-injury (Nock & Kessler, 2006).

As mentioned (cf. p. 41), it is not always straightforward to determine whether an act of self-injury had suicidal intent or not, since the intention may be ambivalent or unconscious. The best method is to address the topic openly in the conversation with the patient in an explorative, non-judging manner.

Functional behavioural analysis

Completing a functional behavioural analysis of, for example, the most recent episode of NSSI can be helpful because it gives both the patient and the clinician invaluable information about the process and context of the episode. For example, a chain analysis (see Chapter 11, p. 203) teaches the person a way to gather information about an NSSI episode. Ask the person to describe what happened, using his or her own words. What happened before the episode? (Allow time for identifying distal as well as proximal antecedents.) What happened after the episode? What were the immediate and long-term consequences? It is important to conduct the chain analysis in an atmosphere of trust and understanding: *Here we are, the two of us standing in front of the whiteboard (or sitting down with a blank sheet of paper) trying to understand what NSSI means to you. NSSI is the problem. You are not the problem. You are an expert in your own life, and you are the one who knows what you want. As a clinician, I will do whatever I can to help you get better at living the life you want to live without needing to use NSSI.*

With help from the clinician, the person conducts a chain analysis with the purpose of grasping the big picture. Start with the NSSI episode and examine the

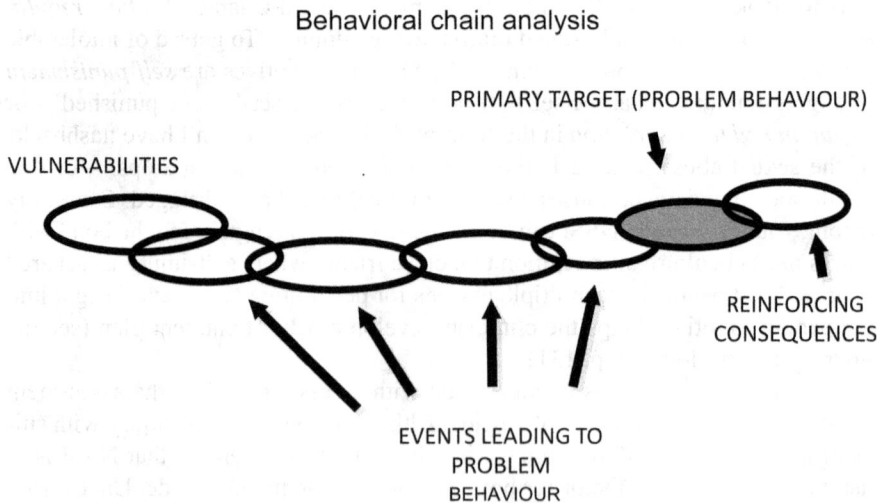

Figure 9.1 Behavioural chain analysis.

emotions, thoughts and behaviour before and after the NSSI episode, and talk about the consequences of the episode and about the specific vulnerabilities that decreased the patient's impulse control (for example, a sleepless night, not eating enough, stress, too much alcohol the day before). After completing the analysis, the patient can take a photo of the whiteboard (or paper) as a reminder or as something to work on for the next session. The chain analysis is a good opportunity for the clinician to validate the patient. It also forms an important part of the next step, the case formulation.

Case formulation

A case formulation is a theoretically based conceptualization of the background and dynamics of the person's NSSI. Based on a hypothesis that is tested in a dynamic approach, the case formulation may be revised based on continuous assessment and the patient's response to treatment. The case formulation can serve as a guide for the treatment and psychotherapy process. It will often be appropriate to include a vulnerability-stress model and to address predisposing, precipitating and maintaining factors.

Predisposing factors may include the vulnerability factors that were described earlier (p. 91 f.), such as genetic disposition for high emotional reactivity, attachment disorders, sexual traumas, neglect and so forth.

Precipitating factors may include, for example, parental divorce, invalidating childhood experiences, bullying and rejection from peers, a broken relationship, sexual abuse, stress associated with exams, tests or other academic requirements, associating with peers who perform NSSI, learning about NSSI from the internet.

Maintaining factors may include the feeling of calm and relief that the person experiences in connection with self-injury or the reaction that others show in connection with self-injury. Maintaining factors are the perceived positive outcome of NSSI.

Information about the patient's NSSI is obtained during the initial assessment (described above). Among other things, the assessment includes information about NSSI methods, age of onset, number of NSSI episodes, other forms of self-injury (such as eating disorders, suicidal ideation and behaviour), risk factors and triggers for NSSI and the functions of NSSI that maintain the behaviour and the person's strengths and assets, including motivation for treatment and support from family and friends.

The case formulation is a working hypothesis of the specific person's symptoms and behaviour and how they relate to the predisposing, precipitating and maintaining factors. Due to the diverse clinical presentations of persons who engage in NSSI, assessments and interventions must be flexible enough to accommodate a range of presentations, contributing individual factors and functions of the behaviour. The case formulation is an ideographic theory of a client's symptoms that can be used to guide the treatment planning and further assessment. (For an example of a case formulation for NSSI, see Andover, 2012.)

The HIRE model is a mnemonic device, where each letter of the acronym calls attention to a different domain of assessment: History, Interest in change, Reasons behind the behaviour and Exposure to risk. The model is designed to assess patients in relation to the proposed DSM-5 diagnosis Non-Suicidal Self-Injury Disorder but can be used to get a systematic description of NSSI in all patients.

H – History

H stands for History, which refers to the patient's past use of NSSI. The focus is on identifying the frequency, duration, intensity and severity of the self-injuring behaviour: how often have you injured yourself during the past year? How many different methods have you used in the past? What is your favourite/usual method? It is always relevant to get an exact description of the NSSI behaviour: how did you injure yourself? Where on the body do you usually injure yourself? What was the trigger for your last NSSI? What was the consequence of the behaviour? Under what circumstances do you injure yourself? Have you ever needed medical help after self-injuring?

I – Interest in change

This domain refers to the patient's motivation to cease or reduce engagement in NSSI – to change the situation. Motivation for change may be driven by the patient's awareness of the negative consequences of the behaviour, such as increased shame, scars or negative reactions from others after engaging in NSSI. Examples of relevant questions: what would you like to be different about your NSSI? What are the negative aspects of your NSSI? Have you ever tried to stop injuring yourself? What happened then? On a scale from 0 to 100, how important do you consider NSSI to be for you?

R – Reasons behind the behaviour

This domain refers to the purpose or function of the behaviour. What motivates the patient to self-injure and what are the consequences? It is important to assess the intentions behind and the functions of NSSI because intentions and functions indicate what the patient seeks to achieve with NSSI. The next step then is to teach him or her better, less destructive skills to achieve that. Do you perform NSSI to reduce negative emotions? Do you perform NSSI to gain attention from others? Do you perform NSSI to punish yourself? – or to get a kick? Do you perform NSSI to affect other people? The patient may be unable to describe the purpose of NSSI, either due to a lack of 'words for feelings' (alexithymia) or because there is often more than one purpose (for example, affect regulation and communication to others) (see the Four-Function Model on p. 131).

E – Exposure to risk

The final domain involves assessing the patient's risk of serious harm by performing NSSI. Buser and Buser focus on four major areas of risk: 1) severity of NSSI, 2) sense of control while self-injuring, 3) addictive features of NSSI and 4) associated suicidal ideation or intention.

Among college students who performed NSSI it was found that individuals who used more than three methods, engaged in NSSI often and used methods capable of inflicting a high degree of tissue damage were most likely to experience unintentionally serious injuries. Twenty-five per cent of self-injuring individuals had experienced an unintentionally serious injury due to NSSI (Whitlock et al., 2008). Also, the use of drugs and alcohol in connection with NSSI can result in unintended serious injuries. Some individuals engage in NSSI compulsively and experience cravings or urges to harm themselves. Exploring the addictive features of NSSI is important because addiction can compromise the sense of control. Lack of control may also be due to dissociation during NSSI. Dissociation can cause the individual not to feel pain and may even lead to blackout. To assess the patient's sense of control over NSSI, the clinician could ask whether the patient has ever injured him/herself more than intended? One of the most important aspects to assess in patients performing NSSI is suicidal ideation or plans. NSSI is often used as a means to avoid suicide behaviour *in the moment*, but the subsequent suicide risk is dramatically increased (Buser & Buser, 2013).

'STOPS FIRE' is another acronym that can be used as a way of remembering what to look for when assessing a patient's self-injury, especially to evaluate increased risk of suicide. STOPS FIRE is designed for use in primary-care settings.

- **S**uicidal ideations during or before self-injury
  High risk: intense thoughts about suicide while self-injuring and thoughts about suicide before or after self-injuring
- **T**ypes of self-injury in which the patient engages
  High risk: multiple types; three or more methods
- **O**nset of self-injury
  High risk: early onset and extended duration or history more than six months
- **P**lace (location) on the body that is injured
  High risk: genitals, breasts or face
- **S**everity and extent of damage caused by self-injury
  High risk: hospitalization or suturing required, neglect or reopening of wounds
- **F**unctions of the self-injury for the patient
  High risk: any relationship to suicide (for example, self-injury used to prevent or manage suicidal ideation and behaviour)
- **I**ntensity or frequency of self-injury urges
  High risk: intense urge to self-injure
- **R**epetition of self-injury
  High risk: 11–50 (moderate risk) or more than 50 (high risk) episodes of NSSI
- **E**pisodic frequency of self-injury
  High risk: multiple times per week and more than five wounds per episode

(Kerr et al., 2010)

Assessment instruments

A number of different assessment instruments have been developed, but most of them are for research purposes. Some of the questionnaires, however, are relatively quick and easy to apply in clinical contexts as way of gathering systematic information about NSSI, but it is important to remember that a questionnaire can never replace the clinical interview, as described above.

Below, a few of the many instruments for assessing NSSI are briefly introduced (see Klonsky & Lewis, 2014, for a review of assessment instruments).

Deliberate Self-Harm Inventory (DSHI) focuses exclusively on NSSI and is useful in clinical contexts as a screening instrument (Gratz, 2001). The original version with 17 items covers 15 different types of self-injury; the inventory also includes an open-ended question asking if the respondents have done anything else to hurt themselves. For each method, the respondents are asked to provide information about age of onset, number of lifetime incidents, most recent incident, whether the respondents have stopped and whether the NSSI has ever resulted in hospitalization or medical treatment. A brief version of DSHI with 9 items has been developed by Lundh et al. (2007).

Self-Injurious Thoughts and Behaviour Inventory (SITBI) was originally developed as a structured interview for research purposes to assess the presence, frequency and characteristics of a wide range of self-injurious thoughts and behaviours, including suicidal ideation, suicide plans, suicide gestures and suicide attempts, as well as NSSI methods, age of onset, frequency, functions, severity, consumption of substances, social influence and impulsivity. SITBI exists in a standard version and in a parent-report version where the parent answers the same questions about their child. The parent version can be used when working with young people. SITBI is comprehensive, and even in a short form with 72 items it takes time and is difficult to apply in a clinical context; however, it does provide valuable in-depth information on a broad range of self-harming behaviour (Nock et al., 2007). Even if the clinician chooses not to use SITBI, the interview guide is a good source of ideas and inspiration for topics and questions to be included in the assessment of patients with NSSI.

Another widely used instrument that covers both suicidal and NSSI is the *Ottawa Self-Injury Inventory* (OSI), which exists in both a clinical and a research version (Nixon et al., 2015). OSI is a thorough measure of NSSI based on a self-report format. OSI specifically addresses 17 different methods of NSSI and includes items on historical and current NSSI behaviour, functions of NSSI, urge to perform NSSI, addictive features of NSSI, motivation to change and suicidal thoughts and behaviour.

The different functions of NSSI have been a focus in research on NSSI for many years. Multiple scales have been developed to assess the functions of NSSI. The most frequently used is probably the *Functional Assessment of Self-Mutilation* (FASM) (Nock & Prinstein, 2004). FASM provides information on recent engagement in different methods of NSSI: cutting/carving, burning, scraping skin to draw blood, hitting self and pulling out hair as well as the frequency of the behaviour, age of onset and history of NSSI. FASM also assesses the function of NSSI, asking about 22 possible reasons for the behaviour (including *To stop bad feelings*, *To punish yourself*, *To feel relaxed*, *To be like someone you respect*) followed by an opportunity to report unlisted reasons. The different reasons can be grouped into the Four-Factor Model, comprised of automatic-negative versus automatic-positive reinforcement and social-negative versus social-positive reinforcement (see p. 131).

Motivation for treatment

Many persons who come into contact with the healthcare system because of NSSI do not see the behaviour as a problem. Most of them are highly ambivalent about getting treatment for NSSI, and their treatment motivation varies over time, which underscores the importance of persistent efforts to motivate the patient for continuing treatment. It is important to take this ambivalence seriously and to validate the patient's effort to 'take care of him/herself' by using NSSI as a coping strategy (albeit a dysfunctional one). One option is to use the principles from Motivational Interviewing (Miller & Rollnick, 2013), where the therapist does not pressure the patient but works with him or her to examine the short-term and long-term pros and cons of the behaviour. If the patient does not regard NSSI as a problem, it is understandable that he or she would feel unmotivated to work with NSSI in therapy. Any perceived pressure from the therapist will likely make the patient defensive and risks increasing the occurrence of NSSI as a way for the patient to maintain control over his or her life situation. The therapist must show empathy, avoid confrontations and roll with the resistance, based on the idea that pressure will only increase the patient's resistance to change. The therapist should support the patient's confidence and faith in the possibility of change and help the patient take a realistic view of the distance between his or her current position and his or her end goal. Motivational Interviewing is often described as a six-stage process of change, where each stage with its own specific characteristics (Prochaska & Norcross, 2001).

1   The *precontemplation stage*, where the patient does not perceive NSSI as a problem and hence has no plans of giving it up. At this stage, there is no point in trying to persuade the person to give up the NSSI. Instead, it is important to offer empathy and to validate the patient's feelings, using the principles of Motivational Interviewing.
2   The *contemplation stage*, where the patient does experience NSSI as a problem but has made no commitment to stop, either because the patient does

not think it is possible, or because the benefits of NSSI seem to outweigh the costs. The patient is ambivalent and has contradictory feelings about NSSI. At this stage, the most constructive approach for the therapist is to acknowledge and validate the ambivalence.

3   The *preparation stage*, where the patient commits to giving up NSSI but may find it difficult to imagine precisely how to go about it. Information about the functions and consequences of NSSI can be constructive at this stage. There may still be a considerable degree of ambivalence, which may vary in strength from day to day, depending on how the patient feels. In situations where the patient does well, he or she may be determined to stop, while the opposite is true when the patient is distressed and thus feels a need to self-injure. Here, it may be helpful to use the pros/cons table from DBT (cf. p. 197) and to work with the patient's motivation by initiating a dialogue about how the patient imagines his or her life five years from now if the self-injury continues, versus how it might look if the patient stops self-injuring.

4   The *action stage*, where the patient engages actively in an effort to stop the self-injury behaviour and to develop alternative affect-regulation strategies. Here it is important that the therapist remains optimistic and supports the patient's belief in him/herself during a difficult phase where the urge to self-injure may be strong. At this stage, the key focus areas are making an active effort, improving one's mentalizing capacity and developing skills to replace self-injury (cf. Chapters 11 and 12).

5   The *maintenance stage*, where the patient has successfully changed, giving up the self-injury behaviour, but may still experience occasional relapses. It can take some time before the desire and the urge to self-injure go away completely. Here, the therapist should validate the difficulties and continue to support the patient in remaining optimistic. When the patient relapses and self-injures again, it is important not to get caught up in either/or thinking and give in to a sense of futility. The positive quality of a relapse is that it offers an opportunity to refresh alternative techniques and skills.

6   At the *termination stage* the patient no longer feels the need for or thinks of self-injury. Normally, the active therapy is less intensive at this stage, with the patient showing up once a month or as needed, or it may have been terminated entirely, but ideally with the reassurance that the patient can contact the therapist if the need arises. Some patients feel that they have put the self-injury behind them completely, so they may be alarmed if they feel the urge resurface in a crisis situation. It is important to explain the risk of relapse to the patient in a way that does not give him or her the impression that it is unavoidable or proof of failure. Even if the urge to self-injure returns, that is not the same as acting on it, and if the patient does self-injure, it is constructive to help him or her resume the use of the acquired skills. This may involve a booster session with the therapist.

Research (Klonsky & Glenn, 2008) has shown that about 90% of people who self-injure have tried to stop, and that the range of methods they have tried includes more than 16 different techniques; this confirms that the vast majority of people who self-injure have some degree of motivation for quitting. The point of Motivational Interviewing and of the six stages of change is to help the patient develop and maintain motivation for change in the right, stage-specific way.

Levels of treatment

The purpose of the assessment is to gather knowledge with a view to planning whether the patient should be offered treatment and if so, which treatment. The severity of NSSI varies considerably, and the treatment should be matched to the patient's needs. A study of NSSI among university students found that 25.4% had had just a single self-injury incident, another 33.2% reported having 2 to 5 incidents, while 24.9% had had more than 10 incidents (Whitlock et al., 2006). Few individuals who have only engaged in NSSI once or twice go on to develop severe NSSI behaviour, and although as a principle, NSSI should always be taken seriously, it would not make sense to offer therapeutic treatment to someone who has only self-injured a couple of times, unless the person has other clear signs of psychological distress or psychopathology.

A *wait-and-see* stance without any formal treatment is indicated if the person has self-injured once or twice for the sake of experimentation or as part of a social activity in a peer group, provided the act of NSSI has not caused severe physical harm, that there was no suicidal intent and that there are no signs of additional psychopathology. If there are signs of relapse or of a worsening of the patient's condition, he or she should be offered actual treatment.

Outpatient treatment is indicated if NSSI has occurred repeatedly, if the incidents have a more severe character, if the person did it while alone (not in a social setting), if affect regulation or self-punishment were the dominant motives, if there are signs of severe psychological distress or psychiatric symptoms or if there is suicidal ideation or intent.

Hospitalization or *day-patient treatment* is indicated if the NSSI has a more severe character, if thoughts about or urges for self-injury are near-constant, if there are intrusive suicidal thoughts, intentions or impulses, and if self-injury occurs frequently and using multiple methods (Klonsky et al., 2011).

Thus, decisions about the level of treatment depend on concerns for the patient's safety and need for contact. Generally, outpatient treatment is preferable because it preserves the patient's autonomy and avoids the risk of regression that may be associated with hospitalization, but in connection with crises, attempted suicide or severe deterioration of the patient's condition, hospitalization may be necessary. If possible, it should be of short duration, unless the patient is treated in a specialized ward or section with a strong focus on preserving the patient's autonomy and interpersonal relationships (cf. Chapter 13).

Prioritizing treatment focus

Another issue in treatment planning is whether the main focus should be on NSSI, or whether some of the underlying problems that may be contributing factors in the patient's NSSI should take priority.

Often, patients with NSSI present additional psychological problems, such as personality disorders, relational issues, depression, anxiety or flashbacks due to childhood sexual abuse, and it is well-documented that NSSI is often secondary to some of these conditions and to emotional dysregulation and overwhelming negative emotions (Klonsky, 2007). In some cases, it may therefore be rational to consider prioritizing the treatment of these psychological problems over the treatment of NSSI, especially if the self-injury is less severe. However, the patient's safety is always the top priority, and although NSSI rarely results in life-threatening injuries, it is important to give the patient both an awareness of the importance of more adaptive skills and a mastery of them that enables him or her to manage stress and affect regulation without resorting to NSSI. NSSI may be regarded as a coping strategy, albeit one that comes at a high cost to the individual – a cost that contributes to maintaining and, in some cases, reinforcing NSSI (cf. the model of perpetuating self-injuring behaviour, Figure 7.2, p. 140).

NSSI can be compared to other dysfunctional coping strategies, such as substance abuse, where the initial focus in practice will always be on helping the patient deal with the alcohol dependency syndrome before focusing on the underlying causes, such as depression or anxiety. Similarly, it is important to stop the patient's NSSI, because the patient uses NSSI as a way to avoid dealing with difficult emotions and situations. In many ways, direct and indirect self-injury (for example alcohol or drug abuse) serve the same purpose for the person, including as a means of affect regulation, and in some regards, it makes sense to treat self-injury as a dependency condition.

Hence, I would advocate making NSSI the top treatment priority without therefore ignoring the patient's other psychological problems, which naturally also need to be addressed. If the patient suffers from PTSD, depression or anxiety, these conditions require attention as well.

However, making NSSI the most urgent treatment priority does come with the risk of focusing exclusively on the patient's coping strategy and turning that into the problem – as happens with other conditions, such as eating disorders or substance abuse – and thus ignoring that it is in fact a *symptom* of an underlying disorder.

10 Treatment of non-suicidal self-injury – an overview

Literature reviews and clinical guidelines recommend psychotherapy as the primary treatment choice for NSSI, possibly combined with pharmacological treatment of underlying causes, such as depression or anxiety (e.g., Turner et al., 2014; NICE, 2013). However, there is no consensus about which specific form of psychotherapy is recommended, which also reflects that NSSI is a non-specific symptom found in severely disturbed individuals as well as in largely well-functioning young people who have experimented with NSSI on a few occasions. NSSI is not just NSSI. Severe NSSI calls for a more intensive treatment effort than superficial and experimental NSSI. When it comes to treatment, one size does *not* fit all.

Most of the psychotherapeutic models that are used with NSSI address it as a symptom of BPD. Thus, they do not have NSSI as their only or even their primary target but focus on other symptoms of BPD as well. However, the psychotherapeutic effort depends on the underlying theory that frames the understanding of the dynamics of BPD, for example emotion dysregulation (You et al., 2018), interpersonal problems and mentalizing deficit (Bateman & Fonagy, 2004), identity diffusion and dissociation (Ford & Gómez, 2015). The treatment rationale is that once the BDP-specific symptoms, such as a reduced capacity for affect regulation or mentalizing, have improved, the person will no longer need to use NSSI.

The findings are not quite consistent as to which psychotherapeutic treatment models are most effective, but in a systematic review of psychological and pharmacological interventions for NSSI, Turner (2014) concludes that *structured* (my emphasis) psychotherapeutic approaches that focus on collaborative therapeutic relationships and motivation for change, and which directly address NSSI behaviours seem to be most effective in reducing NSSI. Structure and predictability are key in the treatment of NSSI, because a patient who self-injures is often impulse-driven and self-destructive. Hence, he or she will often experience one crisis after another that may disrupt a targeted treatment process. It is therefore important that the therapist and the patient together work out a good case formulation, and that they can maintain a clear treatment focus, so that the effort to help the patient stop the self-injurious behaviour does not slip into the background but remains the primary treatment goal throughout the course of treatment. It is, however, important to note that it is often not sufficient for the patient to give up the self-injurious behaviour. Unless the underlying causes are addressed, there is considerable risk that NSSI will simply be superseded by another symptom, for example an eating disorder, substance abuse or depression.

The effect of different forms of psychotherapy also depends on how severe and disruptive the self-injurious behaviour is, how motivated the patient is for giving up NSSI and the patient's personal resources and social network. Most therapy forms have been tested in clinical trials, which is not quite a match for a clinical real-life setting, where the patient population is usually more diverse. Hence, the effect found in a clinical trial cannot always be replicated in a real-life clinical setting.

In a Cochrane review of psychosocial interventions for self-harm in adults that included both non-suicidal and suicidal self-harm, Hawton et al. (2016) find that cognitive-behavioural psychotherapy (CBT) leads to a reduction of NSSI or self-injury, and that Dialectical Behaviour Therapy (DBT) is effective for persons with multiple episodes of self-injury and/or a presumed personality disorder. The review finds that CBT has an effect on NSSI compared to Treatment as Usual (TAU); however, the quality of the studies is low and the evidence is moderate.

CBTs include DBT (cf. Chapter 11), Problem-Solving Therapy (PST), which according to a meta-analysis (Townsend et al., 2001) has good efficacy for self-injury, and Manual-Assisted Cognitive Therapy (MACT), which incorporates elements from PST and standard cognitive therapy. When used as an add-on to another form of psychotherapeutic intervention, MACT significantly reduces self-injury behaviour (Tyrer et al., 2004).

New short-term therapy forms with a specific focus on NSSI are continuously being introduced, and several of them focus on emotion regulation, based on CBT with elements from DBT, Acceptance and Commitment Therapy (ACT) and Motivational Interviewing (MI). Emotion Regulation Group Therapy (ERGT) is a therapy form that is seeing growing use (Sahlin et al., 2017). ERGT also exists in a model for adolescents (ERITA) that has been used in an online version in Sweden and Denmark with good effect (Bjureberg et al., 2018). Treatment for NSSI in Young Adults (T-SIB) is a new short-term outpatient therapy form specially designed for the treatment of NSSI (Andover et al., 2017); in Germany, initial evaluations of the 12-session outpatient Cutting Down Programme (CDP) show promising results (Fischer et al., 2013).

One psychodynamic therapy that has been examined for effectiveness in relation to BPD, including NSSI, is Mentalization-Based Therapy (MBT) (cf. Chapter 12). In a meta-analysis, Calati and Courtet (2016) found MBT to be the only form of psychotherapy that is effective for NSSI. Finally, Transference-Focused Therapy (TFP) also has a documented effect on self-injury in women with BPD (Clarkin et al., 2006).

The following offers an outline of time-limited therapeutic interventions that can be used as add-on treatments for patients with NSSI. It is thus a selective review of treatment options for self-injury. For comprehensive overviews of self-injury interventions, see Glenn et al. (2015); Ougrin et al. (2015); Hawton et al. (2016); Calati and Courtet (2016); and for adolescents Plener et al. (2018).

Problem-Solving Therapy (PST)

PST was one of the first interventions for self-injury to be investigated in efficacy studies. In a summary of 20 different forms of treatment, Hawton et al. (1998) found that PST was the most promising treatment for self-harm. Nock and Mendes (2008) found that individuals who self-injure are less capable of finding adaptive solutions in problem situations, and that they had a lower self-perceived ability to implement effective solutions than peers who do not engage in NSSI. Further, the study found that their ability to generate adaptive solutions decreased considerably when they were distressed. PST is a form of short-term CBT that has been used in connection with a range of different conditions and is found to decrease suicide behaviour, depression and hopelessness better than TAU (Townsend et al., 2001). Suicide behaviour, depression and hopelessness are often found in people who engage in NSSI, and it thus makes sense to relieve these conditions in order to decrease NSSI; however, in a comparison study with a control group, PST was not found to decrease NSSI.

Within PST, NSSI is considered to be a method of avoidance, and PST is focused on developing safer and more efficient problem-solving skills in order to enable patients to generate adaptive solutions and thus alleviate their need to use NSSI when confronted with problems. PST can be conducted on an individual or group basis and follows a structured seven-stage course:

1   Developing a positive and constructive approach to problems ('challenges').
2   Recognizing and identifying a problem (sensing one's emotions, physical reactions, thoughts and behaviours).
3   Selecting and defining a problem to address. (What is the problem, and why is this problem a problem? When and where does the problem occur?)
4   Generating solutions (brainstorming – finding as many solutions as possible).
5   Making a decision (pros and cons of various solutions to the problem).
6   Developing and implementing a SMART action plan (Specific, Measurable, Achievable, Relevant to the problem and Time-bound).
7   Evaluating the process. (What went well, what was less successful? Does the problem still exist? If so, start over).

PST has produced the best results when it is incorporated into other CBT strategies, such as Manual-Assisted Cognitive Therapy (MACT) (Muehlenkamp, 2006).

Manual-Assisted Cognitive Therapy (MACT)

MACT is a focused therapeutic intervention of three months' duration designed specifically to treat self-harm. MACT integrates PST with cognitive techniques and includes six sessions, supplemented with a comprehensive manual that is handed out to the patients. Each session corresponds to a chapter in the manual, and in addition, the patients receive worksheets and instruction. The themes of the six main sessions are

1   Exploring and analysing the recent episodes of self-harm.
2   Providing PST techniques.
3   Training and assisting the patients in self-monitoring thoughts and feelings.
4   Distress coping strategies.
5   Education in the dangers of substance use and abuse.
6   Revisiting attempts or episodes of self-injury and identifying skills deficits
     and coping strategies for the future.

(Adapted from Evans et al., 1999)

MACT was investigated in a British pilot study where 34 patients with self-injury were randomly assigned to either TAU (N = 16) or MACT (N = 18). At the six-month follow-up, the researchers found fewer incidents of self-injury in the MACT group than in the control group, although the difference was not statistically significant (Evans et al., 1999).

In a larger British multi-centre study (POPMACT), 480 patients were randomly assigned to either MACT or TAU. TAU was not uniform, however, but varied across the centres included in the project. This study, too, failed to find significant differences between the MACT group and the control groups at the one-year follow-up. Nevertheless, MACT is considered to have a positive effect as an add-on treatment, as confirmed by an American study (Weinberg et al., 2006), where both the prevalence and severity of self-injury were significantly lower in the MACT group than in the control group at the six-month follow-up.

Emotion Regulation Group Therapy (ERGT)

Gratz developed the 14-week Emotion Regulation Group Therapy (ERGT) programme, which is focused on emotion regulation and NSSI in BPD patients. The programme was inspired by DBT, ACT and Emotion-Focused Therapy and is intended as an add-on treatment for emotionally dysregulated patients with self-injury who are already receiving psychotherapy. It thus functions as an add-on treatment aimed specifically at NSSI. The ERGT group meets once a week for 90 minutes. ERGT is based on the assumption that emotion dysregulation increases the risk of NSSI, and that improved emotion regulation (reduced emotion dysregulation) should therefore lower the risk of NSSI.

Gratz (2007) summarizes that healthy emotion regulation is an adaptive response to emotional experiences which includes 1) the awareness, understanding and acceptance of emotions, 2) the flexible use of situationally appropriate strategies to modulate the intensity and/or duration of emotional responses rather than to eliminate emotions entirely, 3) willingness to experience negative emotions as part of pursuing meaningful activities in life and 4) ability to engage in goal-directed behaviours and inhibit impulsive behaviours when experiencing negative emotions.

In ERGT, the goal is thus not to avoid or control emotions but rather to develop improved awareness, understanding and acceptance of both positive and negative emotions in order to minimize impulsive reactions. The key is to be able to tolerate the emotions and to use flexible coping strategies to regulate their intensity and duration. The weekly group sessions, which deal with the function of NSSI, the function and expression of emotions and impulse control, among other themes, are described in an outline and a manual (Gratz & Gunderson, 2006).

The first session deals with NSSI and the function it may serve for different individuals. The participants' personal experiences with and reactions to NSSI are addressed; this includes feelings of shame, which Gratz views as a key issue in NSSI. In sessions 2 to 6, the group works on the expressions and functions of emotions. The goal of these sessions is to improve the participants' ability to categorize and distinguish between different emotions and to identify the thoughts, sensations and behavioural urges related to different emotions. This includes discussing the meaning of the primary emotions and the more or less adaptive behaviours that these may activate. The purpose of focusing on the expressions and functions of emotions is to enhance the patients' ability to accept their emotions. In sessions 7 and 8, the focus is on the consequences of accepting versus avoiding emotions, including the paradoxical long-term consequences of avoiding emotions (overregulation), which may exacerbate the experience of emotions as negative and as something to be avoided. There is a difference between emotional pain, which is an unavoidable part of life, and the emotional suffering that comes from maintaining the emotion by failing to accept it and perhaps ruminating. In sessions 9 and 10, the focus is on different affect-regulation strategies, for example distraction and other techniques, which are also used in DBT. The closing sessions, 11 through 14, involve an ACT-inspired approach to consider priorities in life and how to act on them.

ERGT combines psychoeducation with group exercises, and as in DBT, the patients are given homework in the form of exercises and forms to record emotions and self-injury impulses. More studies have found a positive effect of ERGT on NSSI (Gratz & Tull, 2011)

In a multi-site uncontrolled open pilot study of ERGT in Sweden including 95 women with threshold or sub-threshold BPD and NSSI, Sahlin et al. (2017) found that participation in ERGT was associated with a significant 52% decrease in NSSI at post-treatment and a 76% decrease from pretreatment to six-month follow-up. Further, they found significant improvements in other self-destructive behaviours, emotion dysregulation and psychiatric symptoms at post-treatment. These gains were either maintained or further improved at the six-month follow-up. ERGT appears to have a convincing effect on NSSI, which has led to the development of ERITA for Adolescents, which also involves the parents during part of the treatment.

To meet the need for short-term, effective and easily accessible treatment, Bjureberg et al. (2018) developed a 12-week online version of ERITA that seems promising. In a pilot study of 25 adolescents engaging in NSSI, the authors found a significant 55% reduction in past-month NSSI frequency and other self-destructive behaviours. These improvements were further strengthened at the three-month follow-up and maintained at the six-month follow-up. The treatment was completed by 96% of the young patients.

There is an interesting potential in using the internet in the treatment of adolescents with NSSI. Most young people are proficient internet-users, and online treatment approaches offer the individual patients flexibility to work on tasks when it suits them. This helps them engage in therapy without others knowing about it, which can also be an advantage, since many find it shameful to receive psychological treatment for NSSI. Finally, it makes it easier for them to fit the therapy into their schedule and overcomes geographic restrictions for seeking treatment.

Mobile apps

In recent years, mobile phone apps have emerged as a new mode of treatment for NSSI. One example is CalmHarm, a free app that contains a number of exercises inspired by DBT. Today, there is a wide range of apps that can either be used independently or support traditional face-to-face therapy, but few have been subjected to systematic testing. One exception is Therapeutic Evaluative Conditioning (TEC), which is a game-like app designed to increase aversion to self-injury-related stimuli (pairing these stimuli with unpleasant stimuli) and increase liking of self-related words (pairing these words with pleasant stimuli). The treatment has been found to result in a significant reduction of self-cutting episodes (from 32% to 40%), suicide plans (from 21% to 59%) and suicidal behaviour (from 33% to 77%) in comparison with a control group using a similar mobile app that only included neutral stimuli (Franklin et al., 2016).

Another app, developed in the UK, is BlueIce, which can be used by young people with NSSI during the time in between their face-to-face treatment sessions in the child and adolescent mental health service. BlueIce includes a mood diary and a menu of personalized mood-lifting activities, including personalized music and photos, physical activities, relaxation and mindfulness exercises, as well as challenging of negative thoughts and distress tolerance activities. Among the young people who used the app, the majority found it helpful, and as many as 75% achieved a decrease in NSSI (Grist et al., 2018).

These findings and the easy access of mobile apps make it a very attractive mode for the treatment of NSSI.

Family therapy

Family therapy or supplementary family sessions may offer a constructive add-on treatment, especially with younger patients. Self-injury inevitably affects the family and often plays a dynamic role for the homeostasis and dynamic of the family. Everyone is affected when a family member self-injures, and it can be difficult for the family members to maintain a validating, non-judging stance towards the primary patient (Waals et al., 2018). Many need help to improve the communication within the family, develop strategies for affect regulation, build trust, preserve their mentalizing capacity, manage stress and so forth. Wedig and Nock (2007) found that parents of adolescents who self-injure are more critical and hostile, which has a negative effect on the mood in the family in general and, not least, on the mood of the young person. Studies show that poor communication between parents and adolescents is associated with a risk of self-injury, and that young people who feel that they cannot talk to their parents about their problems also have an increased risk of self-injury. A close and cohesive family situation is a protective factor against self-injury (Arbuthnott & Lewis, 2015).

The rest of the family can be involved in the therapy in a variety of ways. For example, regular family sessions can supplement the individual intervention as a way of keeping the family up to date on the progress of the primary patient and addressing the destructive communication patterns that often develop in a family when a family member practices self-injury, which argues in favour of offering family therapy (Aggarwal & Patton, 2018). Family members often struggle to find the right way to deal with the primary patient and may therefore need psychoeducation, support and help to improve communication in the family. Both MBT and DBT include specific family programmes, where the family is educated about self-injury and receives help to develop and train skills that may be necessary both for the primary patient and for the family in general.

The following case illustrates some familial problems that explain why Beth chose NSSI as a coping strategy. It also conveys how crucial it can be to bring the family together to change their communication pattern.

Fourteen-year-old Beth had already been cutting herself for a few months when her mother found out. Frightened, the mother contacted her ex-husband, Beth's father. He suggested that they all get together to talk about what was happening. After this initial family meeting, they made an appointment with a therapist who agreed to see them all, including Beth's sister, who a few months earlier had moved to the United States, but who was back in England for a few days. They all showed up at the therapist's office, and he was able to form an impression of the family. The parents had divorced about a year before Beth began cutting; Beth's mother had been diagnosed with cancer but was receiving treatment and expected to have a full recovery; her father was a in a new relationship with a woman Beth did not like; and Beth's sister, whom she was very attached to, had moved to the United States. The many changes in Beth's closest family had put her under pressure. As a further stress factor for Beth, her mother was 'constantly' monitoring and checking her for any signs of self-injury. When she showered, her mother would find excuses to come into the bathroom 'to see if I've cut myself', as Beth put it, clearly annoyed. She also found it stressful that her parents argued as much as they did.

Finally, Beth said that she had made friends with a girl from her class who was also a cutter. She felt very close to the girl and saw her as a confidante who really understood her. Occasionally, the girls would cut themselves during the break at the school lavatory. This strengthened Beth's bond with the other girl.

After Beth and her family had seen the therapist a few times, Beth was able to stop NSSI behaviour, and both her parents confirmed that she was doing much better. She was happier and had also developed a closer relationship with both parents. The story of Beth and her family illustrates some of the factors that may cause a young person to begin to self-injure as well as the way self-injury functions in a family. It also illustrates the importance of shifting the focus away from the individual (Beth) to the family system. Although the parents were still divorced and lived apart, the family got together to help Beth deal with her self-injury. The parents' mutual communication improved, the father had become aware of Beth's troubled relationship with his new girlfriend and Beth had regained her parents' attention. In a sense, Beth's self-injury brought the family problems to the surface and led to them being 'resolved', since the family's response to her self-injury was to pull together. The function of the self-injury was obvious.

It is likely that the reason why Beth recovered so quickly and stopped self-injuring was that she was able to bring the family together – in the therapist's office – without resorting to self-destructive means; another important factor was that the family received help to understand Beth's behaviour and find a language for dealing with the difficult issues. Beth's self-injury became meaningful to her parents when they found a way to verbalize their problems. Although the family was in a difficult situation, they had many resources to draw on and were able to find a constructive way to help themselves and their daughter.

Physical exercise

Patients who are in treatment for NSSI often use physical exercise – running, doing sports or working out at a fitness centre – as a means of resisting the urge to self-injure (Klonsky & Glenn, 2008). In a study where patients who self-injure were asked to rate 43 different ways of resisting a self-injury urge, physical exercise came out on top. Of the study participants, 65% found 'doing sports or exercise recreationally' 'very helpful', 30% found it 'somewhat helpful' and only 4% found it 'not helpful at all'. Physical exercise involves contact with the body, deregulates high levels of mental tension and offers an active way for the person to feel better; as such, it undoubtedly promotes integration and affect regulation. The use of exercise as a treatment for self-injury has not been systematically studied, but Wallerstein and Nock (2007) have published a case involving a 26-year-old woman who used exercise as a way to reduce both her urges and her active need for self-injury, which she had lived with for 13 years. In the case study, Wallerstein and Nock found that exercise has a positive effect in two areas, as it both lifts the person's mood and reduces the urge to self-injure. The effect of exercise may stem from the release of beta-endorphins in connection with physical activity; this increases endogenous opioid levels, which may reduce the need or urge to perform NSSI (Bresin & Gordon, 2013). Jarvi et al. (2017) found that people who never engaged in NSSI seem to exercise more than individuals who recently performed NSSI, and they regard physical activity and exercise as a way to manage urges to engage in NSSI.

Medical treatment

Many people who self-injure receive psychotropic medication, but mostly due to other symptoms, such as anxiety or depression. There is no consensus on any single efficacious pharmacological treatment, and the evidence for effect is mixed: some studies find no effect, while others find that medication may have a limited effect on NSSI. These mixed findings reflect that NSSI is not one well-defined disorder but a manifestation of a variety of underlying disorders. When self-injury occurs in patients with other underlying psychopathology, the pharmacological treatment should primarily target the latter.

In a systematic review of psychological and pharmacological interventions, Turner et al. (2014) found that different types of drugs have been explored. These are SSRIs (e.g., fluoxetine), SNRIs (e.g., venlafaxine), atypical antipsychotics (e.g., ziprasidone), opioids (e.g., buprenorphine) and opioid antagonists (e.g., naltrexone). The authors conclude that medications targeting the serotonergic, dopaminergic and opioid systems have demonstrated some benefits, but this is not the conclusion in a Cochrane review of pharmacological interventions for self-harm in adults. They conclude that there is currently no clear evidence for the effectiveness of pharmacological treatment of self-harm (Hawton et al., 2015).

Since self-injury is a non-specific or transdiagnostic symptom, it is not possible to find a single drug that has a general effect on the practice. In the pharmacological treatment of patients with NSSI it is important to prescribe medication that does not have a sedative effect or otherwise has a negative effect on the psychotherapeutic intervention that is the first choice in the treatment of NSSI. Further, there is a significant risk of polypharmacy, often as the result of therapeutic despair. When the patient does not improve on one type of medication, the therapist adds another, often without discontinuing the former, which reflects the sense of powerlessness that may accompany attempts at stopping NSSI.

Core elements in the psychotherapeutic treatment of NSSI

Several countries have developed clinical guidelines for the treatment of self-harm or NSSI, including the UK, Australia, Germany and Sweden. Several American universities have similarly developed guidelines for dealing with NSSI (e.g., Whitlock et al., 2018).

The following is based on some of the clinical guidelines that have been developed in different countries.

1   Providing a clear treatment structure that provides predictability and continuity for the patient. From the outset, the patient should be informed about his or her diagnosis, the treatment course and what is expected of the therapist and of the patient. This is explicitly stated in both DBT and MBT.
2   Building commitment for treatment, in both patient and therapist. Cancellations, inconsistencies and other kinds of discontinuity should be avoided or minimized.

3   Maintaining continuous efforts to support the patient's motivation for continuing treatment.

4   Adopting an empathic, validating and explorative stance. Listening to the patient, asking about his or her own experience and acknowledging it are *sine qua non* for the therapeutic alliance in the treatment of patients with NSSI. DBT underscores the importance of validation and acceptance, and MBT revolves around the not-knowing curious attitude.

5   Maintaining a focus on building enhanced awareness and understanding of emotions and on developing the capacity for emotion regulation. In DBT, MBT and ERGT, the focus is on emotions and emotion regulation, based on the assumption that one of the primary functions of NSSI is to regulate emotions.

6   Avoiding negative reactions from the therapist towards the patient. NSSI activates many emotions that are difficult to handle, which can cause the therapist to fail to maintain an empathic, validating stance and instead seek to control or even punish the patient. In part as a way to avoid negative reactions from the therapist, DBT and MBT focus on the dynamics within the treatment team.

7   Identifying factors or situations that trigger or maintain NSSI and providing alternative skills or problem-solving strategies.

8   Devoting attention to and treatment of underlying psychiatric disorders or other reasons for NSSI.

9   Offering all patients psychosocial assessment, risk assessment for suicide and clear contacts in case of suicidality.

11 Dialectical Behaviour Therapy

Dialectical Behaviour Therapy (DBT) was developed in the United States during the 1990s by the American psychologist Marsha Linehan and her staff, primarily intended for the treatment of patients with BPD and impulsive NSSI or suicidal behaviour.

DBT draws on elements from cognitive, psychodynamic, humanistic-existential and experiential psychotherapy, but what makes it unique is the specific combination of classical behaviour therapy, mindfulness and dialectical philosophy. These elements are used in a way that is both systematic and pragmatic, and this mix makes DBT an unconventional therapy approach in many regards. As the name indicates, it is inspired by dialectics. The term comes from ancient Greek, where it refers to the art of reasoning and discussing based on considering contrasting arguments with the goal of gaining new insights. Truth is an evolving process that unfolds over time in an interplay of polar opposites – thesis and antithesis – resulting in a synthesis that contains aspects of both perspectives. Dialectics involves the ability to see two sides or views of an issue and thus grasp its full complexity. Reality is not static and absolute but consists of continually evolving opposing forces. Any position contains its own opposite, and hence a key objective of DBT is to avoid getting locked into a particular point of view and instead remain open to the opposite perspective.

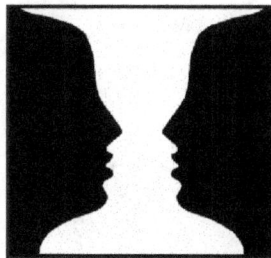

Figure 11.1 Rubin's vase is an example of an ambiguous figure where the viewer can switch between two perspectives, seeing either the white vase or the two black profiles. This illustrates the practice of dialectic thinking in psychotherapy.

Many patients with emotion dysregulation are prone to a polarized black/white mindset, which the dialectical approach challenges. The point is to replace either/or thinking with a both/and mindset which accepts that two opposite positions can be true at the same time, as in the picture of Rubin's vase above (Figure 11.1). A person can be simultaneously beautiful and ugly, good and bad, happy and sad, right and wrong; life can be both painful and joyful; and a behaviour can be both destructive and constructive. Similarly, many self-injuring and suicidal patients have a simultaneous desire to live and to die.

They want both. For example, when a patient says to his or her therapist, 'I don't want to go on living!' that may express a death wish, but at the same time it reflects the patient's desire to live – only, not the life that he or she is living right now. Therapeutic progress is made possible by dissolving the impasse; one solution might be to abandon the life the patient is leading now in favour of a different and better life. DBT aims to generate dialogue, and the alternative to suicide is to build a different life – one worth living – which is the main goal of DBT. The dialectical dialogue always allows for change.

Dialectical dilemmas

An important element in DBT is to balance and work with the dialectical dilemmas that are illustrated in Figure 11.2, overleaf.

The general dialectical opposites that drive the therapeutic approach to patients who self-injure are *acceptance-change* and *validation-confrontation*. To handle these apparent opposites, the therapist must, on the one hand, accept and validate the patient's condition (for example, the fact that the patient may be so distressed that he or she cuts him/herself) and, on the other hand, endeavour to make the patient change and stop cutting.

DBT involves both acceptance and change strategies, and in the therapeutic situation it is essential to be able to balance these strategies in a constructive way. If the therapist demands greater changes than the patient can handle or, conversely,

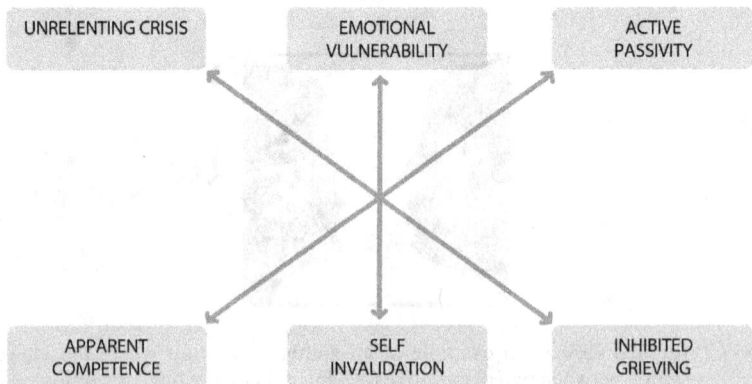

Figure 11.2 Examples of dialectical dilemmas.

relies exclusively on acceptance strategies, the therapy breaks down. A change strategy might involve the use of chain analysis or skills training, where the focus is on insight and behaviour changes, while validation is a therapeutic attitude that permeates the contact with the patient.

Patients will often occupy one of the extreme positions, for example either appear passive and helpless, compelling others to solve their problems, or show apparent competence and reject help from others. It is important to be able to contain and balance these opposites constructively.

Treatment structure

DBT revolves around four components:

1 Individual treatment
2 Group-based skills training
3 Access to telephone coaching
4 Team meetings and supervision for the therapist

Individual treatment

Individual treatment involves weekly sessions of about 50 minutes' duration. The sessions have a regular structure that varies with the current stage of the therapy (see p. 199). In connection with active NSSI, the patient enters into Stage 1, where the patient's safety has priority, and hence the focus of the sessions is on self-injury behaviour.

In the time between the sessions, the patient fills out a diary card that tracks a number of behaviours and experiences, including which forms of NSSI he or she has engaged in as well as when and how (see Figure 11.3). The patient may also register any other failures in impulse control (for example binge eating), vulnerability (on a scale from 0 to 10) and which skills he or she used to refrain from NSSI during the week. Part of the focus in individual therapy is on identifying the situations that cause emotion dysregulation and trigger NSSI as well as the skills the patient might use to handle the situation without self-injuring.

Treatment priorities in the individual session

*   Reducing or eliminating NSSI and life-threatening behaviour
*   Reducing or eliminating behaviour that interferes with therapy (for example nonattendance, noncompliance with homework assignments or other behaviours that undermine the therapy)
*   Reducing or minimizing hospitalization as a means of crisis management
*   Reducing behaviours that reduce the patient's quality of life (for example eating disorders, missing work or school, substance abuse)
*   Increasing or stimulating behaviours that make life worth living
*   Increasing or stimulating skills that help to build relations and efficiently manage emotions and problems

Dialectical Behavior Therapy (DBT) Diary Card	initials	Date Finished	How often did you fill out this card? 1 2-4 5-6 7 Filled out in Session? Y / N Target Behavior:		

Target Behavior		Emotions								Skills		
How strong was your urge to use (or avoid) your target behavior? Did you?		Rate how intense your emotion was each day								*Use this scale to rate how you used your skills. Check "R" if you reinforced yourself for using skills.		
		(0=least intense and 5=most intense)										
Day	Urge	Action	Rx	Pain	Sad	Shame	Anger	Fear	Joy	Skills	R ✔	
Mon												*USED SKILLS 0=Not thought about or used
Tues												1=Thought about, not used, didn't want to 2=Thought about, not used, wanted to
Wed												3=Tried but couldn't use them
Thurs												4=Tried, could do them but they didn't help 5=Tried, could use them, helped
Fri												6=Didn't try, used them, didn't help 7=Didn't try, used them, helped
Sat												
Sun												

Figure 11.3 Example of a diary card the patient is asked to fill out in between the sessions during the week. *Target behaviour* is the problem the patient wants to solve, for example NSSI. *Rx* is prescribed medication. *Used skills* are the skills the patient has learned in the skills training group. Other types of diary cards exist, some with more details than this example.

The point of the structured approach is to maintain focus on the main priority, which is to keep the patient alive and continue the therapy. For example, if the patient has cut him/herself or overdosed, that will always be the top priority in the therapeutic session, while, for example, relationship issues, which may also be very distressing, will have to wait until the more urgent issues have been addressed. Hence, any DBT session begins with writing up an agenda, a prioritized list of topics to be addressed; this ensures that nothing is left out, either due to an oversight or because the time runs out. In between the sessions the patient will often have homework assignments (for example recording the occurrence of the problem behaviour or conducting behavioural experiments).

Group-based skills training

In DBT, NSSI is regarded as a dysfunctional coping strategy that the patient relies on for want of better and more effective skills; hence, the patient needs to learn better skills. Skills training takes place in a group of about eight patients, who meet once a week for about two hours. In the group they learn basic skills that are often underdeveloped in persons who are emotionally dysregulated and rely on NSSI.

The skills training has a modular structure. Each module includes eight sessions, except for the first module (mindfulness), which includes two sessions but is repeated after each of the other modules. An extensive manual has been published with handouts and worksheets for the patients and instructions for the therapists (Linehan, 2015).

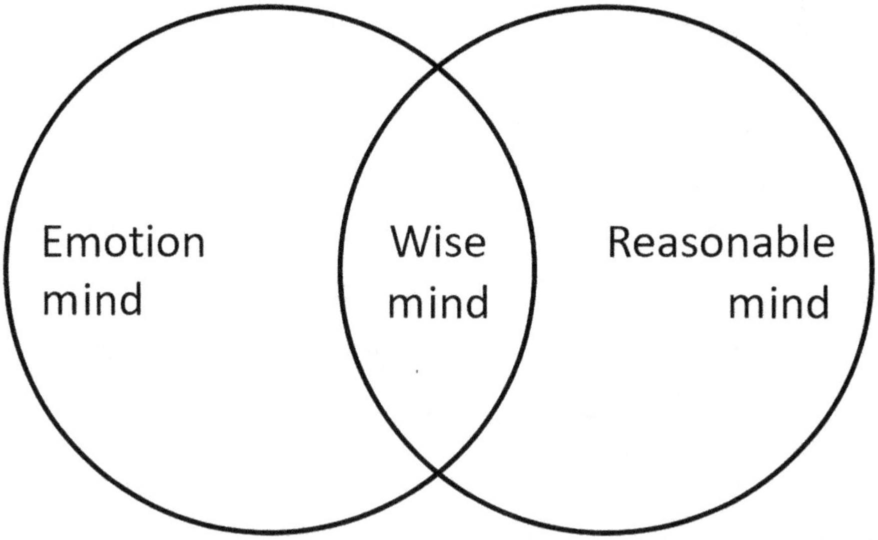

Figure 11.4 Relationship between emotion mind and reasonable mind in wise mind.

Mindfulness

DBT operates with three states of mind (Figure 11.4): *reasonable mind, emotion mind* and *wise mind*. In *reasonable mind*, one's thinking is logical and fact-based and ignores emotions. In *emotion mind*, one's behaviour and thinking are ruled by the current emotions; one is often impulsive, with actions driven by intense feelings and a sense of urgency. Emotion mind disregards logic and reason. *Wise mind* is the synthesis of emotion mind and reasonable mind but also includes intuitive knowing, emotional experiencing and logical analysis. Wise mind is the ideal state of mind that we strive for from which to make our decisions.

We make better, more balanced choices when we are in wise mind. Learning to be more aware of feelings and one's way of thinking is an important component of DBT. The goal is to develop a lifestyle of participating with awareness, and in order to do that, one needs to be able to *observe, describe* and *participate*, the components of practicing mindfulness (the 'what skills' in DBT) (Linehan, 2015).

Observe

- Pay attention to your senses in the present moment.
- Notice what is happening within yourself and without.
- Avoid trying to push the thoughts or emotions away but simply notice that they exist – even if they are painful.
- Imagine having a brain with a non-stick coating that allows thoughts and emotions to glance off and pass through the mind unhindered.

Describe

- Put the experience into words.
- Describe an experience using 'I', 'me', 'my', as in 'I am upset' or 'My heart is pounding' or 'Sadness has just enveloped me'.
- Put a name to your feelings: call a thought just a thought, a feeling just a feeling.
- Describe what you can observe – not what you think is going to happen, or what things were like in the past; your focus should be on the present.

Participate

- Participate in the moment and become one with what you are doing (for example listening to music, dancing, washing up).
- Let yourself get involved in the moment, letting go of ruminating and self-consciousness.
- Listen to and discover your own 'wisdom'; act intuitively from wise mind and go with the flow.
- Mindlessness is participating without attention to the task; mindfulness is participating with attention.

(Linehan, 2015)

The 'how skills' are about *how* to observe, describe and participate. Linehan mentions the importance of 1) being non-judgemental, 2) doing one thing at a time (one-mindfully) and 3) doing what works (effectively). It is extremely important not to avoid the emotions, even if they are negative and unpleasant. Unless one is ruminating, emotions pass quickly, and being in a condition where one is not afraid of certain emotions makes one stronger and more adaptive.

Interpersonal Effectiveness

In this module, patients are taught relevant skills, including effective strategies for asking for what they need (e.g., requesting someone to do something), how to say no assertively and how to manage interpersonal conflict while maintaining self-respect. Effectiveness means doing what works, that is, achieving the desired result without violating one's own or the other's boundaries. The skills taught are intended to maximize the chances of achieving one's goals in a specific situation without damaging the relationship or one's own self-respect.

Emotion Regulation

Emotion regulation is the ability to control or influence what emotions one has, when one has them and how one experiences and expresses them (ibid.). Emotion regulation skills aim to help the patient avoid getting caught up in a storm of emotions and 'hitting the roof' or dropping into a deep hole of depression. The patient needs to learn skills to handle acute crises without, for example, using NSSI, and that there are steps he or she can take to reduce his or her vulnerability, including sleeping and eating right, taking medication as prescribed and avoiding stress and excessive drinking.

- Naming and understanding the functions of emotions
- Identifying obstacles to changing emotions
- Reducing vulnerability to emotion mind by taking care of oneself
- Increasing positive emotional events
- Increasing mindfulness to current emotions
- Taking opposite action
- Applying distress tolerance techniques

Opposite action means doing the opposite of avoidance behaviour and is a way to change or reduce unwanted emotions if they do not fit the facts. If, for example, the patient is depressed and feels like isolating him/herself and staying in bed, opposite action would be to *activate*, getting out of bed and meeting the world. If the patient feels extreme shame, opposite action would be to *engage* with others rather than hiding in isolation. Opposite actions are based on wise mind.

1   The patient examines what emotion he or she is feeling and checks whether it fits the facts.
2   The patient examines what action urge the emotion activates.
3   The patient identifies the opposite action.
4   The patient performs the opposite action.

Table 11.1 Emotions always coincide with an urge to act on the associated impulse. That is why it is important to identify which impulse goes with which emotion.

Emotion	Urge	Opposite action
Fear and anxiety	Avoiding what is perceived as dangerous (for example shopping for groceries or taking the bus)	Confronting what provokes anxiety and doing that repeatedly (exposure)
Depression and sadness	Isolating oneself and turning one's back on the world	Being active and extroverted; contacting others and doing things that create a sense of control and of being effective
Shame and guilt	Withdrawing from contact	Reaching out and contacting others, even if it may feel difficult and awkward (exposure)

Distress Tolerance

Persons with NSSI are often easily overwhelmed by negative emotions that rapidly increase in intensity. Hence, they need skills that improve their ability to manage stress and distress and thus minimize impulsive behaviour as NSSI. Distress tolerance skills constitute a natural development from mindfulness skills, and rely on the ability to accept both oneself and the current situation without evaluating or judging.

In this module, the patient learns to distract him/herself, self-soothe, use sensory awareness, improve the moment, accept the situation, which includes radical acceptance and turning the mind towards acceptance, and consider the pros and cons of, for example, NSSI.

Examples of self-soothing and improving the moment through sensory awareness

- *Vision*: looking at something beautiful or exciting; visiting a museum
- *Taste*: having a nice cup of tea; eating something tasty – without overdoing it: it is the flavour that is essential
- *Hearing*: listening to music, singing along
- *Scent*: wearing perfume or scented lotion that one likes; lighting a scented candle; breathing in the smell of fresh-ground coffee
- *Physical touch or stimulation*: taking a hot bath or shower; petting a dog or a cat; snuggling up in a chair wrapped in a soft throw; holding an ice cube in one's hand
- *Physical exercise*: going for a run; stretching; swaying from side to side

Examples of ways to distract oneself

- Playing a computer game
- Surfing the internet
- Watching a film
- Reading a book
- Ringing a friend to chat

Pro and cons are used to compare the advantages and disadvantages of different options, for example the positive and negative consequences of tolerating distress by resisting the impulsive behaviour and the positive and negative consequences of not tolerating distress by engaging in, for example, NSSI.

Table 11.2 Matrix for analysing pros and cons.

Analysing pros and cons	
NSSI: pros	NSSI: cons
Tolerating distress: pros	Tolerating distress: cons

Other modules focus on other skill sets (for example validating self and others) or skills adapted to a specific patient group (for example eating skills for patients with anorexia).

Telephone coaching

In the time between the sessions, the patients may ring the therapist in order to prevent self-injury and practice the use of some of the skills from their skills training group. The patient may ring if he or she experiences a crisis and does not know which skills to apply. According to Linehan (1993), however, a patient who has already self-injured may not contact the therapist for the following 24 hours.

> Julie rings the DBT coaching telephone late one night because she is upset and worried that she might self-injure by cutting herself. Her boyfriend is out with some of his friends, and she misses him. In a brief phone call, lasting just a few minutes, she talks with the therapist about the options listed on her crisis card (cf. p. 206) and what her options are. She rang one of her close friends but failed to reach her, and she feels abandoned and all alone. The therapist suggests a long shower. Even though Julie is not really motivated for that, she agrees to give it a try, and the therapist promises to ring her in 30 minutes. When they speak again she feels a little better, but not great. She decides to wrap up in her duvet on the sofa and watch a film before going to bed. They also agree that she can ring the therapist later if she still feels bad.

Experience shows that many patients hesitate to use the telephone to reach out for help. On the other hand, many therapists worry about having to take calls at all hours of the day or night. In fact, that rarely happens, and if it is a concern, the therapist can tell the patients that the DBT line is only open during certain hours, for example, until 22.00. However, the time that goes into providing coaching over the phone is well spent. The conversations with Julie only took a few minutes and helped her learn how to apply a more constructive strategy than cutting herself.

Team meetings

In therapeutic work with patients with BPD and NSSI, it can be difficult to maintain realistic goals for the therapy and to preserve the dialectical balance between validation and acceptance, on the one hand, and problem-solving and the desire for change on the other. Hence, team meetings with mutual support and supervision are a necessary part of DBT. The team typically meets once a week for one to one-and-a-half hours; among other topics, the meetings typically include working on some of the skills that the patients are learning. Therapists also need distress tolerance and emotion regulation skills.

The five stages of DBT

DBT follows a set structure, beginning with a pretreatment stage that is followed by four treatment phases, each focusing on specific themes and goals.

During the *pretreatment stage*, the primary goals are to *begin to build a good, trusting working alliance* between patient and therapist, develop *collaborative commitment* and *educate the patient on the underlying treatment principles*, including the biosocial model. The latter aims to give the patient insight into the background and causes of his or her NSSI. The pretreatment stage also involves identifying the problems that will be the focus of Stage 1. At the conclusion of the pretreatment stage, therapist and patient draw up a contract where, among other points, the patient commits to doing whatever he or she can to conclude the therapy, show up for the sessions, work to reduce suicidal and self-injury behaviour and take part in the skills training. The therapist, among other points, commits to doing whatever he or she can to provide effective treatment, avoid therapy-interfering behaviour, act ethically, be respectful, be accessible and receive supervision. With these commitments in place, the actual treatment can begin.

1   The main theme of Stage 1 is the *patient's safety*. Behaviours that put the patient or others at risk are the top priority. By order of priority, the topics are life-threatening behaviours and NSSI, therapy-interfering behaviour (for example that the patient misses sessions or that the therapist cancels) and behaviours that reduce the patient's quality of life (for example by failing to take medication as prescribed, by drinking to excess or by practicing unsafe sex).
    Concurrently with working with these themes in individual therapy, the patient takes part in the skills training group to acquire specific skills, as outlined above. This stage may last about a year, and when the patient is sufficiently stable and able to manage strong and difficult emotions without resorting to self-destructive behaviour, it is time to move on to Stage 2.
2   Stage 2 is about processing *earlier traumas* with the purpose of reducing post-traumatic stress. Many patients with BPD have suffered severe childhood traumas (for example neglect and sexual abuse), which has led to psychological problems in their current life. At this stage, *prolonged exposure therapy* can be used to work with PTSD.
3   Stage 3 aims to *enhance the patient's self-respect* and to help him or her achieve a better quality of life. Many self-injuring patients have very low self-esteem and have difficulty accepting and believing in themselves.
4   Finally, Stage 4 aims to build 'a life worth living'. Among other things, this involves engaging in interpersonal relationships and feeling alive. This stage involves finding meaning in life and pursing self-realization in accordance with one's personal goals and values.

It is important to proceed gradually and to work through one stage at a time. In particular, it is important that Stage 1 is completed successfully, meaning that the patient has developed adaptive strategies for managing stress and NSSI, before moving on to Stage 2, where emotionally upsetting topics will exacerbate mental suffering and thus the risk of NSSI. In practice, most of the treatment process unfolds during Stage 1 and 2. Patients with impulsive NSSI and suicidal behaviour are the primary target group for DBT, but DBT now includes a broad range of disorders e.g., eating disorders, drug abuse, mood disorders.

Validation

A key concept in DBT is validation, which makes sense, considering that Linehan considers growing up in an *invalidating* environment a major factor in the development of emotion dysregulation and, thus, NSSI. An invalidating environment is one where one's emotions are not acknowledged (validated) but instead misinterpreted, dismissed or ridiculed.

Validation comes from Latin (*validare*). From its basic original meaning, 'to make legally valid', in modern English it is used to indicate that something is true, reasonable, meaningful, cogent. Validating someone means communicating that their emotions, behaviour and motives are credible, relevant, understandable, meaningful and reasonable in the given situation. Thus, validation implies affirmation. Validation is not soothing, care or praise but a recognition of the other person's integrity and right to experience the world as he or she does. Validation may also involve *not* comforting or praising and instead challenging the patient, thus signalling confidence in his or her ability to rise to the challenge. That kind of validation signals recognition of the patient as a competent equal. Too much praise can be invalidating, if the therapist praises something that *the patient* perceives as trivial. Validation is also not the same as empathy, although empathy is a condition for validation.

Validation helps build a good connection with another person, whether between parents and child, between adults or between therapist and patient. Validation is a social lubricant that helps to develop and enhance the therapeutic alliance, which is a condition for treating self-injury.

When parents validate the child's behaviour and emotional expressions, thus communicating that his or her reactions are reasonable and relevant in the given situation, the child learns to recognize, contain and manage his or her emotions. That does not mean that the parents necessarily have to agree with the child; the key is that they acknowledge the child's right to have emotional reactions. On the other hand, if the parents ridicule the child's emotions, ignore them, dismiss them or misinterpret them, thus *invalidating* them, the child may grow up to have difficulty sensing and managing his or her emotions. The parents' validation of the child's reactions also teaches the child to self-validate – the opposite of judging and demeaning him/herself, which is a common characteristic among people who self-injure.

What can be validated?

In addition to the basic act of validating the other as a unique and credible person, DBT distinguishes between validation of thoughts, feelings, behaviour and body sensations. It is not always possible to validate all these aspects at once, and it is important only to validate what can be validated. If a patient has cut him/herself, the therapist can validate the emotion that led to it; for example, 'I can understand why you got upset and worried about being abandoned when your girlfriend told you on the phone that she wanted to take a break'. Cutting as a way of dealing with difficult emotions is not a constructive long-term strategy, thus it is not primarily the self-injury behaviour itself that should be validated but the underlying emotions. In addition to thoughts, emotions, behaviour and body sensations, it may be appropriate to validate the patient's desires, reactions, intentions, attitudes, efforts or difficulties in a given situation.

Validation can be verbal as well as nonverbal. Explicitly stating that it is meaningful for the patient to react as he or she does – as in the example above – is verbal validation. Validation can also be nonverbal, conveyed by attention, nodding, facial expressions or, for example, by serving a cup of coffee or tea as a tangible expression of care and recognition of the patient. Many patients feel that actions speak louder than words when it comes to feeling accepted and acknowledged (cf. also the teleological mode, p. 112).

Levels of validation

DBT operates with different levels of validation. The therapist can validate the patient through a variety of behaviours:

1   Listening attentively and maintaining eye contact and responding in other ways that show focus and attention.
2   Mirroring and actively expressing that one understands what the patient is expressing, for example by asking clarifying questions or recapitulating a key point in the conversation.
3   Reading and reflecting on the patient's behaviour: 'I sense that there is something happening inside you right now. Is that right? Is it possible that you. . . ?'
4   Affirming the behaviour and describing it as understandable in light of past circumstances. 'It makes sense that would react strongly to your boyfriend yelling at you, since you grew up with a violent father'.
5   Affirming the behaviour and describing it as understandable in light of the current circumstances. 'It's no wonder that you felt overwhelmed and powerless when you had that argument with your girlfriend. After all, you hadn't slept or eaten for close to 12 hours. That makes you vulnerable'.
6   Treating the patient as a responsible and independent person; addressing him or her, not as a patient in poor health, but as a fellow human being who one can make demands of.
7   The therapist's self-disclosure, where he or she talks about her own response in a situation similar to the patient's, can be a highly effective form of validation by indicating that the patient's behaviour is a normal human response. For example, 'I can certainly understand why you'd be stressed out by leaving home. I remember how tough it was when I moved to the dorms. I think anybody can relate to that'.

Change strategies

In addition to acceptance and validation, change strategies are a key part of DBT. Change strategies include helping the patient to develop and practice skills that are necessary for development and change. However, it is important to maintain the dialectical balance between acceptance and change. When therapeutic progress slows down or stops entirely, it is important to consider whether the balance and synthesis between acceptance and change strategies may have become lopsided. At times, the therapist needs to prioritize *either* acceptance *or* change strategies in order to achieve the right synthesis to ensure that the patient receives the optimal benefit from the therapy.

Change strategies in DBT aim to help the patient change his or her dysfunctional behaviour, including NSSI. Dysfunctional behaviour, such as NSSI, is often perceived as the key problem to be addressed, in part by focusing on learning new skills; however, it could be argued that the opposite is true, that self-injury should really be seen as a *dysfunctional solution* to a problem. The point is that both functional and dysfunctional behaviour have a function that makes it meaningful to the patient.

Problem-solving strategies

Exposure, self-monitoring based on diary cards, systematic skills training, cognitive restructuring and contingency management (working with the consequences of an action) are key elements of DBT. As these techniques are described elsewhere (e.g., Linehan, 1993), the focus in the present context will be on the use of chain analysis, which is a particularly important tool in the treatment of NSSI.

Chain analysis

The purpose of a chain analysis is to uncover connections, identify the underlying factors behind the patient's NSSI and apply problem-solving strategies and skills to help the patient find an alternative to NSSI. Chain analysis is a key part of DBT. It can be conducted on a whiteboard or a sheet of paper, and it is important that the patient can take the analysis home, for example as a mobile phone photo or a photo copy.

Beginning with the act of NSSI, patient and therapist together examine the events as well as the thoughts and emotions that led up to the act. It is important to include vulnerability factors (fatigue, hunger, stress, alcohol, drugs and so forth) that compromise the patient's 'mental immune defence' and thus increase the risk of NSSI or other forms of dysfunctional problem-solving.

DBT applies certain basic principles of behaviour therapy in examining the consequences of a given behaviour. Any benefit of a given behaviour, for example the short-term relief produced by NSSI, will act as natural reinforcement. However, the positive consequences ('Cutting gives me immediate relief') may be accompanied by negative long-term consequences ('but I hate the scars it leaves'). Focusing on the long-term consequences (such as scars, shame, negative reactions from significant others) may activate the patient's motivation for finding ways to deal with mental suffering that are free from negative effects. DBT seeks to reward constructive and adaptive behaviour while making maladaptive behaviour less attractive.

Step 1 in a chain analysis (cf. Figure 11.5) is to describe what happened; often this is based on a diary card where the patient records certain events during the week, including NSSI, since the previous session. It is important to hear – in detail – about the patient's thoughts, emotions and behaviours in all the following steps. (Celine: 'I cut my thigh in three places. I did it in our bathroom at home').

Step 2 is to chart the consequences of the self-injury. (Celine: 'I felt better right away, and later, when my boyfriend came home, I think he felt bad for going out. So he was really sweet and attentive to me the rest of the evening, even into the next day. He could tell that I had been in pain'.) That Celine felt better just after cutting is in itself a factor that reinforces her NSSI, but it is not helpful that her boyfriend gives her additional positive attention when she has cut herself. That may further reinforce her NSSI and is an issue that needs to be addressed in the conversation.

Step 3 consists in reviewing what led up to NSSI (Celine: 'We had planned to go on a picnic, and I had packed a lunch. Just before we were about to leave, one of his friends rang to ask if he wanted to go watch a ballgame'.

Step 4: 'He cancelled our appointment, and I was really angry, but he didn't care. He just left, and I felt abandoned'.

Step 5: 'I rang my friend Rita, but she couldn't talk because she was out with her new boyfriend. That made me feel even worse. Then I tried to ring my boyfriend, but he didn't pick up'.

Step 6: 'I went into the bathroom, where I saw my boyfriend's shaver. I pulled a blade out and decided to cut myself'.)

Step 7 involves identifying vulnerability factors that may compromise the patient's impulse control (Celine: 'I was super-tired, because we had been at a party the night before, so we hadn't slept much. I had also had quite a bit to drink and woke up with a hangover. So, also, I hadn't eaten much'.)

Behavioral Chain Analysis

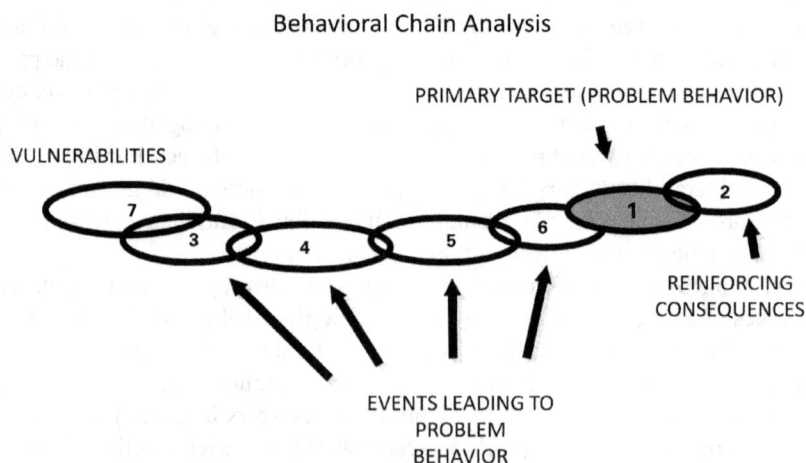

Figure 11.5 Chain analysis. Steps 1–7.

Steps 8–11 (Figure 11.6) are about changing the behaviour and breaking the existing pattern. In this part of the analysis, the patient and the therapist try to determine what the patient could have done instead of cutting him/herself (breaking the existing pattern). This involves identifying the skills that the patient, Celine, lacked in the situation where she needed to cut herself.

Obviously, I was pretty vulnerable because I hadn't had enough sleep and I had too much to drink. I also hadn't had anything to eat because I had a hangover. I had been looking forward to our picnic, but maybe I should have told him that instead of getting so angry and yelling at him. Maybe I should have talked to him more, to make him understand how much I'd looked forward to spending time with him [using interpersonal skills]. Just after he had left I really felt rejected and abandoned. So I rang Rita, but that was a bad idea. It just made matters worse, because she was busy with her new boyfriend. Maybe I should have rung someone else. Or arranged a picnic with a friend? I could also have gone for a run or done something else entirely, like go to the cinema. Or I could have treated myself to a hot bath [emotion regulation skills]. Even though I was angry, maybe I should have planned to have a nice dinner ready when he came home, so that we could still have had a nice time together. But I wasn't sure when he'd be back. I just got so upset, so I went into the bathroom where I found his shaver and took out the blade, which I used to cut myself. I hadn't actually planned to cut myself, but then I saw the shaver. Maybe I should have used mindfulness skills, observe, describe, participate. Or may I should have done a pros-and-cons matrix to remind myself why it's not a great idea to cut myself [distress tolerance skills]. When I look at the cons I know that I regret it afterwards. What I hadn't anticipated was that my boyfriend was so sweet and happy when he came home. He was really sad when he found out I had cut myself, and I think he felt kind of guilty because he had gone to the game when we already had a plan to go on a picnic. So in a sense there were a lot of pros to cutting myself. I felt much better right away, and even though I felt bad later, my boyfriend showed

Behavioral chain analysis / 2
Changing Behavior and breaking the old pattern

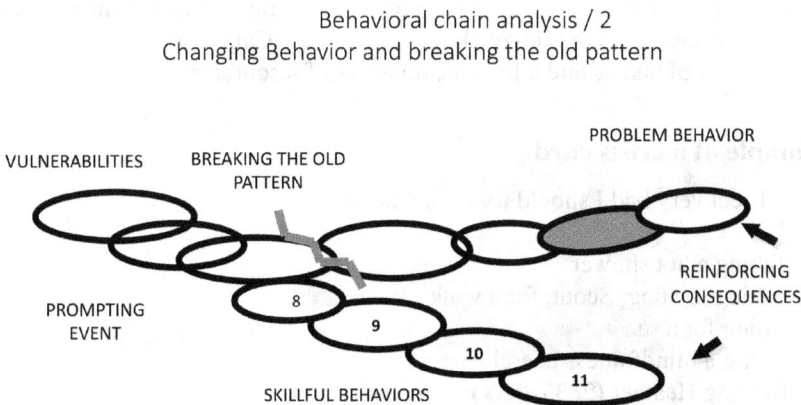

Figure 11.6 Chain analysis. Steps 8–11: using new skills to prevent problem behaviour.

up and comforted me. But of course I'm upset that it happened again. It's embarrassing, both with my boyfriend and when I go to the beach that I've got these big wounds. Everyone can see that I've cut myself. And maybe there will be scars.

Throughout the analysis, it is important to focus on the patient's varying actions, emotions and thoughts without judging them. What happened? What did you do? What did you feel? How could you sense that feeling in your body? What happened to the feeling? What did you think? What do you think your boyfriend/girlfriend thought?

Celine refers to some specific skills she could have used. A review of these skills in DBT would also include talking about 1) what role vulnerability factors (due to a hangover, lack of sleep and lack of food) played in her impulsive act, 2) what interpersonal skills she could have used to react differently when her boyfriend wanted to go watch a ballgame, instead of getting angry, 3) mindfulness skills, which she brought up herself, and which could have helped her manage her emotion better by using *observe, describe, participate* (cf. p. 193 f.), 4) emotion regulation skills, which she could have used when her boyfriend left to be with his friends, when she experienced feeling worse after talking to her girlfriend and, finally, when she went into the bathroom and reacted impulsively by cutting herself. Finally, she could have used 5) distress tolerance skills by being physically active or by improving the moment. Celine mentions that she could have gone for a run or taken a hot bath. It is also important to talk to Celine – and perhaps her boyfriend – about the maladaptive function of him giving her special attention after she has self-injured. The positive attention functions as a positive social reinforcement.

Crisis card

A crisis card is a personalized tool the patient can use when he or she feels powerless and overwhelmed by self-destructive impulses and is therefore unable to think clearly. The crisis card includes ideas for specific skills that can be helpful when things get difficult. The patient and the therapist prepare the crisis card together and revise it throughout the course of therapy. The patient may use a smartphone app as a reminder of skills (for example CalmHarm; see p. 181) or to provide a list of names and telephone numbers of resource persons.

Example of a crisis card

When I feel very bad I should try to feel better by

- Taking a hot shower
- Taking my dog, Scout, for a walk
- Going for a run
- Doing a mindfulness exercise
- Ringing Heather (2833 3xxx)
- Streaming a film

Contact between patient and therapist

DBT underscores the importance of a patient–therapist relationship based on trust, warmth, engagement and the shared responsibility for the treatment outcome. Linehan points out that since patient and therapist share the same existential universe, they have much in common. She recommends occasional self-disclosure if it serves a therapeutic purpose. DBT thus does not advocate the detached, cool therapeutic contact but instead places a priority on spontaneity and vitality in the patient–therapist contact.

During the therapeutic process, the patient exists in a field of tension between accepting things as they are and hoping for change – change that is often hard to attain. As mentioned above, the therapist has to balance acceptance and validation on the one hand with change on the other. Dialectics is also at play in the therapist's communication style, which can be both respectful and humorous at once, despite the serious topics. Irreverent communication is used to get the patient's attention, present an alternative viewpoint or push the patient 'off balance' in order to bring new energy into the therapy. For example, the therapist may use paradox and metaphor or play devil's advocate, mixing seriousness with humour in arguing for an extreme version of the patient's dysfunctional behaviour. For irreverence to be effective it must be genuine and come from a place of compassion and warmth towards the patient (Linehan, 2015).

Rebecca did not want to stop cutting herself, because it helped her to cope with many difficult situations, and she felt that the pros of cutting far outweighed the cons. The therapist chose to play devil's advocate and argued that she ought to teach her little sister the same way of coping with her conflicts and challenges. The purpose of this unusual communication style is to suspend the conventional roles in order, in this case by making Rebecca argue why her little sister should *not* use NSSI to deal with difficult situations in life. Naturally, this form of communication requires both respect for the patient and a good ability to balance between seriousness and humour. In DBT, it is important that the patient regards the therapist as an ally in the effort to change the problem behaviour.

Effect of DBT on NSSI

DBT protocols in various forms have been the subject of many outcome studies. The following mentions a few examples. Most outcome studies that include frequency of NSSI among the outcome measures involve patients with BPD or subclinical BPD. The quality of the studies is not strong, and there are many methodological challenges (for example definition of self-injury, follow-up time, population).

According to a Cochrane review of psychosocial interventions for self-harm in adults compared with TAU, DBT showed a significant reduction in frequency of self-harm at final follow-up but not in the proportion of individuals repeating self-harm. Compared with an alternative form of psychological therapy, DBT-oriented therapy was also associated with a significant treatment effect for repetition of self-harm at final follow-up (Hawton et al., 2016). Included in this review is not just NSSI but also suicidal behaviour. Another review demonstrated that most studies show that DBT outperformed TAU, measured on rates, frequency of and urges to engage in NSSI, suicidal ideation, interpersonal problems, therapy dropout rates, medication use and inpatient days; however, RCT studies of the efficacy of DBT in treating NSSI have shown mixed results. Some studies found that reductions in frequency were not statistically greater than those achieved in active control groups, while other studies conversely demonstrated that DBT led to greater reduction in rates and frequency than TAU (Turner et al., 2014). Finally, in a systematic review and meta-analysis of therapeutic interventions for suicide attempts and self-harm, Ougrin et al. (2015) found that CBT is among the treatment interventions with the biggest effect size.

Some reviews have been made of studies of treatment of *adolescent* patients. For example, a review of studies of outpatient DBT for adolescents engaged in self-harm found promising results in reducing self-harm and associated symptoms up to one year post-treatment, but longitudinal studies are clearly needed to determine sustainability (Freeman et al., 2016). The same reservations due to quality and methodological issues have been noted by Cook and Gorraiz (2016), who reviewed studies of outpatient treatment of depression and NSSI in adolescents with DBT. They conclude that DBT has a large effect size for NSSI. In a multi-site RCT of DBT versus individual and group supportive therapy for reducing repeated suicide attempts and NSSI for adolescents at high risk for suicide, McCauley et al. (2018) found a significant advantage for DBT with regard to NSSI and other forms of self-harm after treatment (see also Wilkinson, 2018).

Some clinicians have *shortened* the programme to six months or even shorter (Brief DBT (DBT-B)). The most focused DBT treatment protocol is for outpatient adolescents diagnosed with BPD; it has a duration of 16 weeks. The treatment included skills training, one hour of individual therapy per week, telephone coaching, two hours of multi-family group skills training and family therapy as needed. NSSI and suicidal behaviour had decreased for all 27 participants by the end of the treatment period, and the frequency had dropped further at the one-year follow-up (Tørmoen et al., 2014). There seems to be a potential for using DBT principles in brief treatments. In addition, group skills training alone has also been shown to have a positive effect on self-harm (Sambrook et al., 2007).

Finally, in *routine* outpatient care (real-life setting), Stiglmayr et al. (2014) found a significant reduction in NSSI and improvement of BPD symptoms after treatment with DBT.

DBT is increasingly used to treat patients with BPD and NSSI, and elements of DBT are included in other therapeutic models for the treatment of NSSI (for example ERGT). In my own clinical experience, many patients with NSSI appreciate learning about and training in the specific DBT skills, and in particular, severely emotion dysregulated patients can profit from specific skills that they can use across a variety of situations.

12 Mentalization-Based Therapy – keeping mind in mind

The development of Mentalization-Based Therapy (MBT) was driven by the clinical and theoretical contributions by Peter Fonagy and Anthony Bateman based on psychoanalysis, neuropsychology, attachment theory and the study of early mother–infant interactions (Fonagy et al., 2002) (cf. Chapter 6, where the concept of mentalizing is presented and discussed). One of the strengths of MBT is the integration of the various theoretical and clinical approaches that give the theory a firm scientific foundation.

Together, Bateman and Fonagy have written numerous articles and books on MBT, including a manual for individual therapy (Bateman & Fonagy, 2004; 2006). Bateman has also co-authored several contributions with the Norwegian Sigmund Karterud, including manuals for individual MBT, MBT group therapy (MBT-G) and mentalization-based psychoeducational group therapy (MBT-I) (Karterud, 2015). New literature is continuously being published on the method (e.g., Karterud, 2018). With characteristic modesty, Bateman and Fonagy (2006, Preface, p. x) emphasize that

> our therapeutic approach lacks novelty and innovation and, to some extent, repackages commonly used therapeutic techniques in an attempt to harness an elemental human capacity, namely mentalizing, that is at the core of our definition of what it means to be human.

MBT is an evidence-based psychodynamic form of psychotherapy that is practiced in both individual and group formats. The primary focus is on the interpersonal processes ('events') that unfold between the patient and others, both in and outside the therapy. Generally, the focus is on the emotional experiences related to an 'event' (such as an argument or a misunderstanding) in order to uncover failures of mentalizing. The effort aims to help patients understand that individuals have different minds, which (often) contain different mental models of the world and which guide our actions. Developing a better appreciation and understanding of our own and others' perceptions of a given situation helps us mentalize. Thus, an improved mentalizing capacity involves an improvement in the patient's self-understanding, sense of coherence and identity and capacity for managing interpersonal interactions. As described in Chapter 6, mentalizing means understanding others from inside and oneself from outside, and it is this process that MBT revolves around.

Unlike DBT, MBT does not focus on NSSI itself but on the underlying mental processes. The rationale is that an improved mentalizing capacity will reduce the person's vulnerability and thus his or her need for NSSI or other forms of self-destructive acting out. An enhanced, more resilient mentalizing capacity also improves interpersonal relations and reduces the need for control and compulsion in relationships. An improved ability to relate with others in turn reduces the occurrence of conflicts and helps the patient develop more lasting and mutually binding relationships. Without such a mentalized understanding of self and others, the person is at the mercy of external influences and unmediated impulses and urges.

MBT is not an insight therapy in the traditional sense; instead, it takes up here-and-now situations in order to train and develop the patients' inherent mentalizing capacity with the purpose of improving their ability to understand their own and others' behaviour, regulate their own emotions and thus prevent a failure to mentalize.

MBT is most effective when it takes place in a secure attachment relationship between patient and therapist. The basic therapeutic stance in MBT is to be supportive and empathic. The therapist adopts a curious, non-judging, not-knowing stance, using dialogue and mirroring to help the patient sense and understand his or her own thoughts and emotions. The interventions are simple and based on attaining and maintaining attention control, affect regulation and mentalizing.

Treatment structure

MBT has three main phases, each containing specific goals and therapeutic processes (Bateman & Fonagy, 2006):

1   The main goal of the *initial phase* is to conduct a clinical assessment of the patient's mentalizing capacity and personality function. The specific processes include history of NSSI, diagnosis, psychoeducation, establishing a hierarchy of therapeutic goals, stabilizing social and behavioural problems and working out a case conceptualization. Moreover, the patient's medication is reviewed, and a crisis plan is drawn up that the patient can rely on when he or she is overwhelmed by impulses to engage in NSSI or attempt suicide.
2   The *middle phase* aims to stimulate the mentalizing capacity and thus help the patient develop a better understanding of self and others. Several specific processes and techniques are used to pursue this goal, including chain analysis. Timing and the assessment of the patient's mentalizing capacity are crucial for the choice of interventions and, ultimately, the treatment outcome.
3   The *final phase* aims to prepare the patient for the end of treatment and for the emotions it gives rise to. It also involves maintaining the therapeutic progress and planning a follow-up programme.

MBT was originally developed as part of a day-hospital programme with low-functioning patients (GAF[1] = 35) with frequent hospitalization, behaviours that put themselves and others at risk, trouble adapting to everyday life, substance abuse and unstable living accommodations. The core of the programme is the interaction between group and individual therapy with a shared focus on mentalizing (Bateman & Fonagy, 2006).

MBT is also offered as an intensive outpatient programme with sessions consisting of one hour of individual therapy and one-and-a-half hour of group therapy. This format, too, emphasizes the crucial interaction between group and individual therapy. When performed correctly, the individual and group therapy components are assumed to have a synergy effect. Participation in group therapy can be challenging for the patients, but it is essential, because a group with seven to eight participants is an excellent setting for working with multiple perspectives on an issue, which promotes the development of the patients' mentalizing capacity. Due to risk of 'social spread (contagion)', and because they are a manifestation of poor mentalizing, NSSI, suicidal ideation, substance abuse and so forth are only addressed during the individual therapy sessions.

Case formulation

One of the first tasks during the initial phase of therapy is to prepare a case formulation and a crisis plan. This is done by the individual therapist in cooperation with the patient and the treatment team. An MBT case conceptualization does not differ significantly from other dynamic case conceptualizations, except for its focus on the mentalizing perspective. The structure may look as follows:

1   The patient's developmental history with relations to attachment persons, traumas, vulnerable personality aspects, coping strategies and the costs of these strategies. If self-injury is present, problems that stem from failure to mentalize and from acting rather than mentalizing are discussed. Some therapists perform a systematic assessment of the patient's attachment style, for example using the Adult Attachment Interview (AAI).
2   Nature and severity of mental problems, their manifestation in interpersonal relationships and the occurrence of failures of mentalizing.
3   Focus on how the above-mentioned problems may play out in therapy in relation to therapists and fellow patients.

Treatment principles

The first goal of MBT is to build a secure and trusting relationship between patient and therapist as a necessary condition for working with the patient's mentalizing capacity. That is facilitated by a regular structure, a consistent, coherent and

---

1 Global Assessment of Functioning is a psychiatric scale used to assess a patient's level of functioning.

genuine approach, a focus on relations and mentalizing and a process- and goal-oriented treatment approach.

The core aim of MBT is to promote the patient's mentalizing capacity by stimulating his or her ability to regain it when it has been compromised and to preserve it when it is active. As mentioned above, the process often revolves around an 'event' (for example a misunderstanding). Rather than striving for insight by interpreting the involved parties' behaviour, the therapists seeks to maintain a mentalizing stance throughout in order to model mentalizing behaviour to the patients. The therapists' mentalizing stance aims to convey

1   Humility deriving from a sense of 'not-knowing'
2   Patience in taking time to identify differences between the patient's and the therapists' perspectives
3   Legitimizing and accepting different perspectives
4   Actively questioning the patient about his/her experience, asking for detailed descriptions of experience ('what questions') rather than explanations ('why questions')
5   Careful eschewing of the need to understand what makes no sense (saying explicitly that something is unclear)

(Bateman & Fonagy, 2010)

As an integral part of the MBT concept, the therapist must remain non-judging, accommodating and open as well as honest about his or her own mistakes and misunderstandings. In group therapy, it is important to facilitate reflections based on the different patients' perception of a given situation in order to promote mentalizing. The purpose of MBT is to develop the patient's ability simultaneously to be in and reflect on an emotional state without being overwhelmed by action urges or dissociation. In the therapy, the focus is on the emotion, thoughts and intention rather than on behaviour.

General intervention

MBT interventions generally aim to build awareness of and support the ability to verbalize mental states. Interventions should be simple, brief and manageable and, as mentioned earlier, should revolve primarily around an interpersonal event, aiming to clear up the misunderstanding or mentalize both parties' perspectives. The focus is on the patient's mental state, not on behaviour, and the emphasis is more on conscious or near-conscious material than on unconscious issues.

In a group session, Nadia says that she had an argument with her boyfriend, which caused her to cut herself with a razor in order to calm down. They had argued because she felt he was being insensitive to the fact the she was feeling unwell and hence had not prepared dinner. In the ensuing discussion, the initial focus is on the event as it unfolded. She describes her perception of the sequence of events, which is that he came home late and began to 'complain' about the fact that she had not shopped and cooked dinner. The other group members express their outrage and say that it is no wonder that she is angry and upset. Nadia begins to cry and clearly needs the group's validation of her emotions. The group asks follow-up questions in a manner that conveys a supportive, accepting stance. The therapists and the group try to identify what emotions were activated. She says that she had been quite angry, but maybe more sad, because she felt that her boyfriend was being completely self-absorbed and selfish and treating her 'like shit', as she put it. These emotions too were generally validated by the group members. At one point, a young woman in the group asks why he had come home so late, and why he had not shopped on the way home. It turned out he had been working on a graduation project that was due two days after the day of their argument. In other words, he had been extremely busy, which makes it easier for the group to understand his behaviour. When it emerges that she had not told him she was not feeling well and hence had not shopped, his behaviour seems to make even more sense to the group. Another young woman asks what Nadia's relationship with her boyfriend is generally like. She begins to cry again and says that she worries that he is 'losing interest in her'. Several group members spontaneously react with sympathy, 'forgetting' to mentalize. The anxiety of being abandoned is a common theme for most members of the group. One of the therapists asks what it is that makes her fear that her boyfriend is 'losing interest in her'. Nadia says he has spent a lot of time away during the past month. She feels that they have lost the close connection they used to have, and in her frustration and anger she has responded by giving him 'the cold shoulder' and rejecting him sexually. Several group members express support for her strategy of 'getting even' by means of rejection. One young woman says that 'men don't react until they're denied sex', in a classic example of a failure to mentalize and resorting to generalization.

One of the therapists tries to get the group to imagine the boyfriend's perspective. What might be the reason for his actions and reactions? Only when one of the other young women in the group mentions that his graduation project might have been keeping him extra busy this past month, making him preoccupied and working late, does Nadia begin to be able to see that the loss of personal and sexual intimacy between them might have other explanations than his 'losing interest in her'. The group rounds off with a constructive reflection on how we can be so preoccupied with our biggest fear – in this case abandonment – that we are unable to come up with alternative explanations.

> Catastrophizing – driven by abandonment anxiety – and Nadia's impotent rage probably contributed to her failure to mentalize and caused her to react by cutting herself.

The case illustrates how the intervention focuses on identifying emotions, validating, exploring the facts of the event and maintaining attention on mental processes. The group does not discuss what specifically happened when Nadia cut herself but tries to understand her motives for doing so, because the focus in MBT is on mental processes.

Characteristically, both Nadia and the rest of the group have difficulty mentalizing when they are 'caught up in' the anxiety of being abandoned. When tension runs too high, a certain degree of tunnel vision sets in, and mentalizing becomes much harder.

Intervention hierarchy

MBT interventions must be adapted to the patient's general and current mentalizing capacity, and the therapist must remain aware of the patient's emotional state. As in DBT, the therapist has to be able to balance between an empathic, validating stance and a not-knowing, explorative and curious one. The patient has to be fairly calm to be able to mentalize, and it is important to strike while the iron is *warm*. If the emotional tension is low (the iron is cold), the patient has no engagement in the current situation, which is often the case in pretend mode. If, on the other hand, the affect level is too high (the iron is hot), as is often the case in psychic equivalence mode, the subcortical brains structures take over and inhibit activity in the prefrontal cortex, resulting in a failure to mentalize (Lieberman, 2007) (cf. p. 117). The therapist thus has to try to *optimize* the level of emotional tension, so that the patient is capable of mentalized affectivity (feeling and thinking at the same time).

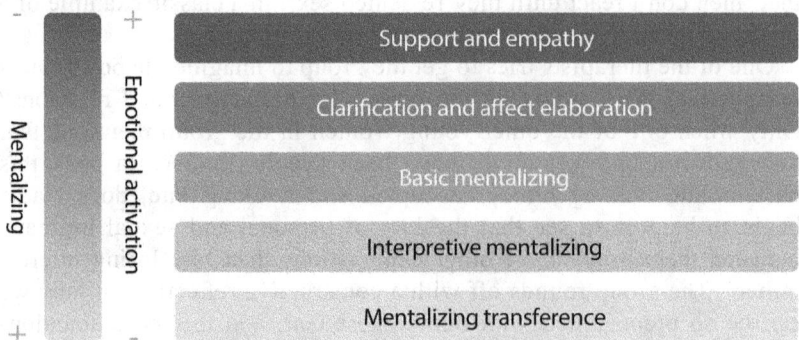

Figure 12.1 Intervention hierarchy. Begin at the top, and do not descend until the current step has been completed.

When emotional tension runs high, the capacity for mentalizing is low. When the mentalizing capacity is low, the therapist needs to use a *supportive* and *empathic* approach to minimize stress and prevent a further increase in emotional tension. Through supportive and empathic validating statements, the therapist conveys understanding for the patient's reactions. When the patient feels validated, the emotional pressure eases, and they can now attempt to move to the next level, *clarification and affect elaboration*. Here, the therapist and patient focus on the interpersonal event and the mental processes that caused the emotional tension to rise. The purpose is to gain more knowledge in order to achieve a better understanding of the event in question. At the next level, *basic mentalizing*, the goal is to help the patient better understand his or her own thoughts and emotions and to see that the other person may have a different perspective and thus a valid motive for acting the way he or she did. This can help the patient better understand the other's behaviour. Basic mentalizing helps us contain and understand that others may perceive a situation differently and have different needs.

Throughout, the therapy will address recurring events, which gives the patient an opportunity to practice mentalizing. At the subsequent level of *interpretive mentalizing*, the effort is to understand individual events in a wider context, as the patient gains insight into recurring problem situations. However, it is important to prioritize process over content in order to develop the patient's mentalizing capacity. As the relationship with the therapist becomes more secure and, ideally, develops into an actual attachment, the relationship between patient and therapist will take on a growing role in the therapy. In *mentalizing transference*, the effort revolves around the patient's unique relational patterns and the interaction between two minds.

Importantly, however, transference is not used to explain the present but to help the patient understand it better.

The therapist initially offers supportive, validating and empathic interventions at the top of the hierarchy and then gradually goes more in depth with a timing that depends entirely on the patient's current mentalizing capacity and ability to contain the emotional intensity. Whenever there is an indication that the emotional tension is becoming too high or that there is a risk of a mentalizing failure, the therapist moves back up the hierarchy and does not begin to descend again until the emotional tension has decreased, and the mentalizing capacity has been restored.

Elements of MBT

Karterud and colleges (2013) have specified 17 interventions that typically characterize MBT. The list is used to rate the therapist's adherence to the MBT model and is a practical tool in connection with supervision, not least to focus awareness on the key aspects of therapy. Several of the elements listed below are not unique to MBT but are also found in other forms of therapy. That pertains, for example, to the first point, *Engagement, interest and warmth*, which probably form the most essential non-specific factor in psychotherapy.

Core elements of MBT

1   Engagement, interest and warmth
2   Exploration, curiosity and not-knowing stance
3   Challenging unwarranted beliefs
4   Adjustment to level of mentalizing
5   Regulation of arousal level
6   Stimulating mentalizing through the process
7   Acknowledging positive mentalizing
8   Handling pretend mode
9   Handling psychic equivalence
10   Focus on affects
11   Focus on emotions and interpersonal events
12   Stop and rewind
13   Validating emotional reactions
14   Focus on transference and the relationship with the therapist
15   Use of countertransference
16   Checking one's understanding and correcting misunderstandings
17   Integration of experiences from concurrent group therapy

(adapted from Karterud et al., 2013)

Apart from 'stop and rewind', the content of these 17 elements will not be reviewed further in the present context. For a more in-depth description, see Karterud et al. (2013).

'Stop and rewind'

'Stop and rewind' is a technique that the therapist can use to re-establish the mentalizing process after it has failed in a therapy session. When a failure to mentalize occurs, both patient and therapist need to stop and rewind in order to understand the process that unfolded. The point is to go back to a point *prior to* the failure to mentalize in order to investigate what happened.

> During a tense group session, Anne is clearly struggling. She does not say anything but begins to cry silently, while two other group members (Beth and Celia) are having a confrontation. One of the therapists pauses to ask what is going on with Anne. Anne does not want to talk about it right now (which would indeed have been difficult while the two other group members are having their heated confrontation), but the therapist insists on examining the process by directing the question to the group at large. Several of the other group members say that they too are negatively affected by the high level of tension, and Anne says quietly that she cannot stand discord. She finds it unsettling and scary. Now the therapists rewind the group process to understand what happened between Beth and Celia, and Anne points out that

the moment she became 'really scared' was when Celia threatened to leave the group unless Beth apologized for calling her domineering and 'deaf to other people's problems'. The remainder of the group session is spent achieving a deeper understanding of the group events that led to Beth's and Celia's failure to mentalize ('understanding the misunderstanding').

The therapists' responsibility is to put the ongoing process on pause and direct the focus to the cause of the failure to mentalize ('stop and rewind'). This involves a detailed examination of who has what emotions towards whom, and how each group member perceives the events from his or her unique perspective (Bateman & Fonagy, 2006). In the case above it was important to clarify what emotions were in play and, not least, to validate and maintain a non-judging stance in order to regulate the emotional tension. It is important to follow the intervention hierarchy and to avoid mentalizing before the mental tension in the group is at a level that allows it.

When one or more of the patients function(s) in a psychic equivalence mode, there is an increased risk of a failure to mentalize and of mutual confrontations that may be difficult to contain and deal with in the group. In that situation, it is important for the therapist to use active validation (perhaps by 'siding with the patient') before exploring the sequence of events: 'That sounds really rough. I'm wondering how it might feel to be Celia right now. If I had been told I was "domineering and deaf to other people's problems", I imagine I would be pretty upset. What are your thoughts on that?' The purpose of this is to validate the individual group members' emotions and to stimulate reflection and curiosity about the experience.

'Stop and rewind' is mainly used when a mentalizing failure occurs, but also when the presentation is hectic, incoherent and influenced by a high level of emotional tension. The therapist adopts a not-knowing stance and is therefore free to interrupt the process by saying, for example, 'I'm having trouble keeping up here, could we just rewind a bit and go over it one more time?' In pretend mode, the problem often stems from a lack of mental tension; in that case, it is up to the therapist to challenge the patient and try to promote affective mentalizing by bringing emotional content into the presentation, for example: 'I don't understand what you mean when you say you don't care what Anne is thinking when Beth and Celia are having a confrontation. Could you tell me a little more about that?'

In some regards, MBT's 'stop and rewind' is similar to a DBT chain analysis, but it is often applied on events in the therapeutic setting, as described above, and is *not* primarily focused on behaviour but on the mental processes behind the behaviour. While the focus in DBT is on examining which skills the patient lacks, the focus in MBT is on mentalizing and understanding the emotions and the motivation behind a given behaviour, both in the patient and in others who are involved in the event.

Effect of MBT on NSSI

Like DBT, MBT was originally developed for the treatment of BPD. During the past decade, numerous MBT effect studies have been conducted, but not all include NSSI or self-harm as an outcome measure, and the studies are not directly comparable, as they involve different MBT protocols. MBT is mentioned in several reviews of effective treatments for NSSI and self-harm with large effect size (Ougrin et al., 2015). In a meta-analysis, Calati and Courtet (2016) found no evidence for the effectiveness of psychotherapeutic interventions other than MBT in the treatment of NSSI, and in a systematic review of MBT and its evidence-base status, Malda-Castillo et al. (2018) found promising results for the treatment of adolescents who self-injure. Another systematic review of the effectiveness of MBT in the treatment of BPD documented that in all studies that reported measures of self-injury, MBT was found to cause a significant reduction superior or equal to other treatments (Vogt & Norman, 2018). The Cochrane review of psychosocial interventions for self-injury in adults found that MBT was associated with significantly reduced repetition when compared to TAU (Hawton et al., 2016).

Like DBT, MBT has been developed as an intervention for adolescents, including monthly family therapy sessions (MBT-A) (Rossouw & Fonagy, 2012). In an RCT (N = 80), MBT-A was more effective than TAU in reducing self-harm and depression. This outcome was explained by improved mentalizing and reduced attachment avoidance (ibid.)

A Swedish naturalistic study of MBT for BPD patients found a significant reduction of NSSI after 12 months' treatment with a combination of individual and group treatment (Löf et al., 2018). Finally, long-term follow-up studies suggest that the effect of MBT is lasting. (For an overview, see Malda-Castillo et al., 2018; Vogt & Norman, 2018).

MBT has been implemented as a treatment of patients with BPD in different countries and is recommended in the Australian Clinical Practice Guidelines for the treatment of BPD but is still not recommended as a first-line treatment in the British NICE guidelines.

MBT is an effective treatment for NSSI but takes longer than other treatments, for example DBT, perhaps because the focus is less on the actual self-injurious behaviour. One important difference between MBT and DBT is that DBT teaches the patient specific skills to be used as an alternative to NSSI here and now. It takes longer to improve one's mentalizing capacity, understood as the capacity for imaginative mental activity about others or oneself and for perceiving and interpreting human behaviour in terms of intentional mental states (such as needs, desires, feelings, beliefs, goals, purposes and reasons). Thus, MBT is aimed more at fundamentally stabilizing the patient's affect and personality management, which is a harder task for patients with a pressing urge to self-injure. In connection with failure to mentalize, such as self-injury, the patient often lacks here-and-now strategies; however, in the long term a stronger and more stable mentalizing capacity will reduce the risk of mentalizing failure and, in turn, of self-injury.

13 Treating self-injury during hospitalization

Patients with NSSI may need hospital treatment during a crisis period due to the severity of their self-injury or their psychiatric condition in general – or both. If the patient is suicidal, inpatient treatment may be necessary. Obviously, it is preferable if the admission is voluntary. Compulsory admission may be indicated if the patient is deemed to pose a risk to him/herself or others. Unless the patient is psychotic or has other severe psychopathology in addition to NSSI, the stay should be as brief as possible, and from the outset, the goal should be to transition to outpatient treatment.

Hospitalizing patients with NSSI has several drawbacks, including that it disrupts the outpatient therapy, that it confronts the patient with stress factors that risk exacerbating the need for self-injury and, not least, that the patient may perceive it as an opportunity to rely on a passive strategy rather than practicing the active coping strategies he or she is learning in outpatient therapy (Swenson et al., 2007). The long-term treatment goal is to enable the self-injuring patient to manage his or her own life, and hospitalization represents a move in the opposite direction.

A condition for establishing a constructive therapeutic environment is to make room for acceptance/validation as well as change/confrontation strategies. Hence, both validation and specific methods such as chain analysis will be a regular part of the treatment during the hospital stay. Ideally, the staff should be familiar with the basic principles of MBT and DBT and thus be able to offer the patient maximum attention and support to avoid self-injury.

Prevalence of NSSI among psychiatric patients is high. In a classic study, Deiter and Pearlman (1998) found that 68% of inpatient and 42% of outpatient psychiatric patients had harmed themselves. An Austrian study of adolescents receiving inpatient psychiatric treatment found that more than half (50.8%) had self-injured at least once in the past, and 38.5% of the sample met DSM-5 criteria for NSSI (Sevecke et al., 2017). Many patients perform NSSI while they are in hospital. Mäkikyrö et al. (2004) found that just under 68% of the patients in a Finnish youth psychiatric ward occasionally self-injured while hospitalized. Some studies have found that hospitalization increases the risk of NSSI. A third of patients who had never engaged in self-injury began to do so while or shortly after being hospitalized (Boxer, 2010).

Studies show that hospital staff often have negative attitudes towards patients who self-injure (Karman et al., 2015) and that they lack knowledge about the practice. Frustration, stress, anxiety, concern, anger and helplessness are some of the emotions reported by staff caring for NSSI patients. The patients are also often perceived as manipulative, aggressive and resistant, and thus, it is little wonder that many patients feel poorly treated (for an overview, see Taylor et al., 2009).

Due to these reactions and emotional pressures, the staff may meet the patients with irrational and negative reactions. Some staff members try to handle these emotions by ignoring and distancing themselves from the self-injuring patient, while others have the opposite reaction and instead provide maximal care and close attention. Neither response is ideal, as detachment may trigger the patient's separation anxiety and sense of betrayal, while excessive care and close attention may act as a positive reinforcement of dysfunctional behaviour and signal an engagement that may be difficult to maintain if the patient fails to make progress (cf. p. 156).

Hospitalized patients are often in crisis and may deteriorate further if they encounter myriad restrictions, rules and other emotional triggers from staff members who may already have a negative attitude towards them. Due to these reactions from the staff, some patients with NSSI can be demanding, and a state of turmoil and chaos often arises around them. BPD patients in particular may find it difficult to be in an inpatient ward that is not especially equipped to deal with emotional dysregulation, self-injury and other forms of acting out.

Emotional dysregulation during hospitalization

Emotion dysregulation means that the patient is hypersensitive, has intense reactions and has difficulty regulating emotions. Emotionally dysregulated patients can be extremely touchy and react with intense anger if they feel threatened or subjected to transgression, verging on a paranoid response where the hypersensitive patient gets tense, standoffish and vigilant.

The patients' interpersonal relations may be chaotic and unstable. Relationships may vary between idealization, with a desire for intense closeness, and devaluation, with aggression and contempt as the dominating feelings. Needless to say, this is difficult for the staff to contain.

A study of nurses' feelings about working with NSSI patients found that two challenges in particular were felt to be stressful and difficult: being overwhelmed by emotions and needing to preserve professional boundaries (Wilstrand et al., 2007). Preserving professional boundaries can be especially hard for the staff when they are subjected to intense irrational reactions that are acted out as self-injury, splitting and projective identification. Emotionally dysregulated patients may also struggle to maintain a stable sense of identity. They may feel empty and lack a firm sense of who they are. This sense of emptiness can be mentally painful, and to achieve relief, the patient may self-injure or provoke a reaction from the staff. The patient thus uses reactions from the staff and the other patients to sense his or her own boundaries and regulate inner tension.

Finally, emotion dysregulation may manifest as a lack of impulse control, caus-ing the patient to act rashly and unpredictably.

The hospital staff is easily affected by the patient's inner chaos, as issues from the patient's relational history are played out and enacted in the multidiscipli-nary team (MDT). In connection with long-term hospital stays, particularly under stress, patients with BPD will often act out their inner anger, for example in the form of splitting.

Anne is a nurse and the contact person for Susan, a patient who is in a closed ward following a suicide attempt. Susan has BPD and sometimes injures herself severely, using anything she can get hold of to cut herself (for example the shards of a broken glass). Anne feels that she has a close and trusting relationship with Susan; for example, Susan always likes to talk with Anne when she begins her shift. Sometimes she says to Anne that she understands her so well, and that she finds it much more helpful to talk to Anne than to the psychologist, who 'doesn't get me the way you do'. Anne begins to look forward to talking with Susan, because it makes her feel competent in a way she is not used to.

In a supervision session Anne says that she almost feels that the patient has 'got under my skin'. Anne thinks of the patient when she is off work, and during her holiday she rang the ward to hear how she was doing. Anne is perturbed by the advice from an older colleague who 'warned' her against becoming overinvolved in the patient. Anne is increasingly annoyed with the older colleague's views about the patient's treatment. One day Susan mentions that she finds the older colleague unprofessional, cold and without empathy – 'the complete opposite of you, Anne'.

At multidisciplinary team meetings, discussions between Anne and the older colleague are becoming increasingly common, and especially when these discussions concern Susan's care, Anne feels a strong commitment and feels herself getting annoyed with the older colleague, finding her unprofessional, cold and completely lacking in empathy – echoing Susan's description precisely. At one point, this gap between their perceptions of the patient culminates, as the older colleague says that the patient is 'manipu-lative and splitting', arguing that the patient would be better off in outpa-tient treatment with the ward's psychologist. Anne, however, finds that the patient is improving and thus profiting from the treatment; for example, she never cuts herself on Anne's shift!

The vignette illustrates how a patient externalizes her black-and-white perception of the world (splitting) and enacts it in the MDT, where it is acted out instead of being contained. In supervision sessions, it became clear that the patient had 'used' Anne by leaning on her and forming an alliance. Naturally, the patient had done the best she could to find security and support; she had found this in Anne, but at the cost of an opportunity to process her stark black-and-white perception of others. Anne also described feeling increasingly constrained by the patient's expectations of her but had difficulty expressing this experience, because she felt that she was 'betraying' the patient.

Thus, NSSI patients with emotion dysregulation NSSI and the staff who treat them are often entangled in complicated and destructive patterns that may be difficult to break, and which may disrupt a targeted, constructive treatment process. The unavoidable differences that exist in any MDT, for example in terms of age, sex, experience and professional perspectives, may produce cracks in the unity and differences of opinion in the MDT, but these differences can also be used therapeutically, provided the team manages to grasp its own role in the group dynamics.

That a patient prefers one team member over another is not necessarily a sign of splitting. We all feel more aligned with or drawn to some people than others, also as members of an MDT, but it is destructive if the team is unable to deal with this process in a reflective manner, instead acting it out in the group. Professional disagreement is not only inevitable but a necessary condition for development, but ideally it should be addressed through mentalizing or reflection as part of a 'culture of inquiry', to borrow the British psychoanalyst Tom Main's term (Main, 1957).

In addition to increasing the risk of conflict and burnout in the MDT, self-injuring and dysregulated patients can also trigger countertransference reactions from team members, which jeopardizes their therapeutic perspective. No one thinks clearly under intense emotional pressure.

At a morning MDT meeting in a psychiatric inpatient ward, the following scene played out:

The night nurse does not normally take part in the morning MDT meeting, because she is off work by then, but today she has made an exception. She describes how Marie, who has BPD, cut herself severely the previous night. Marie smeared blood all over the walls in the bathroom and was clearly in anguish. The night nurse underscores that 'we have to do something for Marie; her condition is deteriorating'. Several of the team members feel that Marie is regressing and using NSSI to maintain her identity and as a means of self-control but also to communicate her suffering. Finally, some team members feel that Marie is using NSSI aggressively in order to take revenge on or punish certain members of the team.

'We have to transfer Marie to a closed ward, where they are better equipped to care for her', says a nurse.

'No way! No one knows Marie better than we do. If we transfer her, there is a risk that she will deteriorate further and become even more self-destructive. We have to place her under permanent watch to stop the cutting', says another team member, who sometimes acts as Marie's contact person.

'Wait a minute! Marie has to be discharged ASAP. Before lunch, ideally. Then we can follow her on an outpatient basis!' says a third team member.

They all agree that Marie is steadily deteriorating with the current treatment, and there are many suggestions about how to stop the self-destructive spiral. Eventually, one of the doctors, who has been looking through Marie's file, brings up that she has tried a wide variety of drugs (SSRIs, mood-stabilizers and antipsychotic medication) and proposes ECT (electroconvulsive therapy). 'Sometimes there appears to be an agitated depression, and since we can't make progress any other way, I suggest we try ECT', she says.

The case illustrates how difficult it can be to treat these patients, and when the treatment is ineffective, as evident in continued NSSI behaviour, the negative countertransference reactions are intensified, and the field around the patient is characterized by defeatism, irritation, anger and anxiety, which may lead to a sort of therapeutic nihilism, where reason and the holistic approach is lost. In very short order, the participants in the MDT meeting made several very different and mutually contradictory suggestions for Marie's treatment, which reflects the sense of frustration that treatment professionals can sometimes feel. They begin to act to escape the feeling of paralysis, suggesting discharge, transfer or permanent observation. Action can also lead to over-medication or neglect, sometimes in a way that appears almost sadistic. ECT is certainly not the treatment of choice for a dysregulated patient with BPD.

The following case shows another example of irrational behaviour that might resemble punishment. It is taken from the magazine *Outsider*, where a former patient describes her experiences with being placed in restraints due to self-injury. Prior to the sequence described below, the patient had self-injured and had therefore been temporarily placed in restraints, strapped to a bed, and put under permanent observation. The person watching her does not speak to her. Moreover, her door is open, so all the other patients can look straight into her room, which she finds very humiliating.

'They observed me for a couple of hours and then checked in on me. I began to cut myself again. My contact person noticed and commented that I was too old for that, and besides, it produced nasty scars. I reacted by barricading my door with a chair so they could not get into my room. Later, the doctor came in and said that if I did not open the door immediately, I would be dismissed. I was unable to react; I just sat on the floor, cutting myself. I just wanted to see blood. Soon after, the doctor says, "You are hereby discharged." '

One clearly senses the frustration of the patient, the contact person and the doctor that results in the patient being discharged.

Sedatives

When self-injuring patients are briefly hospitalized because they need emergency treatment or are in a crisis, they are often prescribed sedatives. This may be rational in an acute phase, but the downside is that the patient may be too sedated to benefit from psychotherapy.

Helen is a 23-year-old woman with BPD, severe NSSI and several suicide attempts. In recent years she has had frequent hospitalizations. These are necessary because she is unable to take care of herself, even with the support she receives at the social-psychiatric residential unit where she lives. The problem is that she takes growing doses of antipsychotic, sedative and mood-stabilizing medication. This has led to a significant weight gain and also makes her too sedated to take part in the skills training group and in outpatient psychotherapy sessions. The outpatient doctor therefore tried to reduce her dose but when she is admitted to hospital due to an emergency, the doctors there prescribe a higher dose or even an additional drug, which undermines her long-term goal. Although her file contains a note that the patient should attempt to use her DBT skills, she is almost invariably discharged with prescription of a higher dose.

Preventing over-medication requires a close and stable cooperation between the various teams and professionals involved in her interdisciplinary treatment. In Helen's case that includes her residential unit, her individual therapist, the therapists in charge of her skills training group, the psychiatrist handling her medication in the outpatient section, the consultant at the psychiatric emergency ward and the consultant at the section where Helen is typically admitted. In addition, Helen's treatment needs to be coordinated with her own general practitioner, the municipal social affairs administration and other agencies and units.

If the coordination between the inpatient ward and the outpatient units is lacking, they risk counteracting each other.

For example, the doctor in charge of the patient's medication during outpatient treatment will have to reduce the dosage to enable the patient to engage in psychotherapy for her self-injury, but if the patient is readmitted due to a crisis or temporary deterioration, the inpatient ward will often increase the dosage, either to sedate the patient or because it is concluded that the patient's deterioration is due to the outpatient team reducing the dosage.

It is thus not unusual that even highly competent and committed treatment professionals disagree about what is the best approach for a patient who continues to deteriorate, as evident from repeated NSSI. They are all specialists in their respective areas and may struggle to maintain a holistic perspective in the work with this specific patient group. Hence, we need a general discussion, ideally resulting in a consensus, about treatment guidelines for this group.

Self-injury by proxy – mechanical restraints

During hospitalization, patients invariably use the people around them and their reactions as a means of affect regulation and of maintaining their identity. Others' reactions to one's behaviour can be therapeutic, which is used in dynamic environmental therapy, but some patients, however, use the reactions of staff and other patients to achieve momentary regulation of their inner tension.

> A 21-year-old woman with BPD and NSSI, including cutting, burning and bloodletting, was prevented from engaging in this behaviour while she was in a closed psychiatric ward. As a result, her inner tension escalated dramatically, and in order to make the staff subject her to force, she had on several occasions attacked them directly or destroyed things in the ward. She had clear insight into her motives and, not least, the staff's reactions: 'It's like pushing a button. They come running, grab me and force me into the restraints. Naturally, I get furious and try to hit and bite them, but I know that I'm going to calm down when I feel the pain and am put into the restraints'. In order to diminish this self-injury by proxy and help her self-regulate her emotions and behaviour, the staff had agreed with her that she would ask to be put in restraints whenever she felt the urge to self-injure. That did not always work, however, because her need for the drama to fill up her inner void and the physical resistance to force was sometimes very powerful. It was not always enough merely to be put into restraints.

The case above outlines an example of self-injury by proxy, where the patient enacts a dramatic incident instead of using NSSI to regulate her inner tension. She arranges a self-injuring act (by proxy) that achieves the same calming effect as more traditional forms of self-injury. This activates the staff, who naturally need to protect both the patient and themselves, but their response inadvertently escalates the tension until it reaches a climax when the patient is placed in restraints. An unpublished study from the Mental Health Services of the Capital Region of Denmark found that BPD is one of the most frequent diagnoses in patients who are placed in restraints, and very often the staff explain that they 'feel provoked by the patient's behaviour: the patient is asking for it'. Placing the patient in restraints can be necessary but is certainly not therapeutic.

Some of the patients, however, had voluntarily subjected themselves to being restrained, which can have a calming effect because it renders them incapable of self-injuring. By externalizing the control and handing it to the staff, the patient avoids having to manage his or her impulse pressure and can thus escape their fear of losing control over his or her urge to self-injure. This may be interpreted as a different, less dramatic form of self-injury by proxy.

The patient who wrote about being restrained in *Outsider* magazine (see above, p. 231) also writes about the calming effect of being placed in restraints due to NSSI:

> 'After a few hours I calmed down slightly. The doctor came in and said the restraints were to be removed. I was not ready for that, because I still had thoughts of self-injury, and now I was sort of getting a break from it. It might sound strange, but it gave me some relief that I was unable to self-injure. The doctor felt otherwise and loosened the restraints'.

The spiral of self-injury – the 'tacit dialogue'

During a hospital stay, a malign dynamic often emerges, where the structure at the ward causes patients to regress and lose their normal skills, making it impossible to lean on a daily routine. To hold on to themselves and their sense of identity and to counteract the regressive process, the patients actively try, in various ways, to take charge, in some cases by means of NSSI. NSSI provides a sense of self-control and of setting personal boundaries.

When the hospital staff are confronted with a patient's self-injury, they will naturally seek to protect the patient by removing sharp objects, increase monitoring, shield the patient and prescribe round-the-clock observation or the use of mechanical restraints. These protective measures are often perceived by the patient as control and a restriction of autonomy. Hence, they may intensify the patient's feelings of anxiety and powerlessness and, in turn, increase the need for NSSI.

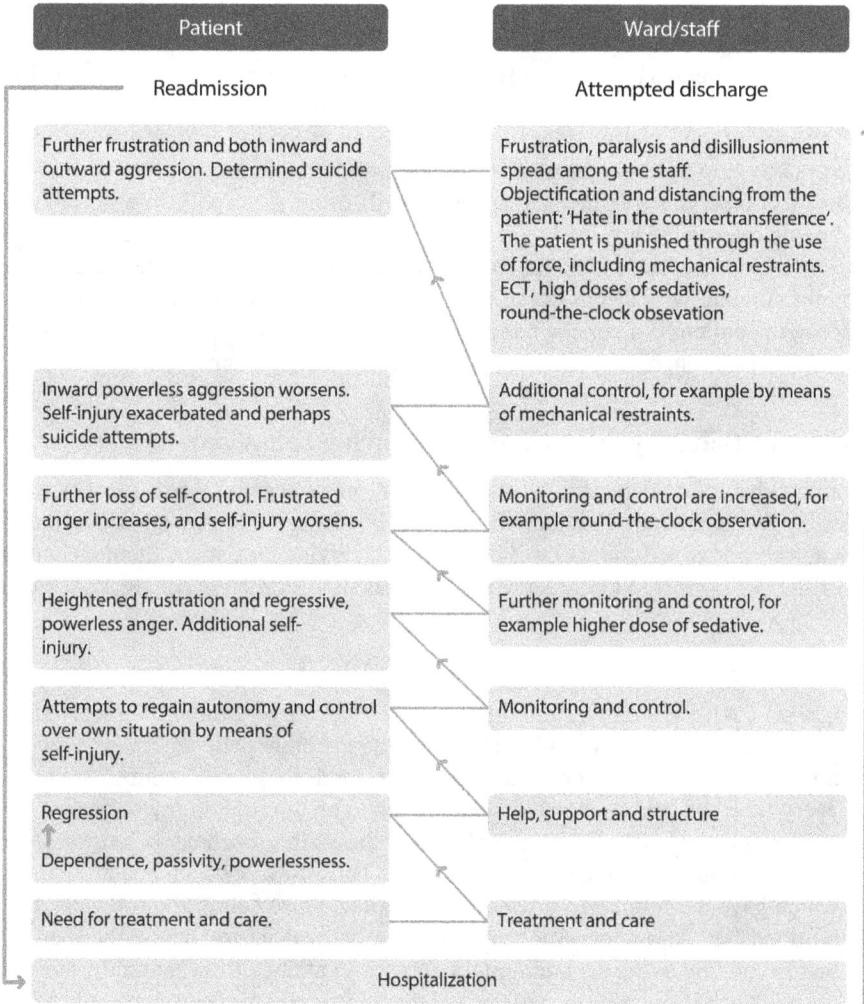

Patient	Ward/staff
Readmission	Attempted discharge
Further frustration and both inward and outward aggression. Determined suicide attempts.	Frustration, paralysis and disillusionment spread among the staff. Objectification and distancing from the patient: 'Hate in the countertransference'. The patient is punished through the use of force, including mechanical restraints. ECT, high doses of sedatives, round-the-clock obsevation
Inward powerless aggression worsens. Self-injury exacerbated and perhaps suicide attempts.	Additional control, for example by means of mechanical restraints.
Further loss of self-control. Frustrated anger increases, and self-injury worsens.	Monitoring and control are increased, for example round-the-clock observation.
Heightened frustration and regressive, powerless anger. Additional self-injury.	Further monitoring and control, for example higher dose of sedative.
Attempts to regain autonomy and control over own situation by means of self-injury.	Monitoring and control.
Regression ↑ Dependence, passivity, powerlessness.	Help, support and structure
Need for treatment and care.	Treatment and care
Hospitalization	

Figure 13.1 The spiral of NSSI.

Source: Møhl (2015).

The treatment risks activating and maintaining a negative process, where the patient regresses and becomes increasingly incapable of taking care of him/herself. Thus, when the patient acts by self-injuring, the staff acts by caring for the patient and intensifying monitoring and control. The staff might also act by objectifying and dehumanizing the patient, distancing themselves from what they struggle to deal with and understand. When the human perspective begins to slip, it becomes easier for the staff to act rather than containing and mentalizing. Action leads to action, and a 'tacit dialogue' may arise, where the escalating process is not verbalized, leading to an added risk that the self-injurious behaviour worsens, and the staff increasingly take control.

Moreover, there is a risk that the staff becomes increasingly frustrated because the patient fails to improve and instead deteriorates with growing frequency and/or severity of self-injury. When the ward becomes aware of this dynamic and attempts to stop it, for example by discharging the patient and transferring him or her to outpatient treatment, the patient will often react with intense anxiety and panic over 'suddenly' being discharged in a condition where he or she, incapacitated by regression, feels far from ready to cope. As a result, the patient may attempt suicide, which will cause the staff to reverse the discharge decision or readmit the patient if he or she has already been discharged. Thus, hospitalization may further entrench the patient's use of NSSI as a coping strategy.

Reactions that may exacerbate self-injuring behaviour

From a behavioural perspective, it is clear that many hospital wards inadvertently intensify dysfunctional behaviour, for example by giving the patient additional attention and care after self-injury. DBT has a focus on giving the patient attention before he or she performs NSSI in order to support non-self-destructive coping strategies.

Cecilia cut herself daily, sometimes very severely. Every time, she received extra interest and care from both the staff and the other patients. A particular doctor, who was very concerned about her condition, would come see her every time she had cut herself, spending up to an hour talking with her.

During supervision it became clear that the staff's reactions to her NSSI reinforced the behaviour: when she had cut herself the staff attended to her, which gave her a sense of power and control and also calmed her down and affirmed her. At a supervision meeting, it was decided to change the regimen, avoiding giving her additional staff contact after cutting. Naturally, they would check if she needed suturing or other physical care. Then she would be left to herself in her room and asked to perform a chain analysis (cf. 203 f). Finally, it was important that she received immediate and empathic contact when she displayed constructive behaviour in order to prevent NSSI.

The staff naturally involved her in the process, informing her about the changes and providing a rational explanation. Nevertheless, and even though the reinforcers were eliminated, there followed a period when the patient intensified both the frequency and the severity of her self-injury. That was to be expected, as the patient wanted to test whether she could still provoke the same behaviour from the staff. It is important for the staff to prepare for this, because their consistency and persistence are what is needed to reduce the patient's self-destructive behaviour.

An American study (Boxer, 2010) found that 33% of hospitalized patients who had not previously self-injured developed NSSI and had a 'critical incident' (for example the staff's use of force in connection with self-injury) on average 60 days after their admission. These Figures show that hospitalization increases the risk of NSSI, also in patients who have not previously self-injured. As mentioned above, one explanation might be that the patients regress during their stay in hospital, lose certain daily living skills and thus use NSSI as a coping strategy in order to regain a sense of having control over their emotions and the situation.

NSSI and peer influence

Due to processes of social influence, NSSI can spread in a peer group or through a hospital ward. School groups and residential schools are places where self-injury can spread like wildfire. 'If one of the cool kids in class begin to self-injure, there is a real risk that others will follow suit'. Social learning which leads to imitation or modelling, is another term that has been used to explain social 'contagion' of NSSI. However, 'contagion' can also happen through mass media, without any direct contact between the person exposing NSSI and the person 'catching the bug' and going on to practice NSSI (Jarvi et al., 2013). Hasking and Boyes (2018) point out that the language often used about NSSI stems from models of infectious disease (including the term 'contagion'), which is inaccurate and stigmatizing.

About 18% of young people who practice NSSI report that they do so with same-age peers or that they began to self-injure after learning that a friend had done it (Heath et al., 2009). Studies show that the risk of NSSI is greater for individuals who have friends who self-injure. This illustrates that NSSI spreads in groups via social learning.

Causes of the spread of NSSI

- The patient sees that others attain relief and wants to try NSSI to achieve the same positive effect.
- The patients compete for time, attention, care and support from the staff, and NSSI helps get this attention.
- Reduced inhibition. Seeing others self-injure lowers the threshold for trying.
- The desire to be part of a group community/subculture with others who self-injure.
- Competing and achieving a higher status in the patient group.

In addition to learning and imitation, a further factor in a psychiatric ward is that the patients are admitted because they are in distress. Many who perform NSSI feel lonely and isolated, and as patients in a psychiatric ward they are willing to do just about anything to get better. When the patient is confronted with others' use of NSSI as a coping strategy that helps them do better and even achieve a sense of community and attention from the staff, it may not seem a big leap to try the method.

Several treatment programmes for patients who use NSSI include group therapy (MBT, DBT). It is well-documented that this may increase the spread of NSSI, and although these are highly structured didactic groups with a focus on skills training, some programmes include rules prohibiting the patients from speaking directly about NSSI or showing in group with visible signs of self-injury (for example wounds from cutting).

Principles of a non-confrontational culture

To avoid a destructive 'power struggle' and the emergence of a 'tacit dialogue' as described above, it is important to support a culture that seeks to avoid confrontations between the patient and the treatment staff. This culture must be based on treatment principles from environmental therapy, including a *culture of enquiry* (Main, 1957) and collaboration between the patient and the MDT based on a not-knowing and not-judgemental stance, mentalizing, validation and a high priority on the patient's autonomy. While ensuring the patients' safety, a key treatment priority should be to engage them as active participants in their own treatment. The treatment should be based on a culture of mentalizing and reflection rather than a passivizing culture of 'tacit dialogue' and action, where the patient's actions lead to actions by the staff and vice versa.

Staff–patient relations in a psychiatric inpatient ward should thus be based on the following assumptions and approaches:

- The patient is doing the best he or she can to cope with his or her difficulties and life. Judgement or criticism is not helpful.
- The staff should deal with NSSI as a meaningful but maladaptive strategy in an attempt to improve life on the ward. NSSI must be perceived as failure to mentalize or due to lack of better skills.
- The staff should validate the emotions behind NSSI, and not the act itself.
- The patient needs to learn different ways of regulating his or her emotions and should receive support to mentalize and to develop skills and alternative strategies.
- The patient should receive support and attention *before* the act of self-injury with a view to developing strategies to prevent NSSI.
- As much as possible, the staff should accept the patient's autonomy, and if the use of force is necessary, they should offer the patient options, whenever possible, and explain the rationale behind the decision.
- As much as possible, the staff should avoid participating in self-injury by proxy.
- The staff should acknowledge the patient's difficulties with managing his or her emotions and talking about NSSI.
- The staff should show concern but avoid providing *secondary gain* and reinforcement of NSSI.
- The staff should minimize their exposure to contagion from the patient's behaviour and remain calm. When the patient's capacity to mentalize fails,

there is an increased risk that the same will happen to the staff working with
the patient.
- The staff should maintain hope for the patient.
- The staff must receive ongoing supervision.

Studies document the importance of having an approach to the patients' NSSI that
is consistent both over time and across staff members, as outlined in the principles
above. That does not mean that disagreement and discussions are ruled out; on the
contrary. What it means is that treatment planning and practices should be based
on a consistent set of principles to prevent the countertransference of individual
staff members from determining the course of the treatment. In dealing with a
behaviour that is as emotionally provoking as NSSI, it is important to have a
containing but consistent attitude and approach to the treatment. If the team fails
to establish a consistent attitude, the staff risks exhaustion and burnout, which
brings internal differences and conflicts to the surface and threatens to undermine
the team spirit. However, it can be difficult to implement consistent principles and
attitudes in the treatment of NSSI.

Several American programmes have developed procedures for taking a systematic approach to acute incidents such as NSSI and attempted suicide while a
patient is hospitalized, most of them inspired by DBT (Swenson et al., 2007). The
individual inpatient ward may use a modified version of DBT as a pragmatic way
of dealing with NSSI. To avoid reinforcing the patient's dysfunctional behaviour,
it is important to help the patient avoid self-injuring. For example, the patient's
contact person can help the patient use a scale to rate his or her inner tension; this
makes it possible to request assistance – such as a sensory stimulation blanket,
support to use specific affect-regulation skills or, ultimately, medication – before
the urge becomes overpowering and compromises mentalizing.

When an act of self-injury occurs at the ward, the first task for the staff is to
look for meaning (that is, to mentalize). After an act of NSSI, the patient's contact
person, in cooperation with the other MDT members who work with the patient,
will determine whether and how the following procedure is to be initiated. If they
initiate the procedure, the contact person informs the patient and hands out the
chain analysis worksheet.

When the patient has self-injured, addressing this becomes a top therapeutic
priority. If the patient is not capable of working with the issue at the moment (cognitive disorder, dissociation, sedation or other issues), it has to be done later, but
as soon as possible. The procedure consists of five steps. They are not necessarily
all required, but steps 1 and 5 are mandatory.

Step 1: Chain analysis

First, the patient performs a chain analysis on the recent act of self-injury.
Initially, this is done in cooperation with the contact person, but later, the
patient should be able to conduct the chain analysis using pre-printed worksheets. The purpose is to identify triggers and vulnerabilities (fatigue, stress

and so forth) and to focus on what the person could have done instead of self-injuring. The therapeutic goal is to help the patient to mentalize and become aware of what happened. (Many patients feel that the urge to self-injure comes out of the blue.) The next step is to examine what skills the patient might have used instead. It is important to support and validate the patient's efforts in a non-judging way.

Step 2: Mentalizing and involving the environment

If the patient has conducted the chain analysis alone, the patient now presents it to his or her contact person or individual therapist. Focus is not on the act of NSSI but on the coping strategies and skills that the patient can use to prevent repetition. If it is possible and appropriate, this may be done in the ward's group therapy or DBT group, where the patient receives feedback. Finally, the patient reviews the sequence of events with his or her contact person and incorporates he perspectives that the other patients contributed.

Step 3: Correction or repair

The patient receives support to conduct an appropriate 'repair', for example meeting with a person who was particularly affected by the patient's act, cleaning the bathroom if it is smeared in blood (cf. the case on p. 230) or anything else that might relieve the patient's guilt, shame or other negative feelings in relation to the act. It is important to reassure the patient that occasionally everyone is slips up – the key thing is to learn from it and move on.

Step 4: Preparing/revising the patient's crisis card

Experiences with handling the act of NSSI can make it relevant to revise the patient's crisis card (a card outlining strategies the patient can use when he or she is approaching a high tension level that involves a risk of self-injury), for example to take a hot shower, play a computer game, reach out to the contact person, lie under a sensory stimulation blanket, take medication prescribed 'per need', go for a run or use other affect-regulation skills.

Step 5: Evaluating the process

Helping patients modify their coping strategies from NSSI to something more constructive can be a lengthy process. Hence, it is important to get continuous feedback from the patient and evaluate the process: what was constructive? What was less constructive or even negative? What can we learn from it? What could we have done differently? This part of the process is important, because it rehearses mentalizing and invites a validation of the patient's reactions and thus strengthens the therapeutic alliance.

When self-injury has occurred, there may be a need for a regular procedure that the patient, the staff and, ultimately, the ward's culture can benefit from. It is important, however, to manage this procedure in a flexible and thoughtful manner and, not least to avoid putting the patient under so much pressure that he or she feels compelled to use NSSI again. Most patients who perform NSSI perceive it as shameful and are thus sensitive to the staff's reactions.

The practical organization of the treatment

Not all members of an MDT are equally motivated for working as contact persons for patients with NSSI. It may therefore be helpful to involve a group of professionals who are interested in acting as contact persons to patients with NSSI. To promote the necessary understanding of patients with NSSI, the ward should offer training to teach the staff about the dynamics of NSSI and about alternative affect-regulation skills, not only in the patients but also in the MDT. Further, the ward should offer continuous clinical supervision and practical training in conflict management and affect regulation of the staff members who agree to be contact persons for patients with NSSI.

In addition to continuous clinical supervision of contact persons in the ward, there may also be a need for ad hoc clinical supervision for the whole staff. It is a well-documented experience that the treatment of patients who use NSSI can be a challenge for everyone involved, and that it may activate conflicts in the MDT. Hence, they may need assistance and support in connection with the treatment of one or more severely disturbed patients.

When a patient with NSSI is discharged from an inpatient ward, it is important to have therapists who can take on psychotherapeutic contact with the patient, ideally with a view to facilitating the transition to targeted outpatient treatment. The transition from inpatient to outpatient status can be challenging for the patient. Often, there is a significant loss of information, and as mentioned above, it is important to maintain close cooperation between the inpatient ward and the outpatient unit that takes over responsibility for the treatment. That is both due to the risk of splitting and because the patient may need to be readmitted in case of a future crisis.

14   When a loved one self-injures

I dedicate this closing chapter to those close to the person who self-injures because parents, partners, children and close friends are a crucial part of the person's universe, and they are all affected by NSSI. Sometimes, they contribute unwittingly to the emotional pain of the person and thus cause or exacerbate NSSI, but their actions and demeanour also hold a significant treatment potential. For better and worse, the parents in particular play a major role in the development and cessation of NSSI. Many of the risk factors for NSSI are related to family: insecure attachment (Wrath & Adams, 2018), childhood maltreatment and sexual abuse (Liu et al., 2018), high levels of expressed emotions and conflict (Hack & Martin, 2018), invalidating environment (Musser et al., 2018) and separated/divorced parents (Carter et al., 2016). A study found that family support was the most important factor for onset, maintenance and cessation of NSSI (Tatnell et al., 2014).

Having a child with NSSI causes feelings of anxiety, helplessness, inadequacy, guilt, shame and anger, concern and a sense of being manipulated as well as a desperate desire to help. These are all stressful and exhausting emotions (Whitlock & Lloyd-Richardson, 2019). The tension in the family often results in the avoidance of any discussion of NSSI and can sometimes lead to severe communication problems, power struggles and extreme reactions in the family, which can push parents to despair. In a desperate desire to prevent further self-injury, parents may act in extreme ways, including threatening the child with being hospitalized or thrown out of the family home. Of course, this is likely to trigger an equally extreme response from the child and can result in a high level of conflict (Waals et al., 2018).

Some parents perceive a child's NSSI as a repudiation of their parenting and may even develop feelings of hate towards a child with persistent NSSI. The hate is not directed at the daughter or son they used to know, but rather at the family's extreme situation. Parents often judge themselves harshly for having these negative feelings.

A mother and a father both say that they feel their severely self-injuring daughter is 'ruining our lives'. The father states explicitly that he has begun to 'hate her': with her self-injury, suicide attempts and numerous hospital stays, he felt that she was holding the entire family in an iron grip, in which there was room for no one but her. The mother chastises him. She says that no one should hate their own daughter, and as a result the father now also feels shameful, which only exacerbates his feelings of powerlessness and of being a terrible father.

As parents or partners, we never feel better than our loved ones allow. When they are happy, so are we, and when they suffer, so do we. When someone self-injures, close friends or relatives risk being emotionally overwhelmed by feelings of guilt, doubt, self-recrimination, inadequacy and failure. Some friends or relatives are well aware what has gone wrong, but most people find it incomprehensible and thus emotionally excruciating.

The self-injuring person too is struggling with difficult emotions, some of them as a result of NSSI. Shame, guilt, self-loathing and helplessness are common feelings for most people who engage in NSSI. Hence, many attempt to hide NSSI to those around them, who may therefore be unaware of it. The first people to know that someone self-injures are often the person's peers, and it may take a very long time before a young person's parents, for example, become aware of the problem (Arbuthnott & Lewis, 2015). Thus, it is not always easy to discover that one's child or partner is engaging in NSSI.

Classic specific signs of NSSI include always wearing clothes that cover the whole body, even on hot days, avoiding sport or other activities that expose the body or the presence of cuts, bruises and other lesions. Non-specific signs of psychological distress include low mood, lack of interest in life, depression or outbursts of anger, self-blame for problems or expressing feelings of failure, uselessness or hopelessness, withdrawal and sloppy school work. However, these factors are not necessarily indications of NSSI. If parents suspect that their child has begun to self-injure, they obviously need to tread carefully, asking concerned questions that express care and a desire to help. Recriminations or punishment will only exacerbate the situation.

Walking on eggshells

Many relatives have no idea how to respond. Often, the mood at home is tense, and the family risks going from crisis to crisis. Many parents have described the situation as walking on eggshells, echoing Mason and Kreger's (2010) book about living with an emotionally dysregulated child with BPD, *Stop Walking on Eggshells*. The self-injuring teenager or partner becomes extremely sensitive to friends' and family members' reactions and is likely to respond with intense emotional outbursts. These may be infectious because their loved ones cannot contain them and thus respond with similar intensity, for example in the form of anxiety and anger. There is also considerable risk of misunderstandings, as in the following example:

Rita's parents had overheard an argument between Rita and her boyfriend on the phone. Rita was about six months into her treatment for NSSI. The row made them worry that she might cut herself, and so they were watchful when she came down for dinner. Although it was a hot day, Rita wore a long-sleeved blouse. Rita's mother had a hunch that she had been cutting and confronted her with this suspicion in a way that Rita perceived as brusque. Rita was furious with her parents' interference, and the result was a big fight where everybody was very agitated. In a subsequent family therapy session, it became clear that in their anxiety, her parents often reacted in a way that Rita perceived as brusque and angry. She was actually surprised to hear that her parents were primarily worried, scared and sad.

Hollander (2017) points out that parents need to learn some of the same coping skills that their child learns in therapy. The rationale is that they need to be able to look after themselves before they can help their child. Hollander's specific focus is on DBT, but Bateman and Fonagy (2004) and others who work with MBT point to the need for family members to practice their mentalizing and validation skills in order to help a child who self-injures.

NSSI is a coping mechanism. Your child is doing the best he or she can!

- NSSI is a symptom of an underlying problem and not a mental illness.
- About one in four adolescents has self-injured at least once, so it's quite 'normal'. Take it seriously, but don't panic. This can be hard if you are upset about what your child is doing, but the most helpful thing to do is to talk about the issue calmly and show your child that you care for him or her.
- Use 'I' statements when you talk to your child to ensure a non-threatening and non-blaming communication style. Anger or ultimatums are likely to make your child feel worse and increase the risk of self-injury.
- Keep the lines of communication between yourself and your child open. Try to listen and don't overwhelm your child with a whole host of questions.
- Pay attention your child but don't monitor him or her closely.
- Don't expect your child to be able to stop self-injuring from one day to the next.

Accepting the difficult situation

It is essential for the family to accept the difficult situation they are in. DBT operates with the technique of 'radical acceptance', which is not the same as resigning oneself to the situation. The opposite of accepting reality is to deny or object to it. Many parents respond to their child's NSSI with denial. Denial is a defence mechanism. The fact that their child attacks his or her own body is simply too much and too difficult to understand. The inner struggle that a lack of acceptance can activate may perpetuate or intensify the feeling of desperation, powerless rage or mental fatigue. Thus, our suffering is often exacerbated when we fail to accept the pain in our life, investing considerable energy into pushing back against the facts as they are.

In order to survive and continue to engage in the good parts of life, it is important not to let despair over a self-injuring family member dominate one's life. In addition to 'radical acceptance', the best thing to do is to let go of one's pain and enjoy the positive aspects of life without being overwhelmed by guilt or shame. Although it is no easy task, while taking care of the self-injuring child parents should also try to continue their normal life without depriving themselves of the everyday pleasures that help the recharge their batteries and give them the strength to deal with the crisis at hand.

Survivor's guilt

When a child has NSSI, the entire family is affected, including any siblings. Siblings of children who self-injure often experience a kind of survivor's guilt. They have a completely irrational feeling of guilt because they are not the ones suffering and self-injuring instead of their sister or brother. Survivor's guilt may manifest itself in thoughts and rumination but also in behaviour, for example by choosing not to do things one would normally enjoy.

Brit is the younger sister of Janice, who suffers from severe NSSI and who has been hospitalized in the psychiatric ward repeatedly. Brit is deeply worried for her older sister and has decided not to have a party on the occasion of her confirmation because she does not want to 'take attention away from Janice and make her upset'.

Parents need to pay attention to how the other children in the family are doing and sometimes prioritize spending time with them alone, without the self-injuring brother or sister.

Neutral topics

Although worrying and, perhaps, anger over a family member's NSSI play a prominent role in the family's life, it is important to continue to engage the self-injurious person on neutral topics that he or she is interested in and enjoys talking about. If most conversations revolve around the topic of self-injury, the self-injuring person is bound to feel that he or she is under attack, useless, wrong, a failure. This is obviously not conducive to building self-esteem. Most people who engage in NSSI are shameful and prefer to avoid talking about their NSSI, but everyone needs contact, and the best way to support a family member who self-injures is to be non-judging, to listen and to be open to the other's thoughts and emotions. The prescription is simple, although that does not mean it is easy: listen, withhold judgement, use open questions, invite the person into a dialogue, and use every opportunity to validate his or her emotions, for example: 'I can understand how upsetting it must be for you to hear your dad and me arguing'.

As mentioned earlier, validation is a relational 'lubricant', and feeling validated makes it easier for the person to validate him/herself as well as his or her concerned family members. It may be difficult to validate the other when emotions run high, but it is the most helpful response to a self-injuring family member.

Talk about it

Although it is important to engage the self-injuring person on neutral topics, it is also important to talk explicitly about what is happening. Self-injury is a tacit language, which the person uses for want of a better option. If it were possible, he or she would address the issue explicitly, but that may be difficult.

> Anita is 22 years old, has been cutting herself for the past seven years and has been hospitalized after suicide attempts. Anita is obviously in pain, but she has not had the courage to talk about the underlying themes with the numerous psychiatrists and psychologists she has met during her hospital stays. Only after establishing a stable, long-term contact with a psychologist is she able to talk about the sexual abuse she had been subjected to by her uncle. She has not spoken out earlier, in part because she feels shameful about what happened, in part because she worries that others will not believe her. Hence, she has dealt with these emotions and her NSSI alone for all these years.

Educate yourself online and via the literature

Psychoeducation about NSSI is extremely important, and if the family is not in contact with a professional, they should use the internet or books to get information on NSSI. Understanding that NSSI is a coping strategy can make it easier to understand and validate the self-injuring person. People who use NSSI do so for lack of a better option.

It is also important for family members not to keep their knowledge and worries about a self-injuring child or partner to themselves. It is helpful to involve others, ideally with the self-injuring person's consent. This could be the general practitioner, the school psychologist, a social worker or perhaps a teacher. Information about NSSI and self-harm can be found on the following websites:

- The Children's Society: www.childrenssociety.org.uk/mental-health-advice-for-children-and-young-people/self-harm
- The Royal College of Psychiatrists: www.rcpsych.ac.uk/mental-health/problems-disorders/self-harm
- Mind UK: www.mind.org.uk/information-support/types-of-mental-health-problems/self-harm

Parental burnout

The American psychiatrist Michael Hollander, who has many years' experience working with teenagers who engage in NSSI and their parents, has written about parental burnout syndrome (Hollander, 2017). Parents of self-injuring teenagers, who live with constant worries and anxiety, eventually burn out. Some parents withdraw from the child, using work or other activities as a distraction from feelings of despair and desperation. Others focus on their child's difficulties to the point of neglecting everything else, including their work and any other children, with marital or relationship problems as an almost inevitable consequence. If one of the parents blames the child for the behaviour while the other is caring and supportive, the parents risk drifting apart.

Signs and symptoms of parental burnout

- Increased difficulties in significant relationships
- Increased irritability and/or lack of patience
- Significant decrease in pleasurable activities
- Increased alcohol use
- Changes in appetite
- Sleep difficulties
- Increased sense of loneliness and isolation
- Persistent anxiety and rumination

(Hollander, 2017)

Parental relations – GIVE

Hollander (2017) underscores that the parents' mutual relationship affects their risk of burnout. Psychological distress and NSSI in a child will almost inevitably reactivate old conflicts. A search for the causes of the current problems risks leading to mutual accusations and recriminations: 'She's cutting because you were always too soft and never disciplined her!' 'What are you talking about; she's in pain and cutting because you've always been so harsh and demanding'.

Stressful times place high demands on the parents' ability to communicate constructively and keep conflicts from getting out of control. The greater the pressure on the family members, the greater the risk of a failure to mentalize and of 'either-or thinking': 'Either you're right, or I'm right' or 'If I win this discussions, that means you lost'. It is important to maintain one's mentalizing capacity and to remember the dialectical principles, according to which there is always more than one side to any issue, and two parties can both be right. Maybe the daughter is cutting because right now, that is the best way for her to handle the fact that one of her parents is 'too soft', while the other is 'too demanding'. Either-or thinking often turns conversations into a struggle to be right – to win. The risk is that both parents – and, not least, their daughter – lose. Rather than thinking in terms of winning or losing, it is more constructive to look for what works and to search for the best way forward. For example, it is not helpful to argue over the causes of the daughter's self-injury. It is far more helpful to determine how she might give up this practice and develop more effective and sustainable coping strategies. A helpful approach involves looking forward, setting a goal and being willing to compromise.

Hollander (2017) recommends following the principles of GIVE – (be) Gentle, (act) Interested, Validate and Easy manner – in dialogues. Although that might sound obvious, sadly it is not always the case, especially when people are under emotional pressure.

Be gentle

When the parents talk to each other, they should strive to be kind and polite. Everybody reacts more positively to someone who is friendly and forthcoming than to someone who is unfriendly. When we feel that someone is being patronizing or aggressive, we tend to become defensive and stop listening to what the person is saying. Constructive conversations have to be based on respect.

Act interested

When the parents talk to each other, they should seek to signal that they are interested in what the other is saying. They should try to listen actively, ask follow-up questions and strive to understand the background for what the other is saying. They should avoid interrupting and allow the other person to make his or her point. That also allows for greater nuance and makes it easier to understand the other. Feeling heard and understood is an important part of any conversation.

Validate

Validating means confirming that the other's emotions, opinions, ideas, wishes, difficulties or actions make sense and are understandable. One does not have to agree with the other's assessments. Validating implies that the other is entitled to state his or her opinion, and that his or her points are valid and reflect at least a part of reality. It is a condition for a good conversation that both parties feel recognized and validated.

Easy manner

Having an easy manner means helping each other maintain a good flow in the conversation, even if it is serious. A light tone is not incompatible with serious topics. Humour, tolerance and kindness are important ingredients of a good conversation. It is not about being right but about finding the best solution to a common problem. It is a classic rule of diplomacy that a negotiation should never result in a winner and a loser. A loser will almost inevitably feel shameful, helpless, violated or defeated, which easily leads to aggression and vindictiveness.

Scars

Both the person who self-injures and their loved ones are, naturally, concerned about the bodily harm caused by NSSI. NSSI usually leaves marks, some of them lasting. A bruise or other signs of physical harm may fade in a matter of days or weeks, while scars from cutting or burning may remain, an enduring reminder of self-injury.

In an MBT group of young women with BPD who had self-injured, at one time or another, the conversation turned to scars after self-injury. One of the women said she had had an argument with her boyfriend because he wanted her to have the scars on her arms and legs removed. She regarded the scars as a reminder of the tough times she had gone through. 'All my scars are signs of how tough my life has been. Now I've moved on, and I want to keep them as reminders'. Some of the women in the group agreed with her boyfriend that she should have the scars removed; others agreed with her that they were testimony to the conflicts and emotional turmoil that she had survived.

Injuries to the body can leave scars, which often spark reactions from others. The young women in the group discussed whether one should hide one's past or 'own it as a way of letting others know that you don't have to be crazy to be a cutter'.

People who self-injure have different views of the marks it leaves behind. Many cut or burn themselves on parts of the body that are easy to hide, while others choose the most accessible places, often the lower arm or the wrist. Some do what they can to hide their self-injury, while others do not care or even flash it. Naturally, the person's view of scars may change in the course of time.

A study by Lewis and Mehrabkhani (2016) identified four different perceptions among patients of their own NSSI scars. A little over one-third (36%) perceive scars as part of a self-narrative, for example, 'They are like my story – they remind me how much I've been through and how strong I've had to be to survive that.

I wouldn't want to be without them now'. One-quarter (26%) did not accept their scars and felt repulsed by them, for example, 'I know when each scar was made and how I felt, or didn't feel, at that moment. If I think about them I can feel the pain resurface and it makes me feel ugly'. One-fifth (20%) experienced gradual acceptance after initial difficulty. Shame seems to hamper initial scar acceptance. For example, 'I have come to terms that they will always be there so I might as well accept them'. Finally, one-fifth (18%) was ambivalent about their scars. For example, 'I always had a love/hate relationship with mine'.

Scars develop when the body repairs the skin after an injury. The damaged tissue is replaced with stronger collagen fibres, which look different than the epidermis. These fibres have no pigmentation, so over time, scars turn white. Some people form 'ugly' keloid scars, a permanent bulky or fibrous scar that extends beyond the originally damaged area. Keloid scarring is probably genetically determined and is more frequent in people with darker skin. Keloid scarring occurs regardless how the wound was treated.

Generally, to diminish scarring it is important to clean the fresh wound and, not least, to close it. In simple cases, a plaster will do, while bigger injuries require strips, surgical glue or suturing, either at the doctor's or in an emergency room. The risk of scarring is biggest for gaping wounds, and to optimize healing, the wound should be held together and closed as soon as possible after the injury. Deep wounds or wounds bleed heavily require professional care.

To minimize tissue damage burns should be held under cold water until the burning sensation is reduced or goes away.

Scars can never be fully removed, but cosmetic improvement is possible by means of a silicone or aloe vera gel, which also has a healing and pain-reducing effect, or vitamin E lotion. All of these are available over the counter. For optimal results, it is important to use the gel or lotion continuously for 3–6 months. Medically prescribed treatments include steroid cremes, laser treatment or surgery. Surgery removes keloid tissue and replaces the scar with a new cut while ensuring optimal healing. It has to be carried out by a plastic surgeon and can only happen after the self-injury has stopped.

Finally, some people choose to get a tattoo to cover up their scar tissue, but this is not risk-free, as scar tissue reacts differently to the ink than normal skin. It is thus important to seek professional advice before choosing one of the more invasive methods.

For several years, Maria had performed NSSI, cutting and burning herself. This had left scars, particularly on her left lower arm. When she had gone a full year without self-injuring, she celebrated by getting a tattoo of a dove on her arm. She determined that whenever she looked at it, she was to think about doing something nice for herself and thus avoid self-injuring. She was proud of her dove and liked to show it off as a sign that she moved through and past a major crisis in her life.

References

Adler, P. A., & Adler, P. (2007). The demedicalization of self-injury: From psychopathology to sociological deviance. *Journal of Contemporary Ethnography, 36*(5), 537–570.

Adler, P. A., & Adler, P. (2010). *The tender cut: Inside the hidden world of self-injury.* New York, NY: New York University Press.

Aggarwal, S., & Patton, G. (2018). Engaging families in the management of adolescent self-harm. *Evidence Based Mental Health, 21*(1), 16–22.

Ainsworth, M. D. S., Blehar, M. C., Waters, E., & Wall, S. (1978). *Patterns of attachment: A psychological study of the strange situation.* Hillsdale, NJ: Lawrence Erlbaum Associates.

Ali-Sharifi, A., Krynicki, C., & Upthegrove, R. (2015). Self-harm and ethnicity: A systematic review. *International Journal of Social Psychiatry, 61*(6), 600–612.

Allen, J. G. (2013). *Restoring mentalizing in attachment relationships: Treating trauma with plain old therapy.* Arlington, VA: American Psychiatric Publishing.

American Psychiatric Association. (1987). *Diagnostic and statistical manual of mental disorders, DSM-III-R.* Washington, DC: American Psychiatric Publishing.

American Psychiatric Association. (2013). *Diagnostic and statistical manual of mental disorders, DSM-5.* Washington, DC: American Psychiatric Publishing.

Ammerman, B. A., Jacobucci, R., Kleiman, E. M., Muehlenkamp, J. J., & McCloskey, M. S. (2016). Development and validation of empirically derived frequency criteria for NSSI disorder using exploratory data mining. *Psychological Assessment, 28*(2), 221–231.

Andover, M. S. (2012). A cognitive-behavioral approach to case formulations for non-suicidal self-injury. *Journal of Cognitive Psychotherapy, 26*(4), 318–330.

Andover, M. S., Pepper, C. M., Ryabchenko, K. A., Orrico, E. G., & Gibb, B. E. (2005). Self-mutilation and symptoms of depression, anxiety and borderline personality disorder. *Suicide and Life-Threatening Behaviors, 35*(5), 581–591.

Andover, M. S., Primack, J. M., Gibb, B. E., & Pepper, C. M. (2010). An examination of non-suicidal self-injury in men: Do men differ from women in basic NSSI characteristics? *Archives of Suicide Research, 14*(1), 79–88.

Andover, M. S., Schatten, H. T., Morris, B. W., Holman, C. S., & Miller, I. W. (2017). An intervention for non-suicidal self-injury in young adults: A pilot randomized controlled trial. *Journal of Consulting and Clinical Psychology, 85*(6), 620–631.

Andrewes, H. E., Hulbert, C., Cotton, S. M., Betts, J., & Chanen, A. M. (2017). Relationships between the frequency and severity of non-suicidal self-injury and suicide attempts in youth with borderline personality disorder. *Early Intervention in Psychiatry, 22*(476), 1–8. DOI: https://doi.org/10.1111/eip.12461

Angelotta, C. (2015). Defining and refining self-harm: A historical perspective on non-suicidal self-injury. *Journal of Nervous and Mental Diseases, 203*(2), 75–80.

Arbuthnott, A. E., & Lewis, S. P. (2015). Parents of youth who self-injure: A review of the literature and implications for mental health professionals. *Child and Adolescent Psychiatry and Mental Health, 9*(1), 35. DOI: https://doi.org/10.1186/s13034-015-0066-3

Atwood, M. (1989). *Cat's eye*. London: Bloomsbury.

Barrocas A. L., Hankin B. L., Young J. F., & Abela J. R. (2012). Rates of nonsuicidal self-injury in youth: Age, sex, and behavioral methods in a community sample. *Pediatrics, 130*(1), 39–45.

Bass, C., & Halligan, P. (2014). Factitious disorder and malingering. *Lancet, 383*(9926), 1422–1432.

Bastian, B., Jetten, J., Hornsey, M. J., & Leknes, S. (2014). The positive consequences of pain: A biopsychosocial approach. *Journal of Personality and Social Psychology, 18*(3), 256–279.

Bateman, A. (2012). Mindfulness: In 100 words. *British Journal of Psychiatry, 201*(4), 297.

Bateman, A., & Fonagy, P. (2004). *Psychotherapy for borderline personality disorder: Mentalization-based treatment*. Oxford, England: Oxford University Press.

Bateman, A., & Fonagy, P. (2006). *Mentalization-based treatment of borderline personality disorder: A practical guide*. Oxford, England: Oxford University Press.

Bateman, A., & Fonagy, P. (2010). Mentalization based treatment for borderline personality disorder. *World Psychiatry, 9*(1), 11–15.

Bauman, Z. (1997). *Postmodernity and its discontents*. London, England: Polity.

Bennum, I. (1984). Psychological models of self-mutilation. *Suicide and Life-Threatening Behavior, 14*(3), 166–186.

Bettelheim, B. (1955). *Symbolic wounds: Puberty rites and the envious male*. London, England: Thames and Hudson.

Bille-Brahe, U. (1982). Persons attempting suicide in the Danish welfare system. *Social Psychiatry, 17*(4), 181–188.

Bion, W. R. (1970). *Second thoughts*. London, England: Karnac Books.

Bjärehed, J., Wångby-Lundh, M. D., & Lundh, L.-G. (2012). Non-suicidal self-injury in a community sample of adolescents: Subgroups, stability and associations with psychological difficulties. *Journal of Research on Adolescence, 22*(4), 678–693.

Bjureberg, J., Sahlin, H., Hedman-Lagerlöf, E., Gratz, K. L., Tull, M. T., Jokinen, J. . . . Ljótsson, B. (2018). Extending research on Emotion Regulation Individual Therapy for Adolescents (ERITA) with non-suicidal self-injury disorder: Open pilot trial and mediation analysis of a novel online version. *BMC Psychiatry, 18*(1), 326. DOI: https://doi.org/10.1186/s12888-018-1885-6

Bowes, L., Carnegie, R., Pearson, R., Mars, B., Biddle, L., Maughan, B. . . . Heron, J. (2015). Risk of depression and self-harm in teenagers identifying with Goth subculture: A longitudinal cohort study. *The Lancet Psychiatry, 2*(9), 793–800.

Bowlby, J. (1973). *Attachment and loss: Separation*. New York, NY: Basic Books.

Bowlby, J. (1988). *A secure base: Clinical applications of attachment theory*. London, England: Routledge.

Boxer, P. (2010). Variations in risk and treatment factors among adolescents engaging in different types of deliberate self-harm in an inpatient sample. *Journal of Clinical Child and Adolescent Psychology, 39*(4), 470–480.

Bracken-Minor, K. L., & McDevitt-Murphy, M. E. (2014). Differences in features of non-suicidal self-injury according to borderline personality disorder screening status. *Archives of Suicide Research, 18*(1), 88–103.

Bresin, K. (2014). Five indices of emotion regulation in participants with a history of non-suicidal self-injury: A daily diary study. *Behavior Therapy, 45*(1), 56–66.

Bresin, K., & Gordon, K. H. (2013). Endogenous opioids and non-suicidal self-injury: A mechanism of affect regulation. *Neuroscience and Biobehavioral Reviews, 37*(3), 374–383.

Bresin, K., & Schoenleber, M. (2015). Gender differences in the prevalence of non-suicidal self-injury: A meta-analysis. *Clinical Psychology Review, 38*, 55–64.

Briere, J., & Gil, E. (1998). Self-mutilation in clinical and general population samples: Prevalence, correlates, and functions. *American Journal of Orthopsychiatry, 68*(4), 609–620.

Brown, M. Z., Linehan, M. M., Comtois, K. A., Murray, A., & Chapman, A. L. (2009). Shame as a prospective predictor of self-inflicted injury in borderline personality disorder: A multi-modal analysis. *Behaviour Research and Therapy, 47*(10), 815–822.

Brown, R. C., Fischer, T., Goldwich, A. D., Keller, F., Young, R., & Plener, P. L. (2018a). #Cutting: Non-suicidal self-injury (NSSI) on Instagram. *Psychological Medicine, 48*(2), 337–346.

Brown, R. C., Heines, S., Witt, A., Braehler, E., Fegert, J. M., Harsch, D., & Plener, P. L. (2018). The impact of child maltreatment on non-suicidal self-injury: Data from a representative sample of the general population. *BMC Psychiatry, 18*(181), 1–8.

Brown, R. C., & Plener, P. L. (2017). Non-suicidal self-injury in adolescence. *Current Psychiatry Reports, 19*, 20. DOI: https://doi.org/10.1007/s11920-017-0767-9

Buser, T. J., & Buser, J. K. (2013). The HIRE model: A tool for the informal assessment of non-suicidal self-injury. *Journal of Mental Health Counseling, 35*(3), 262–281.

Calati, R., & Courtet, P. (2016). Is psychotherapy effective for reducing suicide attempt and non-suicidal self-injury rates? Meta-analysis and meta-regression of literature data. *Journal of Psychiatric Research, 79*, 8–20.

Caldji, C., Tannenbaum, B., Sherma, S., Francis, D., Plotsky, P. M., & Meaney, M. (1998). Maternal care during infancy regulates the development of neural systems mediating the expression of fearfulness in the rat. *Proceedings of the National Academy of Science of the United States of America, 95*(9), 5335–5340.

Carter, G., Page, A., Large, M., Hetrick, S., Milner, A. J., Bendit, N. . . . Christensen, H. (2016). Royal Australian and New Zealand College of Psychiatrists clinical practice guideline for the management of deliberate self-harm. *Australian & New Zealand Journal of Psychiatry, 50*(10), 939–1000.

Cerutti, R., Zuffianò, A., & Spensieri, V. (2018). The role of difficulty in identifying and describing feelings in non-suicidal self-injury behavior (NSSI): Associations with perceived attachment quality, stressful life events, and suicidal ideation. *Frontiers in Psychology, 9*, 318.

Chamberlain, S. R., Leppink, E. W., Redden, S. A., & Grant, J. E. (2017). Associations between self-harm and distinct types of impulsivity. *Psychiatry Research, 250*, 10–16.

Chaney, S. (2017). *Psyche on the skin*. London, England: Reaktion Books.

Chapman, A. L., Gratz, K. L., & Brown, M. Z. (2006). Solving the puzzle of deliberate self-harm: The Experiential Avoidance Model. *Behaviour Research and Therapy, 44*(3), 371–394.

Chesin, M. S., Galfavy, H., Sonmez, C. C., Wong, A., Oquendo, M. A., Mann, J. J., & Stanley, B. (2017). Non-suicidal self-injury is predictive of suicide attempts among individuals with mood disorders. *Suicide and Life-Threatening Behavior, 47*(5), 567–579.

Christensen, A. I., Davidsen, M., Ekholm, O., Pedersen, P. V., & Juel, K. (2014). *Danskernes sundhed: Den nationale sundhedsprofil 2013*. Copenhagen, Denmark: Danish Health Authority.

Christoffersen, M. N., Møhl, B., DePanilis, D., & Vammen, K. S. (2014). Non-suicidal self-injury: Does social support make a difference? An epidemiological investigation of a Danish national sample. *Child Abuse & Neglect, 44*, 106–116.

Cipriano, A., Cella, S., & Cotrufo, P. (2017). Non-suicidal self-injury: A systematic review. *Frontiers in Psychology, 8*, 1946. DOI: https://doi.org/10.3389/fpsyg.2017.01946

Claes, L., Luyckx, K., Baetens, I., Van de Ven, M., & Witteman, C. (2015a). Bullying and victimization, depressive mood, and non-suicidal self-injury in adolescents: The moderating role of parental support. *Journal of Child and Family Studies, 24*(11), 3363–3371. DOI: https://doi.org/10.1007/s10826-015–0138-2

Claes, L., Luyckx, K., Bijttebier, P., Turner, B., Ghandi, A., Smets, J. . . . Schoevaerts, K. (2015). Non-suicidal self-injury in patients with eating disorder: Associations with identity formation above and beyond anxiety and depression. *European Eating Disorders Review, 23*(2), 119–125.

Claes, L., Vandereycken, W., & Vertommen, H. (2007). Self-injury in female versus male psychiatric patients: A comparison of characteristics, psychopathology and aggression regulation. *Personality and Individual Differences, 42*(4), 611–621.

Clarkin, J. F., Yeomans, F. E., & Kernberg, O. F. (2006). *Psychotherapy for borderline personality: Focusing on object relations* (2nd edition). Washington, DC: American Psychiatric Publishing.

Clendenin, W. W., & Murphy, G. E. (1971). Wrist cutting: New epidemiological findings. *Archives of General Psychiatry, 25*, 465–469.

Cook, N. E., & Gorraiz, M. (2016). Dialectical behavior therapy for non-suicidal self-injury and depression among adolescents: Preliminary meta-analytic evidence. *Child and Adolescent Mental Health, 21*(2), 81–89.

Cucchi, A., Ryan, D., Konstantakopoulos, G., Stroumpa, S., Kaçar, A. Ş, Renshaw, S. . . . Kravariti, E. (2016). Lifetime prevalence of non-suicidal self-injury in patients with eating disorders: A systematic review and meta-analysis. *Psychological Medicine, 46*(7), 1345–1358.

Daigle, M.-P., Lafontaine, M. F., Levesque, C., Bureau, J. F., Wehbe, H. W., & Caron, A. M. (2018). The relationship between perfectionism and non-suicidal self-injury in a student sample of young adults. *Journal of Interpersonal Relations, Intergroup Relations and Identity, 11*, 53–64.

Darche, M. A. (1990). Psychological factors differentiating self-mutilating and non-self mutilating adolescent inpatients females. *Psychiatric Hospital, 21*(1), 31–35.

Deiter, P. J., & Pearlman, L. A. (1998). Responding to self-injurious behavior. In P. M. Kleespies (Ed.), *Emergencies in mental health practice: Evaluation and management.* New York, NY: Guilford Press.

Dick, K. (1996). *Sick: The life and times of Bob Flanagan, supermasochist.* Documentary.

Dickey, L. M., Reisner, S. L., & Juntunen, C. L. (2015). Non-suicidal self-injury in a large online sample of transgender adults. *Professional Psychology: Research and Practice, 46*(1), 3–11.

Doctors, S. (1981). The Symptom of delicate self-cutting in adolescent females: A developmental view. In S. C. Feinstein, J. G. Looney, A. Z. Schwartzberg, & A. D. Sorosky (Eds.), *Adolescent psychiatry: Developmental and clinical studies* (Vol. 9). Chicago, IL: University of Chicago Press.

Doctors, S. (1999). Further thoughts on 'self-cutting': The intersubjective context of self-experience and the vulnerability to self-loss. *Psychoanalytic Review, 86*, 733–744.

Douglas, M. (2003). *Purity and danger: An analysis of concepts of pollution and taboo.* Abingdon, England: Routledge.

Edmondson, A. J., Brennan, C. A., & House, A. O. (2016). Non-suicidal reasons for self-harm: A systematic review of self-reported accounts. *Journal of Affective Disorders*, *191*, 109–117.

Emerson, L. E. (1913). The case of Miss A: A preliminary report of psychoanalytic study and treatment of a case of self-mutilation. *Psychoanalytic Review*, *1*, 41–52.

Evans, K., Tyrer, P., Catalan, J., Schmidt, U., Davidson, K., Dent, J. . . . Thornton, S. (1999). Manual-Assisted Cognitive-Behavior Therapy (MACT): A randomized controlled trial of a brief intervention with bibliotherapy in the treatment of recurrent deliberate self-harm. *Psychological Medicine*, *29*(1), 19–25.

Favazza, A. R. (1996). *Bodies under siege: Self-mutilation and body modification in culture and psychiatry* (2nd edition). Baltimore, MD: Johns Hopkins University Press.

Favazza, A. R. (1998). The coming of age of self-mutilation. *Journal of Nervous and Mental Disease*, *186*(5), 259–268.

Favazza, A. R. (2012). Non suicidal self-injury: How categorization guides treatment. *Current Psychiatry*, *11*(3), 21–27.

Favazza, A. R., & Rosenthal, R. J. (1993). Diagnostic issues in self-mutilation. *Hospital and Community Psychiatry*, *44*(2), 134–140.

Figueroa, M. D. (1988). A dynamic taxonomy of self-destructive behavior. *Psychotherapy: Theory, Research, Practice, Training*, *25*(2), 280–287.

Firestone, R. W., & Seiden, R. H. (1990). Suicide and the continuum of self-destructive behavior. *Journal of American College Health*, *38*(5), 207–213.

Fischer, G., Brunner, R., Parzer, P., Resch, F., & Kaess, M. (2013). Short-term psychotherapeutic treatment in adolescents engaging in non-suicidal self-injury: A randomized controlled trial. *Trials Journal*, *14*, 294. Retrieved from https://www.trialsjournal.com/content/14/1/294

Fonagy, P. (1989). On tolerating mental states: Theory of mind in borderline patients. *Bulletin of the Anna Freud Centre*, *12*(2), 91–115.

Fonagy, P., Gergely, G., Jurist, E. L., & Target, M. (2002). *Affect regulation, mentalization and the development of the self*. New York, NY: Other Press.

Ford, J. D., & Gómez, J. M. (2015). The relationship of psychological trauma and dissociative and posttraumatic stress disorders to non-suicidal self-injury and suicidality: A review. *Journal of Trauma Dissociation*, *16*(3), 232–271.

Forrester, R. L., Khowla Jomar, H. S., Mitzman, S., & Taylor, P. J. (2017). Self-esteem and non-suicidal self-injury in adulthood: A systematic review. *Journal of Affective Disorders*, *221*, 172–183.

Fox, K. R., Franklin, J. C., Ribeiro, J. D., Kleiman, E. M., Bentley, K. H., & Nock, M. K. (2015). Metaanalysis of risk factors for non-suicidal self-injury. *Clinical Psychology Review*, *42*, 156–167.

Fox, K. R., Toole, K. E., Franklin, J. C., & Hooley, J. M. (2017). Why does self-injury improve mood? A preliminary test of three hypotheses. *Clinical Psychological Science*, *5*(1), 111–121.

Frances, A. (1987). Introduction (to the section on self-mutilation). *Journal of Personality Disorders*, *1*, 316.

Franklin, J. C., Fox, K. R., Franklin, C. R., Kleiman, E. M., Ribeiro, J. D., Jaroszewski, A. C. . . . Nock, M. K. (2016). A brief mobile app reduces non-suicidal and suicidal self-injury: Evidence from three randomized controlled trials. *Journal of Consulting and Clinical Psychology*, *84*(6), 544–557.

Franklin, J. C., Lee, K. M., Hanna, E. K., & Prinstein, M. J. (2013). Feeling worse to feel better: Pain-offset relief simultaneously stimulates positive affect and reduces negative affect. *Psychological Science*, *24*(4), 521–529.

Fraser, G., Wilson, M. S., Garisch, J. A., Robinson, K., Brocklesby, M., Kingi, T. . . . Russell, L. (2018). Non-suicidal self-injury, sexuality concerns, and emotion regulation among sexually diverse adolescents: A multiple mediation analysis. *Archives of Suicide Research, 22*(3), 432–452.

Freeman, K. R., James, S., Klein, K. P., Mayo, D., & Montgomery, S. (2016). Outpatient dialectical behavior therapy for adolescents engaged in deliberate self-harm: Conceptual and methodological considerations. *Child and Adolescent Social Work Journal, 33*(2), 123–135.

Freud, S. (1955). Beyond the pleasure principle. In J. Strachey (Ed. and Trans.), *The standard edition of the complete psychological works of Sigmund Freud* (Vol. 18, pp. 1–283). London, England: Hogarth. (Original work published 1920)

Friedman, M., Glasser, M., Laufer, E., Laufer, M., & Wohl, M. (1972). Attempted suicide and self-mutilation in adolescence: Some observations from a psychoanalytic research project. *British Journal of Psychoanalysis, 53*(2), 179–183.

Gabbard, G. O., & Wilkinson, S. M. (1994). *Management of countertransference with borderline patients.* Lanham, MD: Rowman and Littlefield Publishers.

Gandhi, A., Luyckx, K., Baetens, I., Kiekens, G., Sleuwaegen, E., Berensd, A. . . . Claes, L. (2018). Age of onset of non-suicidal self-injury in Dutch-speaking adolescents and emerging adults: An event history analysis of pooled data. *Comprehensive Psychiatry, 80*, 170–178.

Gatta, M., Dal Santo, F., Rago, A., Spoto, A., & Battistella, P. A. (2016). Alexithymia, impulsiveness, and psychopathology in non-suicidal self-injured adolescents. *Neuropsychiatric Disease and Treatment, 12*, 2307–2317.

Germain, S. T., & Hooley, J. M. (2012). Direct and indirect forms of non-suicidal self-injury: Evidence for a distinction. *Psychiatry Research, 197*(1–2), 78–84.

Geulayov, G., Casey, D., McDonald, K. C., Foster, P., Pritchard, K., Wells, C. . . . Hawton, K. (2018). Incidence of suicide, hospital-presenting non-fatal self-harm, and community-occurring non-fatal self-harm in adolescents in England (the iceberg model of self-harm): A retrospective study. *The Lancet Psychiatry, 5*(2), 167–174.

Giddens, A. (1991). *Modernity and self-identity: Self and society in the late modern age.* Stanford, CA: Stanford University Press.

Gillies, D., Christou, M. A., Dixon, A. C., Featherston, O. J., Rapti, I., Garcia-Anguita, A. . . . Christou, P. A. (2018). Prevalence and characteristics of self-harm in adolescents: Meta-analyses of community-based studies 1990–2015. *Journal of the American Academy of Child and Adolescent Psychiatry, 57*(10), 733–741.

Gilman, S. L. (2013). From psychiatric symptom to diagnostic category: Self-harm from the Victorians to DSM-5. *History of Psychiatry, 24*, 148–165.

Glenn, C. R., Franklin, J. C., & Nock, M. K. (2015). Evidence-based psychosocial treatments for self-injurious thoughts and behaviors in youth. *Journal of Clinical Child and Adolescent Psychology, 44*(1), 1–29.

Glenn, C. R., & Klonsky, E. D. (2013). Non-suicidal Self-Injury Disorder: An empirical investigation in adolescent psychiatric patients. *Journal of Clinical Child and Adolescent Psychology, 42*, 496–507.

Gould, R. M., & Pyle, W. l. (1897). *Anomalies and curiosities of medicine.* London & Philadelphia Retrieved from http://www.searchengine.org.uk/ebooks/09/23.pdf

Graf, H., & Mallin, R. (1967). The syndrome of the wrist cutter. *American Journal of Psychiatry, 124*(1), 36–42.

Gratz, K. L. (2001). Measurement of deliberate self-harm: Preliminary data on the deliberate self-harm inventory. *Journal of Psychopathology and Behavioral Assessment, 23*(4), 253–263.

Gratz, K. L. (2007). Targeting emotion dysregulation in the treatment of self-injury. *Journal of Clinical Psychology: In Session, 63*(11), 1091–1103.

Gratz, K. L., Conrad, S. D., & Roemer, L. (2002). Risk factors for deliberate self-harm among college students. *American Journal of Orthopsychiatry, 72*(1), 128–140.

Gratz, K. L., & Gunderson, J. G. (2006). Preliminary data on an acceptance-based emotion regulation group intervention for deliberate self-harm among women with borderline personality disorder. *Behavior Therapy, 37*(1), 25–35.

Gratz, K. L., & Roemer, L. (2004). Multidimensional assessment of emotion regulation and dysregulation: Development, factor structure, and initial validation of the difficulties in emotion regulation scale. *Journal of Psychopathology and Behavioral Assessment, 26*(1), 41–54.

Gratz, K. L., & Tull, M. T. (2011). Extending research on the utility of an adjunctive emotion regulation group therapy for deliberate self-harm among women with borderline personality pathology. *Personality Disorders: Theory, Research, and Treatment, 2*(4), 316–326.

Grist, R., Porter, J., & Stallard, P. (2018). Acceptability, use, and safety of a mobile phone app (BlueIce) for young people who self-harm: Qualitative study of service users' experience. *JMIR Mental Health, 5*(1), e16. DOI: https://doi.org/10.2196/mental.8779

Grossman, K. E., Grossman, K., & Waters, E. (Eds.) (2005). *Attachment from infancy to adulthood: The major longitudinal studies.* New York, NY: Guilford Press.

Grunebaum, H. U., & Klerman, G. I. (1967). Wrist slashing. *American Journal of Psychiatry, 124*(4), 527–534.

Guerry, J. D., & Prinstein, M. J. (2010). Longitudinal prediction of adolescent non-suicidal self-injury: Examination of a cognitive vulnerability-stress model. *Journal of Clinical Child and Adolescent Psychology, 39*(1), 77–89.

Gunnell, D. (2018). The adolescent mental health in crisis. *British Medical Journal, 361,* k2608. DOI: https://doi.org/10.1136/bmj.k2608

Hack, J., & Martin, G. (2018). Expressed emotion, shame, and non-suicidal self-injury. *International Journal of Environmental Research and Public Health, 15*(5), 890; pii: E890. DOI: https://doi.org/10.3390/ijerph15050890

Hammen, C. (2018). Risk factors for depression: An autobiographical review. *Annual Review of Clinical Psychology, 14,* 1–28. DOI: https://doi.org/10.1146/annurev-clinpsy-050817-084811

Hankin, B. L., & Abela, J. R. (2011). Non-suicidal self-injury in adolescence: Prospective rates and risk factors in a 2(1/2) year longitudinal study. *Psychiatry Research, 186*(1), 65–70.

Hasking, P., & Boyes, M. (2018). Cutting words: A commentary on language and stigma in the context of non-suicidal self-injury. *Journal of Nervous and Mental Disease, 206*(11), 829–833.

Hasking, P., Whitlock, J., Voon, D., & Rose, A. (2016). A cognitive-emotional model of NSSI: Using emotion regulation and cognitive processes to explain why people self-injure. *Cognition and Emotion, 31*(8), 1543–1556. DOI: https://doi.org/10.1080/02699 931.2016.1241219

Hawton, K., Arensman, E., Townsend, E., Bremner, S., Feldman, E., Goldney, R. . . . Traskman-Bendz, L. (1998). Deliberate self-harm: A systematic review of the efficacy of psychosocial and pharmacological treatments in preventing repetition. *British Medical Journal, 317*(7156), 441–447.

Hawton, K., Saunders, K., Topiwala, A., & Haw, C. (2013). Psychiatric disorders in patients presenting to hospital following self-harm: A systematic review. *Journal of Affective Disorders, 151*(3), 821–830.

Hawton, K., Witt, K. G., Taylor Salisbury, T. L., Arensman, E., Gunnell, D., Hazell, P. . . . van Heeringen, K. (2015). Pharmacological interventions for self-harming adults. *Cochrane Database of Systematic Reviews, 7*. Art. No.: CD011777. DOI: https://doi. org/10.1002/14651858.CD011777

Hawton, K., Witt, K. G., Taylor Salisbury, T. L., Arensman, E., Gunnell, D., Hazell, P. . . . van Heeringen, K. (2016). Psychosocial interventions for self-harming adults. *Cochrane Database of Systematic Reviews, 5*. Art. No.: CD012189.

Heath, N. L., Schaub, K., Holly, S., & Nixon, M. K. (2009). Self-injury today: Review of population and clinical studies of adolescents. In M. K. Nixon & N. L. Heath (Eds.), *Self-Injury in youth: The essential guide to assessment and intervention*. New York, NY: Routledge.

Hesse, E., & Main, M. (2000). Disorganized infant, child, and adult attachment: Collapse in behavioral and attentional strategies. *Journal of the American Psychoanalytic Association, 48*(4), 1097–1127.

Hilt, L. M., Cha, C. B., & Nolen-Hoeksema, S. (2008). Non-suicidal self-injury in young adolescent girls: Moderators of the distress-function relationship. *Journal of Consulting and Clinical Psychology, 76*(1), 63–71.

Hodgson, S. (2004). Cutting through the silence: A sociological construction of self-injury. *Sociological Inquiry, 74*(2), 162–179.

Hollander, M. (2017). *Helping teens who cut: Using DBT skills to end self-injury*. New York, NY: Guilford Press.

Honneth, A. (2009). *Pathologies of reason: On the legacy of critical theory*. New York, NY: Columbia University Press.

Hooley, J. M., & Franklin, J. C. (2018). Why do people hurt themselves? A new conceptual model of non-suicidal self-injury. *Clinical Psychological Science, 6*(3), 428–451.

Jarvi, S. M., Hearon, B. A., Batejan, K. L., Gironde, S., & Björgvinsson, T. (2017). Relations between past-week physical activity and recent non-suicidal self-injury in treatment-seeking psychiatric adults. *Journal of Clinical Psychology, 73*(4), 479–488.

Jarvi, S., Jackson, B., Swenson, L., & Crawford, H. (2013). The impact of social contagion on non-suicidal self-injury: A review of the literature. *Archives of Suicide Research, 17*(1), 1–19.

Joiner, T. E. (2005). *Why people die by suicide*. Cambridge, MA: Harvard University Press.

Jones, S. (2008). *The outcast*. London, England: Random House.

Kahan, J., & Pattison, E. M. (1984). Proposal for a distinctive diagnosis: The deliberate self-harm syndrome (DSH). *Suicide and Life-Threatening Behavior, 14*(1), 17–35.

Kafka, J. S. (1969). The body as a transitional object: A psychoanalytic study of a self-mutilating patient. *British Journal of Medical Psychology, 42*(3), 207–212.

Karman, P., Kool, N., Poslawsky, I. E., & van Meijel, B. (2015). Nurses' attitude towards self-harm: A literature review. *Journal of Psychiatric and Mental Health Nursing, 22*, 65–75.

Karterud, S. (2015). *Mentalization-Based Group Therapy (MBT-G): A theoretical, clinical, and research manual*. London, England: Oxford University Press.

Karterud, S. (2018). A high-quality Mentalization-Based Group Therapy session. *Group Analysis, 51*(1), 18–43.

Karterud, S., Pedersen, G., Engen, M., Selsbakk Johansen, M., Niklas Johansson, P., Schlüter, C. . . . Bateman, A. W. (2013). The MBT Adherence and Competence Scale (MBT-ACS): Development, structure and reliability. *Psychotherapy Research, 23*(6), 705–717.

Kernberg, O. (1995). *Love relations: Normality and pathology*. New Haven, CT: Yale University Press.

Kerr, P. L., Muehlenkamp, J. J., James, M., & Turner, D. O. (2010). Non-suicidal self-injury: A review of current research for family medicine and primary care physicians. *Journal of the American Board of Family Medicine, 23*(2), 240–259.

Kessel, N. (1965). Self-poisoning. *British Medical Journal, 2*(5474), 1336–1340.

Kettlewell, C. (1999). *Skin game: A cutter's memoir*. New York, NY: St. Martin's Press.

Klonsky, E. D. (2007). The functions of deliberate self-injury: A review of the evidence. *Clinical Psychology Review, 27*(2), 226–239.

Klonsky, E. D. (2009). The functions of self-injury in young adults who cut themselves: Clarifying the evidence for affect-regulation. *Psychiatry Research, 166*(2), 260–268.

Klonsky, E. D. (2011). Non-suicidal self-injury in United States adults: Prevalence, sociodemographics, topography and functions. *Psychological Medicine, 41*(9), 1981–1986.

Klonsky, E. D., & Glenn, C. R. (2008). Resisting urges to self-injure. *Behavioural and Cognitive Psychotherapy, 36*(2), 211–220.

Klonsky, E. D., & Lewis, S. P. (2014). Assessment of non-suicidal self-injury. In M. K. Nock (Ed.), *The Oxford handbook of suicide and self-injury*. Oxford, England: Oxford University Press.

Klonsky, E. D., Muehlenkamp, J., Lewis, S. P., & Walsh, B. (2011). *Non-suicidal self-injury: Advances in psychotherapy, evidence-based practice*. Cambridge, MA: Hogrefe.

Klonsky, E. D., & Olino, T. (2008). Identifying clinically distinct subgroups of self-injurers among young adults: A latent class analysis. *Journal of Consulting and Clinical Psychology, 76*(1), 22–27.

Klonsky, E. D., & Weinberg, A. (2009). Assessment of non-suicidal self-injury. In M. K. Nock (Ed.), *Understanding non-suicidal self-injury: Origins, assessment, and treatment*. Washington, DC: American Psychological Association.

Kreitman, N., Philip, A. E., Greer, S., & Bagley, C. R. (1969). Parasuicide. *British Journal of Psychiatry, 115*, 746–747.

Lane, R. C. (2002). Anorexia, masochism, self-mutilation, and autoerotism: The spider mother. *Psychoanalytic Review, 89*(1), 101–123.

Laukkanen, E., Rissanen, M.-L., Tolmunen, T., Kylma, J., & Hintikka, J. (2013). Adolescent self-cutting elsewhere than on the arms reveals more serious psychiatric symptoms. *European Child and Adolescent Psychiatry, 22*, 501–510.

LeDoux, J. (1996). *The emotional brain*. New York, NY: Simon and Schuster.

Levenkron, S. (1998). *Cutting: Understanding and overcoming self-mutilation*. New York, NY: Norton.

Lewis, S. P., & Baker, T. G. (2011). The possible risks of self-injury web sites: A content analysis. *Archives of Suicide Research, 15*(4), 390–396.

Lewis, S. P., & Mehrabkhani, S. (2016). Every scar tells a story: Insight into people's self-injury scar experiences. *Counselling Psychology Quarterly, 29*, 1–15.

Lieberman, M. D. (2007). Social cognitive neuroscience: A review of core processes. *Annual Review of Psychology, 58*, 259–289.

Lindgren, B.-M., Svedin, C. G., & Werkö, S. (2018). A systematic literature review of experiences of professional care and support among people who self-harm. *Archives of Suicide Research, 22*(2), 173–192.

Linehan, M. M. (1993). *Cognitive-behavioral treatment of borderline personality disorder*. New York, NY: Guilford Press.

Linehan, M. M. (2015). *DBT skills training manual*. New York, NY: Guilford Press.

Liu, R. T., Scopelliti, K. M., Pittman, S. K., & Zamora, A. S. (2018). Childhood maltreatment and non-suicidal self-injury: A systematic review and meta-analysis. *Lancet*, *5*(1), 51–64. DOI: https://doi.org/10.1016/S2215-0366(17)30469-8

Löf, J., Clinton, D., Kaldo, V., & Rydén, G. (2018). Symptom, alexithymia and self-image outcomes of mentalization-based treatment for borderline personality disorder: A naturalistic study. *BMC Psychiatry*, *18*, 185.

Lundh, L.-G., Karim, J., & Quilisch, E. (2007). Deliberate self-harm in 15 year-old adolescents: A pilot study with a modified version of the deliberate self-harm inventory. *Scandinavian Journal of Psychology*, *48*(1), 33–41.

Madge, N., Hewitt, A., Hawton, K., de Wilde, E. J., Corcoran, P., Fekete, S. . . . Ystgaard, M. (2008). Deliberate self-harm within an international community sample of young people: Comparative findings from the Child & Adolescent Self-Harm in Europe (CASE) Study. *Journal of Child Psychology and Psychiatry*, *49*(6), 667–677.

Mahtani, S., Melvin, G. A., & Hasking, P. (2018). Shame proneness, shame coping, and functions of non-suicidal self-injury (NSSI) among emerging adults: A developmental analysis. *Emerging Adulthood*, *6*(3), 159–171.

Main, M., Hesse, E., & Kaplan, N. (2005). Predictability of attachment behavior and representational processes at 1, 6, and 19 years of age. In K. E. Grossmann, K. Grossmann, & E. Waters (Eds.), *Attachment from infancy to adulthood: The major longitudinal studies*. New York, NY: Guilford Press.

Main, T. F. (1957). The ailment. *British Journal of Medical Psychology*, *30*(3), 129–145.

Mäkikyrö, T., Hakko, H., Timonen, M. J., Lappalainen, J. A. S., Ilomäki, R. S., Marttunen, M. J. . . . Räsänen, P. K. (2004). Smoking and suicidality among adolescent psychiatric patients. *Journal of Adolescence Health*, *34*(3), 250–253.

Malcove, L. (1933). Bodily mutilation and learning to eat. *Psychoanalytic Quarterly*, *2*, 557–561.

Malda-Castillo, J., & Browne, C. (2018). Mentalization-based treatment and its evidence-base status: A systematic literature review. *Psychology and Psychotherapy: Theory, Research and Practice*, 1–34. DOI: https://doi.org/10.1111/papt.12195

Manca, M., Presaghi, F., & Cerutti, R. (2014). Clinical specificity of acute versus chronic self-injury: Measurement and evaluation of repetitive non-suicidal self-injury. *Psychiatry Research*, *215*(1), 111–119. DOI: https://doi.org/10.1016/j.psychres.2013.10.010

Mannarino, V. S., Pereira, D. C. S., Wagner, S., Gurgel, W. S., Costa, C. B. F., Alexandre, M. . . . Mendlowicz, M. V. (2017). Self-embedding behavior in adults: A report of two cases and a systematic review. *Journal of Forensic Sciences*, *62*(4), 953–961.

Marchant, A., Hawton, K., Stewart, A., Montgomery, P., Singaravelu, V., Lloyd, K. . . . John, A. (2017). A systematic review of the relationship between internet use, self-harm and suicidal behaviour in young people: The good, the bad and the unknown. *PLoS One*, *12*(8), e0181722.

Marshall, E., Claes, L., Bouman, W. P., Witcomb, G. L., & Arcelus, J. (2016). Non suicidal self-injury and suicidality in trans people: A systematic review of the literature. *International Review of Psychiatry*, *28*(1), 58–69.

Martin, G., & Swannell, S. (2016). Non-suicidal self-injury in the over 40s: Results from a large national epidemiological survey. *Epidemiology (Sunnyvale)*, *6*, 266.

Mason, P. T., & Kreger, R. (2010). *Stop walking on eggshells: Taking your life back when someone you care about has borderline personality disorder* (2nd edition). Oakland, CA: New Harbinger Publications.

Matney, J., Westers, N. J., Horton, S. E., King, J. D., Eaddy, M., Emslie, G. J. . . . Stewart, S. M. (2018). Frequency and methods of non-suicidal self-injury in relation to acquired capability for suicide among adolescents. *Archives of Suicide Research*, *22*, 91–105.

McCauley, E., Berk, M. S., Asarnow, J. R., Adrian, M., Cohen, J., Korslund, K. . . . Linehan, M. (2018). Efficacy of dialectical behavior therapy for adolescents at high risk for suicide: A randomized clinical trial. *JAMA Psychiatry*, *75*(8), 777–785. DOI: https://doi.org/10.1001/jamapsychiatry.2018.1109

Meins, E., Fernyhough, C., Wainwright, R., Das Gupta, D., Fradley, E., & Tuckey, M. (2002). Maternal mind-mindedness and attachment security as predictors of theory of mind understanding. *Child Development*, *73*, 1715–1726.

Menninger, K. (1938). *Man against himself*. New York, NY: Harcourt, Brace.

Menninger, K. (1959). *A psychiatrist's world*. New York, NY: Viking Press.

Michelsen, K. (1989). *Synålejomfruen* [The Needle Girl]. København: Munksgaard.

Millard, C. (2015). *A history of self-harm in Britain*. Hampshire, England: Palgrave Macmillan.

Miller, W. R., & Rollnick, S. (2013). *Motivational interviewing: Helping people change* (3rd edition). New York, NY: Guilford Press.

Møhl, B. (2015). *Selvskade: Teori og behandling*. Copenhagen, Denmark: Hans Reitzel.

Møhl, B., & Kjølbye, M. (2013). *Psykoterapiens ABC*. Copenhagen, Denmark: PsykiatriFonden.

Møhl, B., La Cour, P., & Skandsen, A. (2014). Non-suicidal self-injury and indirect self-harm among Danish high school students. *Scandinavian Journal of Child and Adolescent Psychiatry and Psychology*, *2*(1), 11–18.

Møhl, B., & Rubæk, L. (submitted). *Genital self-injury as a sign of childhood sexual abuse*.

Møhl, B., & Skandsen, A. (2012). The prevalence and distribution of self-harm among Danish high school students. *Personality and Mental Health*, *6*(2), 147–155.

Monto, M. A., McRee, N., & Deryck, F. S. (2018). Non-suicidal self-injury among a representative sample of US adolescents, 2015. *American Journal of Public Health*, *108*(8), 1042–1048.

Moran, P., Coffey, C., Romaniuk, H., Degenhardt, L., Borschmann, R., & Patton, G. C. (2015). Substance use in adulthood following adolescent self-harm: A population-based cohort study. *Acta Psychiatrica Scandinavia*, *131*(1), 61–68.

Morgan, C., Webb, R. T., Carr, M. J., Kontopantelis, E., Chew-Graham, C. A., Kapur, N., & Ashcroft, D. M. (2018). Self-harm in a primary care cohort of older people: Incidence, clinical management, and risk of suicide and other causes of death. *Lancet Psychiatry*, *5*, 905–912.

Morgan, C., Webb, R. T., Carr, M. J., Kontopantelis, E., Green, J., Chew-Graham, C. A. . . . Ashcroft, D. M. (2017). Incidence, clinical management, and mortality risk following self-harm among children and adolescents: Cohort study in primary care. *British Medical Journal*, *359*, j4351. DOI: https://doi.org/10.1136/bmj.j4351

Morgan, H. G., Burns-Cox, C. J., Pocock, H., & Pottle, S. (1975). Deliberate self-harm. *British Journal of Psychiatry*, *127*(6), 564–574.

Muehlenkamp, J. J. (2006). Empirically supported treatments and general therapy guidelines for non-suicidal self-injury. *Journal of Mental Health Counseling*, *28*(2), 166–185.

Muehlenkamp, J. J. (2014). Distinguishing between suicidal and non-suicidal self-injury. In M. K. Nock (Ed.), *The Oxford handbook of suicide and self-injury*. Oxford, England: Oxford University Press.

Muehlenkamp, J. J., Brausch, A. M., & Washburn, J. J. (2017). How much is enough? Examining frequency criteria for NSSI disorder in adolescent inpatients. *Journal of Consulting and Clinical Psychology*, *85*(6), 611–619.

Muehlenkamp, J. J., Claes, L., Havertape, L., & Plener, P. L. (2012). International prevalence of adolescent non-suicidal self-injury and deliberate self-harm. *Child and Adolescent Psychiatry and Mental Health*, *6*(1), 10.

Muehlenkamp, J. J., Hilt, L. M., Ehlinger, P. P., & McMillan, T. (2015). Non-suicidal self-injury in sexual minority college students: A test of theoretical integration. *Child and Adolescent Psychiatry and Mental Health, 9*, 16.

Musser, N., Zalewski, M., Stepp, S., & Lewis, J. (2018). A systematic review of negative parenting practices predicting borderline personality disorder: Are we measuring biosocial theory's 'invalidating environment'? *Clinical Psychology Review, 65*, 1–16.

NICE Guidelines. (2013). *Quality standard for self-harm.* National Institute of Health and Care Excellence. Retrieved from https://www.nice.org.uk/guidance/qs34

Nixon, M. K., Cloutier, P. F., & Aggarwal, S. (2002). Affect regulation and addictive aspects of repetitive self-injury in hospitalized adolescents. *Journal of the American Academy of Child and Adolescent Psychiatry, 41*(11), 1333–1341.

Nixon, M. K., Levesque, C., Preyde, M., Vanderkooy, J., & Cloutier, P. F. (2015). The Ottawa self-injury inventory: Evaluation of an assessment measure of non-suicidal self-injury in an inpatient sample of adolescents. *Child and Adolescent Psychiatry and Mental Health, 9*, 26.

Nock, M. K. (2008). Actions speak louder than words: An elaborated theoretical model of the social functions of self-injury and other harmful behaviors. *Applied Preventive Psychology, 12*(4), 159–168.

Nock, M. K. (2009). Why do people hurt themselves? New insights into the nature and functions of self-injury. *Current Directions in Psychological Science, 18*(2), 78–83.

Nock, M. K., Holmberg, E. B., Photos, V. I., & Michel, B. D. (2007). Self-injurious thoughts and behaviors interview: Development, reliability, and validity in an adolescent sample. *Psychological Assessment, 19*(3), 309–317.

Nock, M. K., & Kessler, R. C. (2006). Prevalence of and risk factors for suicide attempts versus suicide gestures: Analysis of the National Comorbidity Survey. *Journal of Abnormal Psychology, 115*(3), 616–623.

Nock, M. K., & Mendes, W. B. (2008). Psychological arousal, distress tolerance, and social problem-solving deficits among adolescent self-injurers. *Journal of Consulting and Clinical Psychology, 76*(1), 28–38.

Nock, M. K., & Prinstein, M. J. (2004). A functional approach to the assessment of self-mutilative behavior. *Journal of Consulting and Clinical Psychology, 72*(5), 885–890.

Nock, M. K., & Prinstein, M. J. (2005). Contextual features and behavioural function of self-mutilation among adolescents. *Journal of Abnormal Psychology, 114*(1), 140–146.

Noll, J. G., Horowitz, L. A., Bonanno, G. A., Trickett, P. K., & Putnam, F. W. (2003). Revictimization and self-harm in females who experienced childhood sexual abuse. *Journal of Interpersonal Violence, 18*, 1452–1471.

Norman, H., & Borrill, J. (2015). The relationship between self-harm and alexithymia. *Scandinavian Journal of Psychology, 56*, 405–419.

O'Connor, R. C., Wetherall, K., Cleare, S., Eschle, S., Drummond, J., Ferguson, E. . . . O'Carroll, R. E. (2018). Suicide attempts and non-suicidal self-harm: National prevalence study of young adults. *BJPsych Open, 4*(3), 142–148.

Ougrin, D., Tranah, T., Stahl, D., Moran, P., & Asarnow, J. R. (2015). Therapeutic interventions for suicide attempts and self-harm in adolescents: Systematic review and meta-analysis. *Journal of American Academy of Child and Adolescent Psychiatry, 54*(2), 97–107.

Pao, P. R. (1969). The syndrome of delicate self-cutting. *British Journal of Medical Psychology, 42*(3), 195–206.

Patchin, J. W., & Hinduja, S. (2017). Digital self-harm among adolescents. *Journal of Adolescent Health, 61*(6), 761–766.

Pattison, E. M., & Kahan, J. (1983). The deliberate self-harm syndrome. *American Journal of Psychiatry*, *140*(7), 867–872.

Peters, E. M., John, A., Baetz, M., & Balbuena, L. (2018). Examining the role of borderline personality traits in the relationship between major depression and non-suicidal self-injury. *Comprehensive Psychiatry*, *86*, 96–101.

Plener, P. L., Allroggen, M., Kapusta, N. D., Brähler, E., Fegert, J. M., & Groschwitz, R. C. (2016). The prevalence of non-suicidal self-injury (NSSI) in a representative sample of the German population. *BMC Psychiatry*, *16*, 353.

Plener, P. L., Kaess, M., Schmahl, C., Pollak, S., Fegert, J. M., & Brown, R. C. (2018). Non-suicidal self-injury in adolescents. *Deutsches Ärzteblatt International*, *115*, 23–30. DOI: https://doi.org/10.3238/arztebl.2018.0023

Plener, P. L., Schumacher, T. S., Munz, L. M., & Groschwitz, R. C. (2015). The longitudinal course of non-suicidal self-injury and deliberate self-harm: A systematic review of the literature. *Borderline Personality Disorder and Emotion Dysregulation*, *2*, 2. DOI: https://doi.org/10.1186/s40479-014-0024-3

Prochaska, J. O., & Norcross, J. C. (2001). Stages of change. *Psychotherapy: Theory, Research, Training*, *38*(4), 443–448.

Rilke, R. M. (2008/1910). *The notebooks of Malte Laurids Brigge*. London, England: Penguin Classics.

Robinson, J., McCutcheon, L., Browne, V., & Witt, K. (2016). *Looking the other way: Young people and self-harm*. Melbourne, Australia: Orygen, The National Centre of Excellence in Youth Mental Health.

Rosa, H. (2010). Alienation and acceleration: Towards a critical theory of late-modern temporality. In *Summertalk* (Vol. 3). Aarhus, Denmark: NSU Press.

Rosenthal, R. J., Rinzler, C., Walsh, R., & Klausner, E. (1972). The wrist-cutting syndrome: The meaning of a gesture. *American Journal of Psychiatry*, *128*, 1363–1368.

Ross, S., & Heath, N. (2002). A study of the frequency of self-mutilation in a community sample of adolescents. *Journal of Youth and Adolescence*, *31*(1), 67–77.

Rossouw, T. I., & Fonagy, P. (2012). Mentalization-based treatment for self-harm in adolescents: A randomized controlled trial. *Journal of the American Academy of Child and Adolescent Psychiatry*, *51*(21), 1304–1313.

Rotolone, C., & Martin, G. (2012). Giving up self-injury: A comparison of everyday social and personal resources in past versus current self-injurers. *Archives of Suicide Research*, *16*(2), 147–158.

Royal College of Psychiatrists. (2006). *Better services for people who self-harm: Quality standards for healthcare professionals*. London, England: Royal College of Psychiatrists' Centre for Quality Improvement.

Rubæk, L., & Møhl, B. (2016). Ikke-suicidal selv-skade – et afhængighedssyndrom? *Psyke&Logos*, *37*(2), 205–220.

Sahlin, H., Bjureberg, J., Gratz, K. L., Tull, M. T., Hedman, E., Bjärehed, J. . . . Hellner, C. (2017). Emotion Regulation Group Therapy for deliberate self-harm: A multi-site evaluation in routine care using an uncontrolled open trial design. *BMJ Open*, *7*, e016220. DOI: https://doi.org/10.1136/bmjopen-2017–016220

Sambrook, S., Abba, N., & Chadwick, P. (2007). Evaluation of DBT emotional coping skills groups for people with parasuicidal behaviours. *Behavioural and Cognitive Psychotherapy*, *35*(2), 241–244.

Sandman, C. A. (2009). Psychopharmacologic treatment of non-suicidal self-injury. In M. K. Nock (Ed.), *Understanding non-suicidal self-injury*. Washington, DC: American Psychological Association.

Schoenleber, M., Berenbaum, H., & Motl, R. (2014). Shame-related functions of and motivations for self-injurious behavior. *Personality Disorders: Theory, Research, and Treatment, 5*(2), 204–211.

Schore, A. N. (2003). *Affect dysregulation and disorders of the self.* New York, NY: Norton.

Schreiner, M. W., Klimes-Dougan, B., Begnel, E. D., & Cullen, K. R. (2015). Conceptualizing the neurobiology of non-suicidal self-injury from the perspective of the Research Domain Criteria Project. *Neuroscience and Biobehavioral Reviews, 57*, 381–391.

Sevecke, K., Bock, A., Fenzel, L., Gander, M., & Fuchs, M. (2017). Non-suicidal self-injury in a naturalistic sample of adolescents undergoing inpatient psychiatric treatment: Prevalence, gender distribution and comorbidities. *Psychiatria Danubina, 29*(4), 522–528.

Smith, N. B., Kouros, C. D., & Meuret, A. E. (2014). The role of trauma symptoms in non-suicidal self-injury. *Trauma, Violence & Abuse, 15*(1), 41–56.

Stacy, S. E., Bandel, S. L., Lear, M. K., & Pepper, C. M. (2018). Before, during and after self-injury: The practice patterns of non-suicidal self-injury. *Journal of Nervous and Mental Disease, 206*(7), 522–527.

Stanford, S., & Jones, M. P. (2009). Psychological subtyping finds pathological, impulsive, and 'normal' groups among adolescents who self-harm. *Journal of Child Psychology and Psychiatry, 50*(7), 807–815.

Stern, D. N. (1985). *The interpersonal world of the infant: A view from psychoanalysis and developmental psychology.* New York, NY: Basic Books.

Stiglmayr, C., Stecher-Mohr, J., Wagner, T., Meißner, J., Spretz, D., Steffens, C. . . . Renneberg, B. (2014). Effectiveness of dialectic behavioral therapy in routine outpatient care: The Berlin Borderline Study. *Borderline Personal Disorder Emotion Dysregulation, 18*(1), 20.

Stone, M. (1987). A psychodynamic approach: Some thoughts on the dynamics and therapy of self-mutilating borderline patients. *Journal of Personality Disorder, 1*(4), 347–349.

Strong, M. (1998). *A bright red scream: Self-mutilation and the language of pain.* London, England: Virago Press.

Suyemoto, K. L. (1998). The function of self-mutilation. *Clinical Psychology Review, 18*(5), 531–554.

Swannell, S. V., Martin, G. E., Page, A., Hasking, P., Hazell, P., Taylor, A., & Protani, M. (2012). Child maltreatment, subsequent non-suicidal self-injury and the mediating roles of dissociation, alexithymia and self-blame. *Child Abuse and Neglect, 36*(7–8), 572–584.

Swannell, S. V., Martin, G. E., Page, A., Hasking, P., & St. John, N. J. (2014). Prevalence of non-suicidal self-injury in nonclinical samples: Systematic review, meta-analysis and meta-regression. *Suicide and Life-Threatening Behavior, 44*(3), 273–303.

Swenson, C. R., Witterholt, S., & Bohus, M. (2007). Dialectic behavior therapy in inpatient units. In L. Dimeff & K. Koerner (Eds.), *Dialectic behavior therapy in clinical practice: Applications across disorders and settings.* New York, NY: Guilford Press.

Tatnell, R., Kaleda, L., Hasking, P., & Martin, G. (2014). Longitudinal analysis of adolescent NSSI: The role of intrapersonal and interpersonal factors. *Journal of Abnormal Child Psychology, 42*(6), 885–896.

Taylor, P. J., Jomar, K., Dhingra, K., Forrester, R., Shahmalak, U., & Dickson, J. M. (2018). A meta-analysis of the prevalence of different functions of non-suicidal self-injury. *Journal of Affective Disorders, 227*, 759–769. DOI: https://doi.org/10.1016/j.jad.2017.11.073

Taylor, T. L., Hawton, K., Fortune, S., & Kapur, N. (2009). Attitudes towards clinical services among people who self-harm: Systematic review. *British Journal of Psychiatry, 194*(2), 104–110.

The ICD-10 Classification of Mental and Behavioural Disorders (1992). *Clinical descriptions and diagnostic guidelines*. Geneva: World Health Organization.

The International Society for the Study of Self-Injury (ISSS). Retrieved from http://itriples. org

Tørmoen, A. J., Grøholt, B., Haga, E., Brager-Larsen, A., Miller, A., Walby, F., Stanley, B., & Mehlum, L. (2014): Feasibility of Dialectical Behavior Therapy with suicidal and self-harming adolescents with multi-problems: Training, adherence and retention. *Archives of Suicide Research, 18*(4), 432–444.

Townsend, E., Hawton, K., Atman, D. G., Arensman, E., Gunnell, D., Hazell, P. . . . van Heeringen, K. (2001). The efficacy of problem solving treatments after deliberate self-harm: Meta-analysis of randomized controlled trials with respect to depression, hopelessness, and improvement in problems. *Psychological Medicine, 31*(6), 979–988.

Turner, B. J., Austin, S. B., & Chapman, A. L. (2014). Treating non-suicidal self-injury: A systematic review of psychological and pharmacological interventions. *Canadian Journal of Psychiatry/Revue Canadienne de Psychiatrie, 59*(11), 576–585.

Turner, B. J., Cobb, R. J., Gratz, K., & Chapman, A. L. (2016).The role of interpersonal conflict and perceived social support in non-suicidal self-injury in daily life. *Journal of Abnormal Psychology, 125*(4), 588–598.

Turner, C. A., & Lewis, M. H. (2002). Dopaminergic mechanisms in self-injurious behavior and related disorders. In S. R. Schroder, M. L. Oster-Granite, & T. Thompson (Eds.), *Self-injurious behavior: Genes-brain-behavior relationships*. Washington, DC: American Psychological Association.

Tyrer, P., Tom, B., Byford, S., Schmidt, U., Jones, V., Davidson, K. . . . Catalan, J. (2004). Differential effects of Manual Assisted Cognitive Behaviour Therapy (MACT) in the treatment of recurrent deliberate self-harm and personality disturbance: The POPMACT Study. *Journal of Personality Disorders, 18*(1), 102–116.

Victor, S. E., Glenn, C. R., & Klonsky, E. D. (2012). Is non-suicidal self-injury an 'addiction'? A comparison of craving in substance use and non-suicidal self-injury. *Psychiatry Research, 197*(1–2), 73–77.

Victor, S. E., Muehlenkamp, J. J., Hayes, N. A., Lengel, G. J., Styer, D. M., & Washburn, J. J. (2018). Characterizing gender differences in non-suicidal self-injury: Evidence from a large clinical sample of adolescents and adults. *Comprehensive Psychiatry, 82*, 53–60.

VIOSS. (2015). *Selvskade i den danske befolkning* [Self-harm in the Danish population]. Copenhagen, Denmark: Knowledge Center on Eating Disorders and Self-Harm.

Vogt, K. S., & Norman, P. (2018). Is mentalization-based therapy effective in treating the symptoms of borderline personality disorder? A systematic review. *Psychology and Psychotherapy: Theory, Research and Practice*, 1–24. DOI: https://doi.org/10.1111/papt.12194

Waals, L., Baetens, I., Rober, P., Lewis, S., Van Parys, H., Goethals, E. R., & Whitlock, J. (2018). The NSSI family distress cascade theory. *Child and Adolescent Psychiatry and Mental Health, 12*, 52. DOI: https://doi.org/10.1186/s13034-018-0259-7

Wallerstein, M. B., & Nock, M. K. (2007). Physical exercise as a treatment for non-suicidal self-injury: Evidence from a single-case study. *American Journal of Psychiatry, 164*(2), 350–351.

Walrath, R. (2017). Characteristics of adolescents who engage in non-suicidal self-injury. *Psychology and Behavioral Science International Journal, 2*(5). DOI: https://doi.org/10.19080/PBSIJ.2017.02.555596

Walsh, B. W. (2006). *Treating self-injury: A practical guide*. New York, NY: Guilford Press.

Wedig, M. M., & Nock, M. K. (2007). Parental expressed emotion and adolescent self-injury. *Journal of the American Academy of Child and Adolescent Psychiatry, 46*(9), 1171–1178.

Weinberg, I., Gunderson, J. G., Hennen, J., & Cutter Jr., C. J. (2006). Manual Assisted Cognitive Treatment for deliberate self-harm in borderline personality disorder patients. *Journal of Personality Disorders, 20*(5), 482–492.

Weissman, M. M. (1975). Wrist cutting: Relationship between clinical observations and epidemiological findings. *Archives of General Psychiatry, 32*, 1166–1171.

Wester, K. L., Ivers, N., Villalba, J. A., Trepal, H. C., & Henson, R. (2016). The relationship between non-suicidal self-injury and suicidal ideation. *Journal of Counseling and Development, 94*(1), 3–12.

Whitlock, J. L., Baetens, I., Lloyd-Richardson, E., Hasking, P., Hamza, C., Lewis, S., & Robinson, K. (2018). Helping schools support caregivers of youth who self-injure: Considerations and recommendations. *School Psychology International, 39*(3), 318–328.

Whitlock, J. L., Eckenrode, J., & Silverman, D. (2006). Self-injurious behavior in a college population. *Pediatrics, 117*(6), 1939–1948.

Whitlock, J. L., & Lloyd-Richardson, E. (2019). *Healing self-injury: A compassionate guide for parents and other loved ones.* New York, NY: Oxford University Press.

Whitlock, J. L., Muehlenkamp, J., & Eckenrode, J. (2008). Variation in non-suicidal self-injury: Identification of latent classes in a community population of young adults. *Journal of Clinical Child and Adolescent Psychology, 37*(4), 725–735.

Whitlock, J. L., Muehlenkamp, J., Purington, A., Eckenrode, J., Barreira, P., Abams, G. B. . . . Knox, K. (2011). Non-suicidal self-injury in a college population: General trends and sex differences. *Journal of American College Health, 59*(8), 691–698.

Whitlock, J. L., & Selekman, M. D. (2014). Non-suicidal self-injury across the life span. In M. K. Nock (Ed.), *The Oxford handbook of suicide and self-injury.* Oxford, England: Oxford University Press.

Wilkinson, P. O. (2018). Dialectical Behavior Therapy: A highly effective treatment for some adolescents who self-harm. *JAMA Psychiatry, 75*(8), 786–787. DOI: https://doi.org/10.1001/jamapsychiatry.2018.1079

Wilkinson, P. O., Qiu, T., Neufeld, S., Jones, P. B., & Goodyer, I. M. (2018). Sporadic and recurrent non-suicidal self-injury before age 14 and incident onset of psychiatric disorders by 17 years: Prospective cohort study. *British Journal of Psychiatry, 212*(4), 222–226.

Wilstrand, C., Lindgren, B.-M., Gilje, F., & Olofsson, B. (2007). Being burdened and balancing boundaries: A qualitative study of nurses' experiences caring for patients who self-harm. *Journal of Psychiatric and Mental Health Nursing, 14*(1), 72–78.

Winnicott, D. W. (1949). Hate in the counter-transference. *International Journal of Psychoanalysis, 30*, 69–74.

Winnicott, D. W. (1960). Ego distortion in terms of true and false self. In D. W. Winnicott (Ed.), *The maturational processes and the facilitating environment: Studies in the theory of emotional development.* New York, NY: International University Press.

Winnicott, D. W. (1971). Mirror-role of mother and family in child development. In D. W. Winnicott (Ed.), *Playing and reality.* London, England: Tavistock.

Wrath, A. J., & Adams, G. C. (2018). Self-injurious behaviors and adult attachment: A review of the literature. *Archives of Suicide Research,* online July 2018. DOI: https://doi.org/10.1080/13811118.2018.1486251

Yates, T. M. (2004). The developmental psychopathology of self-injurious behavior: Compensatory regulation in posttraumatic adaptation. *Clinical Psychological Review, 24*(1), 35–74.

Yates, T. M. (2009). Developmental pathways from child maltreatment to non-suicidal self-injury. In M. K. Nock (Ed.), *Understanding non-suicidal self-injury: Origins, assessment, and treatment.* Washington, DC: American Psychological Association.

Yates, T. M., Carlson, E. A., & Egeland, B. (2008). A prospective study of child maltreatment and self-injurious behavior in a community sample. *Development and Psychopathology, 20*(2), 651–671.

You, J., Ren, Y., Zhang, X., Wu, Z., Xu, S., & Lin, M.-P. (2018). Emotional dysregulation and non-suicidal self-injury: A meta-analytic review. *Neuropsychiatry, 8*(2), 733–748.

Young, R., Sproeber, N., Groschwitz, R., Preiss, M., & Plener, P. (2014). Why alternative teenagers self-harm: Exploring the link between non-suicidal self-injury, attempted suicide and adolescent identity. *BMC Psychiatry, 14*, 137.

Zetterqvist, M. (2015). The DSM-5 diagnosis of non-suicidal self-injury disorder: A review of the empirical literature. *Child and Adolescent Psychiatry and Mental Health, 9*, 31.

Zetterqvist, M., Lundh, L.-G., Dahlström, Ö., & Svedin, C. G. (2013a). Prevalence and function of non-suicidal self-injury (NSSI) in a community sample of adolescents, using suggested DSM-5 criteria for a potential NSSI disorder. *Journal of Abnormal Child Psychology, 41*(5), 759–773.

Zetterqvist, M., Lundh, L.-G., & Svedin, C. G. (2013). A comparison of adolescents engaging in self-injurious behaviors with and without suicidal intent: Self-reported experiences of adverse life events and trauma symptoms. *Journal of Youth and Adolescents, 42*(8), 1257–1272.

Zetterqvist, M., Svedin, C. G., Fredlund, C., Priebe, G., Wadsby, M., & Jonsson, L. S. (2018). Self-reported non-suicidal self-injury (NSSI) and sex as self-injury (SASI): Relationship to abuse, risk behaviors, trauma symptoms, self-esteem and attachment. *Psychiatry Research, 265*, 309–316.

Zielinski, M. J., Hill, M. A., & Veilleux, J. C. (2018). Is the first cut really the deepest? Frequency and recency of non-suicidal self-injury in relation to psychopathology and dysregulation. *Psychiatry Research, 259*, 392–397.

Index

Note: page numbers in italic indicate figures and page numbers in bold indicate tables on the corresponding pages.

For Product Safety Concerns and Information please contact our EU
representative GPSR@taylorandfrancis.com
Taylor & Francis Verlag GmbH, Kaufingerstraße 24, 80331 München, Germany

www.ingramcontent.com/pod-product-compliance
Lightning Source LLC
Chambersburg PA
CBHW070241290326
41929CB00046B/2272